MW00527765

Critical Thinking and Persuasive Writing for Postgraduates

For a complete listing of all our titles in this area please visit
he.palgrave.com/study-skills

www.palgravestudyskills.com – the leading study skills website

Palgrave Study Skills

Business Degree Success
Career Skills
Cite Them Right (10th edn)
e-Learning Skills (2nd edn)
Essentials of Essay Writing
Get Sorted
Great Ways to Learn Anatomy and Physiology (2nd edn)
How to Begin Studying English Literature (4th edn)
How to Study Foreign Languages
How to Study Linguistics (2nd edn)
How to Use Your Reading in Your Essays (2nd edn)
How to Write Better Essays (3rd edn)
How to Write Your Undergraduate Dissertation
  (2nd edn)
Improve Your Grammar (2nd edn)
Information Skills
The International Student Handbook
The Mature Student's Guide to Writing (3rd edn)
The Mature Student's Handbook
The Palgrave Student Planner
The Personal Tutor's Handbook
Practical Criticism
Presentation Skills for Students (3rd edn)
The Principles of Writing in Psychology
Professional Writing (3rd edn)
Researching Online
The Student Phrase Book
The Student's Guide to Writing (3rd edn)
Study Skills for International Postgraduates
Study Skills for Speakers of English as a Second
  Language
Studying History (4th edn)
Studying Law (4th edn)
Studying Modern Drama (2nd edn)
Studying Psychology (2nd edn)
Studying Physics
Success in Academic Writing
Smart Thinking
The Undergraduate Research Handbook
The Work-Based Learning Student Handbook
  (2nd edn)
Work Placements – A Survival Guide for Students
Write it Right (2nd edn)
Writing for Engineers (3rd edn)
Writing for Law
Writing for Nursing and Midwifery Students (2nd edn)
Writing History Essays (2nd edn)

Pocket Study Skills

14 Days to Exam Success
Analyzing a Case Study
Brilliant Writing Tips for Students
Completing Your PhD
Doing Research
Getting Critical (2nd edn)
Planning Your Dissertation
Planning Your Essay (2nd edn)
Planning Your PhD
Posters and Presentations
Reading and Making Notes (2nd edn)
Referencing and Understanding Plagiarism (2nd edn)
Reflective Writing
Report Writing
Science Study Skills
Studying with Dyslexia
Success in Groupwork
Time Management
Where's Your Argument?
Writing for University (2nd edn)

Palgrave Research Skills

Authoring a PhD
The Foundations of Research (2nd edn)
Getting to Grips with Doctoral Research
Getting Published
The Good Supervisor (2nd edn)
PhD by Published Work
The PhD Viva
Planning Your Postgraduate Research
The PhD Writing Handbook
The Postgraduate Research Handbook (2nd edn)
The Professional Doctorate
Structuring Your Research Thesis

Palgrave Career Skills

Excel at Graduate Interviews
Graduate CVs and Covering Letters
Graduate Entrepreneurship
The Graduate Career Guidebook
How to Succeed at Assessment Centres
Social Media for Your Student and Graduate Job
  Search
Work Experience, Placements and Internships

Critical Thinking and Persuasive Writing for Postgraduates

Louise Katz

palgrave

© Louise Katz 2018

All rights reserved. No reproduction, copy or transmission of this publication may be made without written permission.

No portion of this publication may be reproduced, copied or transmitted save with written permission or in accordance with the provisions of the Copyright, Designs and Patents Act 1988, or under the terms of any licence permitting limited copying issued by the Copyright Licensing Agency, Saffron House, 6–10 Kirby Street, London EC1N 8TS.

Any person who does any unauthorized act in relation to this publication may be liable to criminal prosecution and civil claims for damages.

The authors asserted her right to be identified as the author of this work in accordance with the Copyright, Designs and Patents Act 1988.

First published 2018 by
PALGRAVE

Palgrave in the UK is an imprint of Macmillan Publishers Limited, registered in England, company number 785998, of 4 Crinan Street, London, N1 9XW.

Palgrave® and Macmillan® are registered trademarks in the United States, the United Kingdom, Europe and other countries.

ISBN 978–1–137–60442–2 paperback

This book is printed on paper suitable for recycling and made from fully managed and sustained forest sources. Logging, pulping and manufacturing processes are expected to conform to the environmental regulations of the country of origin.

A catalogue record for this book is available from the British Library.

A catalog record for this book is available from the Library of Congress.

Contents

Introduction

Education at all levels is an animated process produced in the communicative exchanges of teachers and learners. In this spirit, *Critical Thinking and Persuasive Writing for Postgraduates* provides suggestions for postgraduates (and undergraduates looking ahead to higher degrees) and their teachers on how to continually work towards improving on these skills. There is already a fair bit of literature available that is geared towards undergraduate study, but this book deals with the particular concerns of postgraduates – those engaged in coursework who are not yet experienced writers, those in research programmes at master's and doctoral levels, and students and academics involved in independent research projects. It also includes a strong theoretical component. There are two reasons for this. One, to enrich the reader's understanding of processes involved in refining higher learning skills and writing practices; and two, to contextualise notions of critical thinking within a historical and cultural framework.

Often the literature on critical thinking focuses on its application to study and workplace situations or to assist in decision-making and problem-solving, whether professionally or ethically. This is of course vital: thinking well does not begin with a course of study and end with a university degree. Good employers look for people who can make thoughtful decisions and who have the ability to ask the sort of questions that will benefit their institution. To do this, they need to be able to think of those questions in the first place. Such employers also want people who have long-term vision, are at home with complexity, and can not only work out solutions to problems but actively look for problems to solve. ('Problem-finding' requires a much higher order of cognitive ability than solving already identified problems!) Imaginative and independent thinkers are needed – those able to make intelligent inferences and can put all of these attributes to practical use. Sounds like a lot? It is. These are all aspects of critical practice treated in this book, aspects that rely on linking, rather than dividing, criticality and creativity.

However, while considering vocational requirements and also explicating the ethical dimensions of independent, active thinking, *Critical Thinking and Persuasive Writing for Postgraduates* sees being critical firstly as an attitude of mind rather than simply the deployment of analytical tools from an adaptive 'skill set'. In planning stages I have also been mindful of certain assumptions frequently made by both staff and students at universities: that critical practices are somehow 'embedded' in postgraduate curricula. My experience and research show that this really isn't always so. In fact, often enough only limited critical skills are taught for the purposes of interrogating and analysing texts within narrow frameworks while missing the much greater possibilities for criticality available to us when such thinking skills are fully extended and exercised. This is like using the energy of a nuclear reactor to shell a bowl of peas.

The ability to think critically will enhance study and research skills and potentially, exam results and job prospects, but it also makes possible creative change in any given disciplinary field and in broader social, political, and cultural contexts – *if* allied with expressive skill and the confidence to write with clarity and purpose. Postgraduate students and professional researchers have to be able to think insightfully and autonomously about their fields of interest, but without strong communicative ability, ideas that may be of value might get out of your head and onto the page yet fail to interest the reader very much. This is why a central contention of this book is that academic writing, while imparting information, should never be drudgery to read – or to compose. If the ideas or information are worth exploring, then you want to be able to maintain a powerful interest in your topic, no matter how long it takes. And if the ideas are worth relating, they should have the potential to thoroughly engross your intended readers, whether examiners or colleagues or the wider community. Then, if you can also excite, disturb, or even inspire them, so much the better!

Premises upon which this book is based

1. Writing and thinking go together

Critical acumen is essential for writing creditable and compelling essays, dissertations, and theses. Throughout the book we'll be looking at writing, thinking, and researching as aspects of one creative process – for, as sociologist Laurel Richardson (2005) has claimed, writing itself can be a method of enquiry. That said, for the sake of simplicity and streamlining this book has two distinct sections – one on thinking and the other on writing – but you'll notice that throughout they are treated as complementary aspects of learning and academic communication.

2. Thinking critically is a means towards gaining clarity of mind

Today is an age of unprecedented complexity and global connectivity, 24/7 communication channels ceaselessly demanding our (always divided) attention, so that attention itself has arguably become a commodity prized more highly that any other. It is becoming increasingly difficult to achieve the clarity we need, largely because there is simply *so much* information to filter through to work out what we might think about any given topic. Increasingly accelerated and sophisticated means of global intercommunication link us all so that we are constantly made aware of others' predicaments, aspirations, multifarious viewpoints, and needs. All information, contemporary and historical, truthful or twisted, is a click away. We have never known more, but what are we to do with it all? How do we transform data to knowledge, knowledge to understanding? As Diane Halpern (2013, p. 1) mentions, where critical thinking once called for increased understanding of how to think well and to live well within a particular society, today it's a global enterprise involving the interests of all of us on this planet – in fact, of the earth itself. Never before has the need to think critically been so, well ... *critical*. 'For the first time in the history of the human race, we have the ability to destroy all life on earth. The decisions that we make as individuals and as a society regarding the economy, conservation of natural resources, and the development of nuclear weapons will affect future generations of all people around the world.' Since Halpern wrote this five years ago, intellectual inquiry in general and expertise specifically has come under consolidated attack.

We are considered by some to inhabit a 'post-truth' era, where so-called 'alternative facts' are accepted uncritically and unreflectively by many. It has never been more crucial to mount 'a case for facts as they are grounded in evidence, not as fluid points of convenience employed to cover or distort a proposition' (Glover cited in Grattan 2017).

What choices will we make? And who is the 'I' making them?

- The student? (Critical thinking will help me get good marks but I know there's more to it than that. How do I focus in enough to get the grades I need while also extending my reach, testing the abilities of my intellect?)
- The employee? (My employer wants me to work on a particular project but I don't see its value. Where should my loyalties lie – with my individual critical interpretation of the issue/scenario/data, or with the hand that feeds me?)
- The citizen? (I favour the policies of this politician – as far as I can gauge them in this roadshow of an election. And how can I judge whether he'll act upon his apparent principles or dump them as soon as he's in office? And how can I be sure I'm actually making my own decision and not being coerced – can't tell if I'm jumping or being pushed …)
- The consumer? (Not sure how I came to be reading this book/watching this show/buying this shirt. How strong was the influence of algorithmically engineered predictive analytics? Or: Growing organic food takes up valuable space in an overpopulated world but is purportedly better for you; agribusiness takes up less but over-cultivates a planet with limited resources. How do I work out what to *eat*?)

A skilled critical mind will be in a better position to cope with the information onslaught we deal with daily, to be able to tell the difference between information and misinformation, news and propaganda, a lovely piece of rhetoric and slick sophistry, time-wasting ephemera, or a fleeting but brilliant vision.

3. Critical thinking is a central aspect of thinking well – but it is not the only one

Whether watching a documentary or reading the news or a scholarly text, browsing through Google Scholar or surveying opinions from other online platforms, the critically adept thinker proceeds through a number of phases well beyond recognising stated meanings: analysis and interpretation (identifying inferences of speakers or authors and the rhetorical strategies they employ), evaluation (assessing the validity of evidence and explanations), and synthesis (identifying relationships between ideas, between texts). It then becomes possible to apply the knowledge that's been acquired to filter out some of the clamouring voices and attend to those of true value, and from there to create new knowledge, and to communicate it in writing that is both rigorous and vigorous.

However, we do have to be aware that there are limits to this paradigm. There are ways of thinking other than critical – for example, somatic (involving body awareness) or instinctive (the kind you need to drive a car or fight a battle) – but these are not particularly relevant to the aims of this book. Intellectual sympathy is though. This is where you thoroughly immerse yourself in a text before standing back to critique it. It is closely related to the particular critical ability of open-mindedness and the 'disposition' of curiosity (Ennis 1985, p. 45; Facione 2013, p. 11). We also need to develop the ability to think speculatively and imaginatively, as new knowledge does not emerge without the exercise of creativity which allows us to move 'through "the known" to "the unknown"' (Pope 2005, p. 11) and thus opens up the possibility of a fresh or insightful perception. This is why this book will recommend experimenting with certain more divergent writing and learning styles alongside traditional ones, and suggest ways these can be integrated into your cache of scholarly skills.

I'd argue that critical thinking that seeks to replace, rather than work with, sympathetic engagement does itself a disservice and if scepticism is allowed to trump inquisitiveness or to override imagination – this too impoverishes criticality. This book seeks to address such deficiencies and also to provide an understanding of critical thinking that focuses not only on the intellectual dimension of textual analysis but also on self-reflection, and to link theory with critical action.

4. Fundamental critical approaches are not necessarily discipline-specific

It seems a bit odd to write such a sub-heading in the introduction to a book about critical thinking, but it needs to be mentioned that there are arguments against attempting to teach cross-disciplinary or generic critical skills. Some theorists hold to the idea that the critical habits of mind required in one field are not transferable to another, as each is anchored in domain-specific forms of knowledge. I agree that it is essential to acquire the language and a strong understanding of the concepts and facts in one's discipline, and that there may be critical strategies that are appropriate to some fields but not to others. Also, I have to concede that the examples and discussion points in this particular book are likely to be more readily accessible to those in the arts, humanities, and social sciences because those are areas in which I have some experience. Nevertheless, regardless of my own academic interests, students from diverse disciplines have in fact elected to take my course on critical thinking at the university where I teach (and happily, have reported that they have enjoyed and benefited from the experience). There are certain generic critical skills which definitely are transferable. Peter Facione found that these include skills of interpretation, whether of experiences, data, procedures, or events; both reflective and analytical capability; power of inference; and evaluative proficiency. Facione also refers to critical dispositions that each of us may have to a greater or lesser degree: a desire to be well informed, for instance, or intellectual flexibility; the ability to change one's mind when faced with convincing evidence; the ability to truthfully appraise one's own limitations, biases, and egocentric tendencies (2013, pp. 9–11). We might also consider how strictly discipline-focused critical thinking might miss links between criticality and creativity, or critical thinking and perceptiveness, inventiveness, adaptability, and ethics – as will be discussed in Chapter 2.

The above abilities and attributes can be fostered among scientists, businesspeople, and economists as much as historians, film-makers, and linguists. *Critical Thinking and Persuasive Writing for Postgraduates* attempts to contribute to ongoing scholarly conversations about thinking and writing through discussion, practical guidelines, and exercises to help readers sort the gold from the dross during the research process to come up with new ideas, or at the very least, refreshed perspectives in their own work, and to communicate these thoughts with eloquence.

How is this book organised?

Each chapter briefly theorises the ideas to be explored before offering practical 'how-to' suggestions and exercises that are designed to help the information settle and become integrated into your academic practice. Because the concept of critical thought has a long history, for those readers interested in contextualising today's ideas about critical thinking, Chapter 1 surveys a range of theories and practices from Classical to contemporary thinkers and writers to support the following working definition of critical thinking: 'reasonable reflective thinking that is focused on deciding what to believe or do' (Ennis 1985). There are many definitions to choose from that both pre-date and post-date this one, and I'll refer to several of those in due course, but I favour this one for now for its succinctness. After reading Chapter 1's brief history of critical thinking you may want to amend it to suit your own conceptualisation, but I think this is a good starting point because, first, it is open-ended. As Ennis points out, it also readily accommodates creative aspects of thinking, like forming hypotheses or planning how to go about any given task. Second, it encapsulates the concept of reflectiveness – the cultivation of self-awareness within the critical process. Third, it supports the idea that the critical business of making decisions about how to act or why to believe this argument rather than that are *practical* activities. Criticality, like creativity, ultimately demands action.

Chapter 2 looks at where thinking critically fits into the broader notion of thinking well and, following Ronald Barnett, examines three critical modes: the analytical, the reflective, and the role of criticality in social engagement. The main practical focus of this chapter is advice on how to keep a reflective journal as a means towards fostering critical awareness. Journaling is presented as a metacognitive tool by means of which analytical, interpretive, and particularly reflective skills are developed. Not only is the intellect engaged, but also intuition and imagination. A reflective journal requires that you attempt to query your own thinking and motivations to establish how and why it is that you arrive at the conclusions you draw. Without self-awareness, true critical thought is not possible, as this chapter will demonstrate.

Chapter 3 moves on from reflectiveness to survey several techniques of logic, another indispensable tool of the critical thinker. It is by means of logic that we develop and evaluate theories and texts and see relationships between concepts. This chapter also looks at how to use analogy and generalisation, at premises and arguments, and how to '[try] on a theory for size' by viewing it both from the inside, empathetically, and from the outside, objectively (Restall 2013, p. 11). This leads us into discussion of authorial position and point of view, thence to questions at the heart of critiquing any text to do with truth, usefulness, and value.

In higher education, pedagogical theories and practices are frequently seen as dichotomous: critical/creative; teaching/learning; thinking/writing. Chapter 4 reconnects these concepts. As previously mentioned, *Critical Thinking and Persuasive Writing for Postgraduates* presents teaching and learning as a communicative exchange. This is not a new idea in all cultures. For instance, in the Maori tradition there is one word for both learning and teaching: 'Ako'. Following this precedent, I'll be linking the two wherever possible, supplying recommendations and exercises that are appropriate for both learners and teachers. As I mentioned earlier, in this book thinking and writing too are approached together, and are allied with other creative processes. These concepts inform this chapter's practical experimentation with sympathetic reading, mindmapping, and freewriting as preliminary stages towards developing essay outlines which are both clear and original. These practices set the scene for the focus of the following chapter, which explores ways of integrating writing and research.

Chapter 5 explains how, historically, writing and research became separated, shows how this separation is unhelpful to both scholars and students, and provides exercises based on a more integrated approach. We look at writing itself as a method of enquiry and consider also the subjectivities which affect the way we carry out research. Advice, examples, and exercises are provided for undertaking literature searches involving both wide and close readings. Instruction on how to do a critical literature review, how to annotate your bibliography, and how to review articles are also included.

Now, after having contextualised critical thinking historically, introduced reflective journaling, discussed the role of logic, process of critique and analysis, and reflected upon the relationship of reading, writing, and thinking, of teaching and learning, Chapter 6 shows how all of this combines to form a mode of thinking and working I like to call 'creative criticality'. In order for this to be possible, we need to take 'fallow time', a vital part of the practice of any writer, whether student or professional, novelist or scholar: stop, draw breath, and take the time you need to think and reflect, quietly, soberly, and methodically so as, in due course, to make discerning judgements from among the 'mess of information' (Marshall 2013) that dominates this day and age. Advice is provided in this chapter to foster strong rest-and-study habits, including time-management tips – some of which may seem at first glance to be counterintuitive, and which make an argument against some of the advice often proposed by time-management 'gurus'. Chapter 6 concludes by linking notions of mindfulness with the broader cultural and political purposes of critical thinking, that is, of becoming – following Barnett (2000) – a 'critical being', and how everyday criticality comes into play in academic and professional contexts.

Chapter 7 proposes practical ways to develop one's own scholarly voice in academic writing, that is, how to write well *and* encourage a strong individual voice – because good style is not just a matter of buffing up mediocre prose. The reason that a text isn't working is often to do with the fact that the writer is either unclear on what they mean or unwilling to write what they mean clearly. The latter is often based on a sense of writerly insecurity. Exercises are provided to help deal with these problems. Chapter 7 then examines ideas developed so far about the profound connections between reading critically and writing persuasively. Following Iris Vardi's (2012) fascinating research on the role of referencing as a critical thinking tool, ways to transform your use of sources into a highly workable engagement with research material are explored in some detail.

Chapters 8 and 9 deal with both the theory and the mechanics of persuasion. Chapter 8 begins by asking why it is important to be able to write persuasively. It then explains and contextualises rhetorical techniques, linking traditional forms with contemporary critical writing practices. It also discusses ways of creating a credible writerly persona, and shows how the presentation of authorial 'character' can enable or disable an argument, and why a failure to maintain intellectual integrity is likely to mean losing the trust of your readers. Rhetorical strategies are dealt with in detail and potential stylistic pitfalls are highlighted in activities which are playful but intellectually rigorous.

Chapter 9 is concerned with rhetoric also, but here we consider how the persuasiveness of essays can be increased by taking a storytelling approach. It emphasises the peculiar sociability of academic discourse: it always takes place in the context of research by others. In this sense it is conversational, so it makes sense to become aware of aspects of narrative style that can be transferred to an academic context. Some of the advice and exercises that follow employ devices that are both critical and conversational, such as metacommentary – the creation of a parallel subtext that runs with your line of argument, clarifying your main points – and invoking 'imaginary friends' (or combative enemies if you prefer!) as you write. Many of the examples and exercises in this chapter will involve using stylistic strategies borrowed from fiction, which can be useful in strengthening the persuasiveness of your scholarly writing by augmenting your rhetorical clout.

There are certain conditions under which many writers work which are sometimes overlooked in texts on academic writing. These are doubt and uncertainty. Both are essential to the critical thinker, as we'll see in Chapter 10. This chapter consists almost entirely of practical exercises that highlight divergent or experimental writing genres and styles, ending the book by looking at ways that playfulness and doubt can enrich both the writing process and the results.

Everyday Criticality and Thinking Well

Chapter overview

This chapter will:

- Survey some of the main theories of critical thinking throughout history, so as to arrive at a working definition
- Focus on select critical thinking theories and practice
- Consider ways to develop critical strength and, conversely, to ruin it
- Provide exercises towards enhancing critical skills.

There is no fixed definition of critical thinking. There are scholars who dislike the idea of attempting to find a generic 'definition' at all. Yet some embrace it and also suggest attributes that a critical thinker exhibits; some will stress traits that another authority on the subject might understate – the emphases vary. There are respected proponents of critical thinking in universities who present it simply as a means of sorting what is true from what is false – looking at it as 'the art of being right'. This is a definition that I see as problematic. While critical thinking is a truth-seeking activity, to describe it this way evokes a level of competitiveness at odds with the spirit of enquiry. It also seems to oversimplify it, implying that criticality begins and ends with analytical work, when it also involves reflection (including self-reflection) and needs to be applicable to the workaday world. This book sees criticality as a mental attitude that can be used to guide both specialised and everyday thinking – far more than a utilitarian argumentation tool or a simple skill set. While the ability to think critically will certainly improve academic results, that's just the tip of the iceberg.

This first chapter locates what we now think of as critical thinking within its historical context. I've chosen notables from a range of disciplines and backgrounds, but the possible list is vast and this one little chapter is no 'catalogue of critical thinkers throughout history'. It simply includes an outline, or survey, that highlights some of those that this writer considers important, and whose work contributes to how we understand and practice critical thinking. Most of the exemplars included possess particular cognitive traits other than critical ability – creativity, imagination, and intellectual sympathy for instance – making these people truly original thinkers. As I briefly mentioned in the introduction to this book, a point that is sometimes overlooked in texts on critical thinking is that it is but one aspect of thinking *well*.

This chapter also considers what is involved in improving critical skills in a very practical sense, specifically in today's world, and provides exercises or intellectual games that clarify notions of critical thinking and strengthen critical acumen.

Please note, before you continue reading, I suggest that you arm yourself with a pencil, because as you read it will be useful for you to take note of any particular details that you think might go towards your own working concept of critical thinking. As some readers may not have a great deal of background in the concept, below are some ideas that will help. Some emphasise its scholarly aspects, others its emancipatory possibilities or social relevance. There are also more definitions and conceptions on page 11. The notes you make now will help you in an exercise suggested towards the end of the chapter.

Author	Critical thinking
John Dewey (1933, p. 118)	'Active, persistent, and careful consideration of any belief or supposed form of knowledge in the light of the grounds that support it and the further conclusions to which it tends.'
Peter Facione (cited in 'Critical Thinking on the Web' 2007, n.p.)	'The ability to properly construct and evaluate arguments.'
The Critical Thinking Community, criticalthinking.org	'Critical thinking is that mode of thinking – about any subject, content, or problem – in which the thinker improves the quality of his or her thinking by skillfully analyzing, assessing, and reconstructing it … It entails effective communication and problem-solving abilities, as well as a commitment to overcome our native egocentrism and sociocentrism.'
Sarah Benesch (1993, p. 546)	'A search for the social, historical, and political roots of conventional knowledge and an orientation to transform learning and society.'
Simon Gieve (1998, p. 126)	'For students to think critically, they must be able to "examine the reasons for their actions, their beliefs, and their knowledge claims, requiring them to defend themselves and question themselves, their peers, their teachers, experts, and authoritative texts".'
John McPeck (cited in Seigel and Carey 1989, n.p.)	'Critical thinking requires the judicious use of skepticism, tempered by experience, such that it is productive of a more satisfactory solution to, or insight into, the problem at hand.'

A necessarily (very) brief survey of critical exemplars

Classical Greece

One of the earliest and most compelling, but little known, figures in 5th-century Greek philosophical dialogue was Aspasia of Miletus. We only know of Aspasia through secondary sources, yet her distinction as a philosopher and as an orator is cited in Plato, Xenophon, Cicero, Athenaeus, and Plutarch (Glenn 1994). Although, like Socrates, she recorded none of her thoughts for posterity, there is evidence that not only was she Pericles' political adviser, but also a teacher of Socrates himself (Henry 1995). Socrates is recognised as an exemplar of rationality, critiquing ideas, drawing distinctions, and encouraging others to do the same. Socratic questioning is a critical thinking tool, and also a teaching method used as a device in classrooms to discourage adherence to unfounded or misconceived ideas, and to encourage students' reasoning faculties. A Socratic dialogue as categorised by Richard Paul could include:

1. questions geared to clarify (achieved by asking why or how)
2. interrogating assumptions
3. evidentiary enquiries (e.g. asking for examples or analogies)
4. questions that require consideration of alternative views or perspectives
5. invitations to examine implications and/or consequences of particular assumptions.

Below is an example of an exchange between 'Anna' and 'Bella' that attempts to use Socratic techniques to complexify a statement that Anna uncritically accepts as true. So as to encourage 'Anna' to engage more carefully with the ideas and possibly even rethink her proposition, 'Bella' tries to focus the discussion by asking questions that will invite consideration of the broader implications of Anna's original and very large claim, and to summarise the discussion at intervals for the sake of clarity.

"**Anna (states her position):** Man-made objects are inferior to the products of nature."

"**Bella (expresses curiosity with a question):** Why do you say that?"

"**Anna (now needs to explain why she thinks natural goods are better than synthetic goods):** Because nature has an elemental wisdom that seeks balance. Humans have selfish desires that throw us off balance. So we can't create things that are perfectly balanced, like nature can. That is why nature, and its works, are essentially superior to humans, and our works."

"**Bella (focuses on a detail – an important one – so that A has to start examining her assumptions):** That's an interesting proposition. I'd never thought of nature having 'wisdom'."

"**A (has probably never doubted this claim, and expresses her certainty):** It is self-evident."

"**B (asks for that evidence):** Can you give me some examples of the wisdom of nature?"

"**A (supplies what she considers evidence of nature's wisdom):** The tides are guided by the moon. The seasons follow a cycle of life. You know the sun will rise each morning."

"**B (questions A's terms of reference, inviting her to reconsider her claim):** Is this actually wisdom, or patterns of natural cycles?"

"**A (backs up her position, yet arguably fails to demonstrate how nature is 'wise'):** These natural cycles enable the existence of life on the planet."

"**B (concedes a point so as not to be arrogant or to cause A to become overly defensive, then asks a question geared to clarify how this can be considered 'wisdom'):** It is true that natural cycles enable life on Earth. But I'm still not convinced that that is the same as wisdom. Wisdom is often considered to be a human attribute, based on thought rather than instinct. Can you say more about what wisdom is, and why nature has it but people do not?"

"**A (is quite articulate in addressing B's question, yet her reasoning may still be flawed):** When I say 'wisdom', I am speaking figuratively. I mean that what is natural is not affected by the pettiness of humanity. In nature, there is no desire to win, to control, to overcome a perceived enemy. Nature just *is*. And therefore the products of nature are superior."

"B (makes a further evidentiary enquiry): For example?"

"A attempts to defend her position with a rhetorical question): Vegetation, animals, rivers ... how can these be faulted?"

"B (now requires A to consider alternative views or perspectives): I cannot fault them. But there is also a lot to be said for unnatural objects produced by human agency, like medicine for curing natural diseases, or knives for pruning natural fruit trees to help them thrive, or human impulses like the love a mother feels for her child that drives her to protect him."

"A: There is virtue in these things, but they can also be used for evil purposes."

"B (asks another question geared to clarify): Can you be more specific?"

"A: Poison instead of remedy, killing rather than pruning, taking advantage of love through bribery and blackmail. Nature doesn't do that. As I said, once a human comes into the equation, corruption follows. It is what we *do*. Look, there's crime, there's war, there's betrayal, there's ..."

"B (attempts to summarise the ideas explored so far for the sake of clarity): Just a minute. Slow down. Let me just try and organise the ideas we've covered: Nature is (figuratively) wise. Humans are essentially corrupt – or at least corruptible. Therefore the products of humans will be inferior to natural ones. But while it's probably fair to say that human actions can be, and often are, tainted by selfish desires – I do agree with that statement – does it follow that humans will inevitably corrupt goodness?"

"A: It is inevitable, because of human nature."

"B (now leads A into territory where she'll have to question certain assumptions she's made): Are you saying that humans, too, are natural?"

"A: I thought you might say something like that. But it is natural for human beings to intend to hurt for selfish reasons. Nature – beyond humans – does not set out to cause pain or damage."

"B (now asks A to consider alternative perspectives): I take your point. Yet, if you attribute 'nature' to humans, then surely our actions, even our bad intentions or 'corruptions' too, might be conceived of as part of the natural order of things?"

"A: Yes, but human nature is profoundly flawed."

"B (persists by continuing to question, never laying down the law, but 'leading'): Still, within nature? That is, humans too are part of the natural world."

"A: I see what you're trying to do. You're trying to demonstrate that nature too is capable of corruption, and is therefore imperfect."

"B (requires Anna to acknowledge complexities she has previously overlooked): Partly. I'm suggesting that rather than an either/or argument ..."

"A: ... Nature is capable of corruption, and humans are capable of goodness ..."

You may have noticed that 'Bella' has tried to voice the thoughts that 'Anna's' inner critic might well be asking her.

Exercise 1.1 Socratic dialogue

Experiment with this form of questioning either alone or with a colleague. I've suggested an opening statement and follow-up, dealing with similar subject matter but starting from a different position. However, you might like to choose an argument from your own discipline with which you're already familiar.

Clive: The products of nature must necessarily be imperfect.

Derek: That's a very large claim.

C: I don't think so. It is self-evident that nature is a blind force, without reason; therefore man-made objects will always have greater utility and grace, because of the human intention that drives their creation.

D: …

Although Socrates is held up as one of the greatest models of rationality and we still use his pedagogic techniques today, there is evidence that he was also irrational. He embraced poetry, myths, and dreams, and James Hans (cited in Miller 2008, pp. 299–303) insists that 'these irrational voices help acquaint Socrates with patterns, rhythms, and contexts that escape rational scrutiny'. Hans points out that before Socrates would begin to analyse an event or an idea critically, he would allow himself an intuitive reaction; only after this would he attempt an interpretation. (This sort of intellectual sympathy is explored in Chapter 4 as a means of getting at the truth of any given situation.) Socrates accorded respect to aesthetic responses, hunches, and instances of sudden insightfulness as well as purely intellectual ones. These cannot be termed 'critical', as they defy logic, but they contribute to understanding ideas and phenomena so that it becomes possible to arrive at truths that might escape purely rational analysis.

Medieval era

Hildegard of Bingen, 12th-century philosopher, natural scientist, and theologian, is thought to be 'the first Western thinker to articulate a philosophical theory that woman is not a deficient form of man but … a distinct type of human being' (Dragseth 2016, p. 4). Truly a groundbreaking analysis for its time! She often referred to herself as uneducated, although this comment is now thought to be an expression of modesty, as her writings demonstrate knowledge of Augustine's ideas as well as those of other accredited and invariably male thinkers. The extraordinary breadth of her writing skills, which ranged from music to drama, to scientific texts on the classification of stones and herbs, to theological speculation, to language games, to the philosophy of psychology, reveals a genius unparalleled by a woman and matched by very few men up to the 12th century (Allen 1997).

A little later, Thomas Aquinas (1225–1274), though arguably less radical in his analyses, emphasised the centrality of reason, insisted upon systematically cultivated reasoning, and endeavoured to address any questioning of his ideas regarding this process as 'a necessary stage in developing [those ideas]' (Paul et al. 1997, n.p.). This attitude of responsiveness is an essential critical attribute that acknowledges the potential power of reason in progressing ideas, rather than allowing oneself to be hindered by closed-mindedness or dogmatism.

In 1997 – post-medieval certainly, but bear with me – Charles Mills (cited in Weiss 2009, p. 30) introduced the notion of an 'epistemology of ignorance' (which he related to racism, but may be transferred to multiple contexts). He claimed that this ignorance comes into being through 'structured blindnesses and opacities, misunderstanding, misrepresentation, evasion, and self-deception'. Conversely, critical thinkers need to challenge assumptions, query opaque statements, and insist upon explanations and evidentiary backup for any claims made. An extremely early historical example of this kind of thinking is exemplified by Christine de Pizan (1364–1430). In her *Book of the City of Ladies*, Pizan challenges the pervasive acceptance of female inferiority in an entirely systematic fashion. Firstly, the ignorance of the questioner (herself) is humbly established. A personified voice of reason points out that she has stunted her intellect even to the point where, after 'thinking deeply [and] … judg[ing] impartially and in good conscience' she has then cowered in the face of authority. 'Lady Reason' insists that it is in fact possible for her, and therefore women generally, to respond to this fallaciousness by contradicting and ridiculing it. Remedies which sound very much like contemporary critical thinking strategies are proposed, including 'self knowledge, enhanced interpretive skills and … skepticism' with regard to authority (Weiss 2009, p. 34).

Renaissance

Four examples of writers and philosophers of this time of burgeoning creative and critical thinking are Tullia d'Aragona, Michel de Montaigne, Francis Bacon, and Niccolo Machiavelli. D'Aragona's 'Dialogue on the Infinity of Love' moves from a discussion of the nature of love, to speculations about communication, to an analysis of the processes and techniques of philosophic discourse itself. In the dialogue, she critiques the essentialist assumption of woman's mental deficiencies, including her perceived inability to engage in speculative reason (now understood to be a hallmark of critical thinking). The dialogic struggle between the two participants is a discourse on a discourse, effectively representing the critically reflective process of 'thinking about your thinking while you are thinking in order to make your thinking better' (Paul et al. 1997, n.p.).

Michel de Montaigne's personal and philosophical essays and, in particular, his scepticism had a profound effect upon the work of later philosophers, such as Descartes – to whom I'll refer again in a moment. Montaigne shocked his readers in several of his essays by pointing out the contingent nature of cultural belief systems. For example, he wondered why one would consider it a mark of cultural superiority for men to pee standing up? Or why is it socially acceptable to condescend to those who do not embrace the practice of burying one's dead, but believe that other ways of disposing of the dead are more respectful – like cannibalism? Montaigne was witty and playful as well as critical, and his criticality was highly reflective.

Championing empirical study of the world, Francis Bacon was concerned that people tend to be misled by what he termed 'idols', or habitual ways of thinking that prevent us from observing the truth of phenomena. His *The Advancement of Learning* 'could be considered one of the earliest texts in critical thinking', according to Paul, Elder, and Bartell of the Foundation for Critical Thinking.

> For myself, I found that I was fitted for nothing so well as for the study of Truth; as having a mind **nimble and versatile** enough to catch the resemblances of things … and at the same time steady enough to fix and **distinguish their subtler differences**; as being gifted by nature with **desire to seek, patience to doubt, fondness to meditate, slowness to assert, readiness to consider, carefulness to dispose and set in order**; and as being a man that neither affects what is new nor admires what is old, and that **hates every kind of imposture**. (Bacon 2011, p. 85, emphases mine)

Note the similarities between the emboldened and italicised attributes Bacon claims, and terms from relatively recent consideration of critical traits in Peter Facione's (2013) 'Critical thinking: What it is and why it counts'.

Critical thinking: past and present	
1603 traits	**2013 traits**
nimble and versatile	flexible
distinguish ... subtler differences	distinguishing a main idea from subordinate ideas
desire to seek	habitually inquisitive
slowness to assert	prudent in making judgements
readiness to consider	willing to reconsider; fair-minded in evaluation
carefulness to dispose and set in order	clear about issues; orderly in complex matters; diligent in seeking relevant information; focused in inquiry
hates every kind of imposture	[which requires] honesty in facing one's own biases, prejudices, stereotypes, or egocentric tendencies

Two other aspects mentioned by Bacon, but less remarked upon by Facione, are:

- 'Patience to doubt.' This is a prerequisite for the critical thinker as explored by Jennifer Hecht (2003) in her *Doubt: A History.* She traces a line from Classical Greek to Cartesian scepticism to modern scientific empiricism, with doubt featuring as the departure point for the critically minded enquirer on their path to understanding. Nicholas Burbules (2000) embraces the possibilities of doubt as an opportunity to learn. The process of arriving at reasoned judgements is initiated by a question, a dispute, a contestable notion – or by doubt. Peter Elbow (2008, p. 1) describes critical thinking as 'the disciplined practice of trying to be as skeptical and analytical as possible with every idea we encounter. By trying hard to doubt ideas, we can discover hidden contradictions, bad reasoning, or other weaknesses in them – especially in the case of ideas that seem true or attractive.'
- 'Fondness to meditate' might be translated into contemporary English with the phrase, 'pleasure in reflection', an aspect I'll say more about in due course.

In case any readers are now equating critical traits with virtue, which sometimes happens, I'd like to point out that critical thinking is 'not synonymous with good thinking' (Facione 2013, p. 26), nor is it necessarily meritorious; it may not always lead to socially beneficial actions. Criticality needs reflection, and to take on board ethical considerations. When restricted to purely objective exploration and analysis of concepts it can become highly problematic when translated into action. Scholars with redoubtable reputations for critical skill have certainly been known to acquiesce in or even take on active roles within totalitarian and corrupt regimes.

An example of a thinker of exemplary critical skill and one of the most influential of the Renaissance writers was Niccolo Machiavelli, now thought of as a paragon of political manipulation. His *The Prince* is a guide on how to take and keep control of nations. Machiavelli exhibited an entirely cynical view of humanity. Here is a sample from *The Prince*: 'a prudent ruler cannot, and must not, honour his word when it places him at a disadvantage.' Compassion and kindness will ruin you, according to Machiavelli; a ruler must learn to be duplicitous, deceitful, ruthless, in order to maintain power. Machiavelli critiqued the commonly held notion of the time that political leaders needed to legitimise their power base by exhibiting moral sense, and argued that the ability to acquire, exercise, and maintain control required the use of coercive force, advocating a kind of realpolitik wherein whoever has the power, regardless of their moral fibre, has the right to authority. This may be why some scholars read *The Prince* as satire, proposing that Machiavelli was attempting to reveal the calculation, corruption, and hypocrisy of those in political control in Italy, the Medici family. The book is certainly a bitter and sardonic tract. Other readings insist that he was trying to curry favour with the Medicis by showing that their iniquitous intrigues were justified and that they were doing an excellent job.

17th and 18th centuries

During these centuries an extraordinary number of intellectual innovators were produced. Rene Descartes' (1596–1650) method was to doubt perceived truths derived from the apparent evidence of the senses and from culturally accepted assumptions, and even the process of reasoning itself. He took the position of scepticism to the greatest of extremes, even raising the possibility of a deceptive god – a potentially life-threatening tack to take in his day. Notably, Descartes also allowed intuition to come into his process – as Socrates is purported to have done and, later, Plato, who insisted that intuition was a superior human faculty. Descartes' famous *cogito ergo sum* (I think, therefore I am) 'is not merely an inference from the activity of thinking to the existence of an agent which performs that activity' (Philosophy Britannica). For him, first-person experience too has its own logic.

Thomas Hobbes (1588–1679) and John Locke (1632–1704) made enormous steps in social contract theory; Isaac Newton (1643–1727) radically changed people's understanding of the reality we inhabit so that today critical thinkers hold that the world can only be understood by means of careful, evidence-based reasoning (Paul et al. 1997). The formidable but rarely cited political thinker, writer, and rhetorician Mary Astell (1666–1731) was working on, among other tracts, *A Serious Proposal to the Ladies, for the Advancement of their True and Greater Interest*. This book included suggestions such as the possibility of women's career options being extended beyond motherhood or religious service. Not only this, in recent times she has been described as '"a forerunner of [philosopher] David Hume" … [who] … provided "not only the first but perhaps the most sustained contemporary critique of … Locke's *Two Treatises*" and that she "combined Christian faith with a sophisticated rationalist construction in a system that paralleled [Rene] Descartes's 'Discourse on Method'"'

(Duran, 2000, Springborg, 1995, and Smith 1982, cited in Weiss 2009, pp. 140–141).

Voltaire (1694–1778), poet, author of neo-classical drama, historian, and philosopher, who is best remembered for his works of social engagement, wrote satirical critiques of religion and advocated the separation of church and state. Voltaire's success is attributed to a great extent to the fact that he addressed his tracts against authority to the people. ('God is not on the side of the heavy battalions, but of the best shots') and because of this, some propose that he actually invented the concept of popular opinion. Armed with irony and sardonicism (among other rhetorical techniques to be discussed in Chapters 7 and 8) and supported by careful critical reason and scepticism, he addressed the citizenry rather than the rulers. John Ralston Saul's *Voltaire's Bastards* (1993) refers to ways in which Voltaire questioned the seemingly impregnable logic of the ancient regime and held up to the public gaze the inconsistencies and egoistic hypocrisies of monarchy and the clergy. However – and this is a *big* however – Saul concludes making his case with a sting: 'So a new sceptical logic was born, liberated from the weight of historical precedent and therefore *even more self-serving than the logic which had gone before*' (emphasis mine).

Taking a moment to reflect

According to Saul, Voltaire heralded an era where different controllers of knowledge became the new elite: those who manage the organisation and distribution of information. 'Rationally organised expertise' (1993, p. 8), in Saul's view, became the new ideology. He wrote this twenty-five years ago, and the situation has intensified since then in our 'information society', and thus is well worth mentioning here. Today, profit-oriented global platform companies dominate the market, and through it, cultural and social life worldwide, enjoying ubiquitous regulatory powers able 'to connect, portray the world around us, express our political allegiances and even forge our visions for the future' (Couldry and Rodriguez 2016). Our 'knowledge culture' is controlled not by royalty or religious leaders, but by technocrats guided by expedience and pragmatism, or what is thought of as reason – at the expense of other essential attributes like intuition, intellectual sympathy, and reflectiveness.

The sort of critical thinking we use in analytical work provides an intellectual structure that helps us to arrange our thoughts and to argue with clarity and coherence. I hope that reading this book will help you to hone your critical reasoning and to use it confidently, but it is also essential to recognise that it is not a replacement for other faculties. Well-rounded criticality which goes beyond instrumental reasoning embraces reflectivity; it cultivates the ability to recognise our habitual thought patterns and prejudices. Strategies for self-reflection are dealt with in detail in the next chapter, but for now I want to stress that reflection in general is part of the critical process whereby we transform mere data to knowledge through understanding it, and recognising ways in which it is or might be translated into actions of benefit to others and to ourselves.

Reflections on critical reflection

Robert Ennis (2015, p. 31) includes reflection in his 'conception' of critical thinking as 'reasonable, reflective thinking that is focused on deciding what to believe or what to do', as does McPeck (1981, p. 8): 'The propensity and skill to engage in an activity with *reflective skepticism*'; Paul (1989, p. 213): 'the art of *thinking about your thinking while you're thinking* in order to make your thinking more clear, precise, accurate, relevant, consistent, and fair'; Elkins (1999) – while expressing a certain ambivalence regarding the use of the term 'critical thinking' – nevertheless claims that: 'The critical thinking oriented teacher tries to focus on what it means to think well, to think in the most productive, careful, disciplined, and *reflective* way possible' (emphases mine).

Reflection, finally, is a way of addressing the gap between rationalism and more humanistic approaches to criticality.

Hindrances to critical thinking

It is actually incredibly difficult to let go of accustomed ways of seeing the world and to appraise phenomena with fresh, uncluttered vision, which is why refining critical skills is a lifelong project requiring a good deal of active intellectual exercise. What follows is a consideration of some of the traps to avoid. After this comes an exercise in disengaging from habitual ways of using one of the most fundamental parts of the English language: the verb 'to be'. We'll then look briefly at Richard Paul's 'imperfections' of thought, with particular emphasis on the implications for the 21st-century networked learning environment.

Confirmation bias

Ignoring conflicting points of view leads to narrowing rather than broadening the mind and to bad scholarship, yet probably one of the commonest hindrances to critical thinking is that of confirmation bias, also referred to as 'myside bias', or the tendency to accept ideas and information that agree with our pre-existing beliefs, prejudices, and viewpoints. Evidence that agrees with our position and that shows we are 'right' is very seductive. It is also increasingly hard to avoid, when website algorithms predict our preferences based on our search histories and show us what it seems we would like to see, effectively alienating us from disagreeable news or ideas and isolating us in our own individual ideological 'bubbles'. Confirmation bias is a cousin of another hindrance to critical thinking:

Overestimation of our own intellectual skills and powers of fair judgement

This is a trap for many, but particularly for those of us who are accustomed to being proven right or to attracting the respect of others. In other words, it can be the pitfall of the powerful.

Being unwilling to query authoritative sources

This sort of problem arises for people who are unsure of their own capabilities, or who are accustomed to following the guidance of others. But while inexperienced students, for instance, are unlikely to be in a position to challenge an expert, they might still raise questions in the spirit of enquiry! This sort of inquisitive stance is perfectly appropriate for a learner.

The question of to be (or not to be)

The premise here is that changing accustomed ways of expressing ourselves can have the effect of changing habitual perceptions, and conduct us towards more original thinking. Following Korzybski's 'E-prime' system (of English without the verb, 'to be'), David Bourland (2004) presents an unusual perspective for dealing with problems in critical thinking that can arise when this particular verb is overused – which is common. Bourland suggests semantic exercises in reconfiguring sentences that depend on 'to be'. At this point, however, you may well be asking: What on earth could possibly be wrong with 'I am' (he is, you are, etc.)?

Critical thinking theorists have pointed out that it conveys a sense of permanence and certainty that can lead us to make premature or simplistic judgements. This is best explained through examples, so here is a fundamental 'for instance': You might introduce yourself by saying, 'I am a researcher'. But this doesn't really say much about you or what you do. It abstracts your profession and simplifies you; you've been abridged, abbreviated, truncated!

Exercise 1.2 'What do you do?'

Try to respond to the question, 'What do you do', without using the verb 'to be'. You might come up with a range of formulations, all of which lead your interlocutor to have a better understanding of you and of how you spend your time. Each should be no more than one sentence in length.

After you've had a go, look at my suggested responses – but *do* try it yourself first.

(And the same instruction applies to the exercise following this one.)

Possible answers:

- I read a lot and write essays.
- I'm really interested in […] and spend most of my time studying it.
- After quitting my job as a […] I enrolled in a postgraduate research degree.
- As a child, my mum introduced me to books and reading and I found I loved both, so that's what I do: research.

Do you see what happened when you avoided 'to be'? Where the 'I am' form fixed you in time and bound you to a static state of existence, the other versions did not. And most importantly, in order to rewrite the simple sentence, you had to click yourself out of automatic, taken-for-granted ways of describing yourself, and click into 'critical mode'. Axing 'to be' required you to be inventive – to think in a slightly different way about a simple question – and also to communicate a fact with greater precision and clarity. Such a strategy is likely to improve the quality of conversation all round!

Bourland further notes the impact of 'to be' on writing and talking about people, things, concepts, and beliefs:

Exercise 1.3 From the grammatical to the philosophical – further experiments in absenting 'to be'

Reformulate the following questions or assertions without 'to be'. You'll find when you do this that the psychological or ethical implications will change; your statements may also become more reasonable or humane by means of this little 'critical turn' than when using the abstract versions that use 'to be'. Again, suggestions follow, but try on your own first.

- What is woman, and what is man?

(Implication: Absolute definitions of sex and gender exist, and you can articulate them.)

- I am a failure.

(Implication: And therefore I will remain so. It is my nature.)

- He is a do-gooder.

(Implications: He's unrealistic and/or a bleeding heart, and/or can't make the necessary tough decisions … and others, none of them good.)

- I am just doing my job.

(Implication: I can't be blamed – my actions are not my responsibility.)

- What you are saying is unclear.

(Implication: You're at fault, or your idea is at fault.)

Possible reformulations:

- What attributes absolutely characterise woman and man?

(This version allows for nuance that the 'to be' version lacks.)

- I have not succeeded.

(This allows for the possibility that I may succeed another time. The horrible 'internal instruction' – the sort that can ruin a life – becomes redundant. Avoiding the certainty of 'I am' exempts the failure condition from implications of permanence. 'Is' sets things in concrete; without 'is', you can move on.)

- He tries to do good.

(The meaning has become quite different now. A do-gooder becomes someone who attempts to live a moral life.)

- I don't feel able to break the rules/I consider myself obliged to do what I'm asked.

(The speaker now has agency and must take responsibility for the decision rather than relying on an abstract notion to exempt them.)

- I don't understand.

(Blame is removed, and the conversation opens up. The speaker admits to requiring further elucidation.)

Another interesting feature of 'E-prime' is that it makes it more difficult to use the passive voice. As will be discussed in later chapters, while the passive in academic writing is meant to encourage objectivity, it can also be misused to obfuscate, to evade the responsibility of making contentious claims, or to veer away from concluding an essay with a judgement – when judgement, after all, is the end result of the critical process.

Exercise 1.4 Maybe 'more research needs to be done', but in the meantime be brave enough to state your intelligent, research-based conclusion, however provisional …

Think of an alternative to the rather escapist phrase, 'more research needs to be done', as if you're writing a conclusion to an essay. Base your response on some problematic issue that you're familiar with in your own field, so that you *are* in fact in a position to make an informed judgement. For instance, here's one from mine: *There is no absolute definition of critical thinking and therefore no simple formula to follow in order to cultivate it. Developing criticality is not a simple industrial 'competency' – not a problem with a ready solution – but an ongoing process of disciplined reasoning and reflective scepticism.*

Now, your turn:

'Imperfections of thought'

A director of the Center for Critical Thinking at Sonoma State University, California, Richard Paul (1990) identifies what he refers to as 'imperfections of thought', all of which stand in the way of critical thought. Below is a list of some of these, plus others of my own.

Exercise 1.5 Imperfections and perfections

Firstly, decide what the opposite of each condition might be. That's the easy bit. Then, list some authors in your field who you think exemplify most of the 'perfections', and why.

Imperfections and impediments	Perfections to aspire to	Who exemplifies such perfections and why?
Vagueness		
Illogicality		
Superficiality		
Triviality		
Bias		
Unexamined assumptions		
Inconsistency		
Ignorance		
A closed mind		

Paul was writing in 1990, and since then the world has changed dramatically, and so has higher education. It is global, massified, often conducted at a distance from the university, and enhanced (or debilitated, depending on your point of view) by new technologies. We now inhabit an informational environment of ceaseless data flows that has largely obliterated geographical distance, vastly accelerated the pace of history, and is changing the very nature of human relationships. The tides of data are unremitting and many people are constantly immersed in this oceanic inundation – I have students who acknowledge that they are *never* offline while awake. To disconnect would cause distressing levels of FOMO. While much of the information is important, fascinating, and some of it is reliable, plenty is superficial and trivial. Checking each opinion, claim, fact, or factoid as it breaks upon our consciousness is impossible. The academic research environment is very much a part of a networked culture, at the heart of the virtual economy of ideas.

However, while you – like me – might conduct much of your research online, use social media, rely heavily on email correspondence, and if you are a teacher, run 'blended learning' courses that combine face-to-face and online teaching and learning practices and so forth, we have to remind ourselves that these resources are only tools, whether devices or repositories of data. We may purchase mind-mapping and critical thinking software ('Reason!Able', or 'Rationale', for instance – probably being superseded as I write) which claim to assist in organising arguments and assist in complex reasoning. We may subscribe to CorporateTrainingMaterials.com, which provides 'fully customizable course kits for trainers' of critical thinkers – and there will be many more updates and new programmes by the time of publication of this book. Recent research, however, indicates that overly enthusiastic use of electronic devices can kill both critical and creative ability in students from elementary through to higher tertiary levels.

Even such a simple process as note-taking on a keyboard, according to Mueller and Openheimer (2014), tends to impede rather than enhance comprehension and retention of information. Taking notes by hand can be slower – and that's the point. The slower pace assists learning and encourages analytical depth. It takes longer, but you'll be retaining more. Keying becomes a sort of false way of economising on time. Also, memory of textual content is improved by physically turning the pages of a book; in fact, tests have shown that students who used e-readers received examination scores that were significantly lower than those who read three-dimensional books. Using screens tends to result in fewer annotations and less rereading, both of which are essential if one is to attempt a critical appraisal of a text. My point is: if you want to increase active, engaged reading, electronic devices – regardless of their convenience – are not necessarily superior and can in fact be counterproductive.

We have to attend to our social media habits. As Alex Soojung-Kim Pang, a researcher at a Silicon Valley think tank, puts it, 'connection is inevitable, but distraction is a choice'. Overly enthusiastic online activity can disturb and fragment our attention, and it takes up time and attention that could be spent in reflection or in rest, both of which we need to do to sustain healthy neurological functioning. Chapter 6 provides advice on how to use rest as fallow time where ideas are allowed to gestate, but in the meantime, if you are reading this book because you want to improve your critical skills – and given the title, you probably are – then it is important also to cultivate an approach to information technologies that enhances, rather than debilitates, your attention and ability to focus.

Digital communication, with its speediness, expedience, and immediacy gives the impression that we have knowledge at out fingertips, available 24/7. All we need to do is click. This is quite untrue. What we have at our fingertips is information. Data. In order for information and data to become knowledge, we need to understand it; understanding is the real meaning of knowledge.

Exercise 1.6 Post Enlightenment to contemporary critical thinkers

In (relatively) recent history the world has undergone radical shifts in political philosophy, some of which you will be familiar with, some not. In this field, Mary Wollstonecraft (1759–1797) is an exemplar; in economic theory the paradigmatic figure is of course Karl Marx (1818–1883); in science and philosophy, Charles Darwin (1809–1882); psychology and educational reform, John Dewey 1859–1952); political theory, Hannah Arendt (1906–1975); social theory, Simone de Beauvoir (1908–1986). In order for each of these thinkers to have made such revolutionary changes within their fields and in the world, it was necessary for them to question tenets which at the time were accepted as unquestionable.

Choose three writers or thinkers you admire from your area of study. Briefly outline their contributions in terms of what you consider to be specifically *critical* practice – based on what you already know and what has been outlined so far in this chapter and the introduction of this book.

Thinker 1:

Thinker 2:

Thinker 3:

Conclusion

This chapter presented critical thinking as a central component of thinking well, supported by discussion of a range of concepts and methods available to assist us in developing a critical attitude of mind. We considered critical thinking as a means of working towards understanding information and ideas, and linked criticality to ethical principles that might be used to guide critical action in the everyday, as well as in an academic context. A very brief survey of attitudes towards critical thought and practice was provided, starting with 5th-century Greece. The suggested critical thinking exercises were generic in nature; those in the following chapters will be more directed. If you take nothing else away with you from this chapter, let it be these five central points. Critical thinking is:

- something that needs to be learned formally, which progresses through ongoing practice
- essential for thinking well, but there are limits to the critical paradigm
- a practice that demands time to reflect
- *not* served well by fragmented attention
- *not* just a theoretical concept or a way of getting better marks, but a way of approaching Socrates' goal of finding out not only how to think well, but how to live well.

Chapter

Critical Reflection

Chapter overview

This chapter covers:

- How and why to develop criticality, including discussion of critical thinking at university and its multiple applications to real-world situations
- Definition of the concept of 'critical being'
- An overview of Ronald Barnett's 'Three Domains' of critical thinking
- The concept of the reflection journal for refining critical skills
- Advice on and examples of how to keep a reflection journal.

> The idea of critical thinking as the defining concept of higher education has to give way to a much larger idea of critical being. (Barnett 1997, p. 171)

As already established, critical thinking provides us with essential tools for analysis and critique which we'll explore further here and in Chapters 3 to 5. More to the point regarding a book concerned with developing criticality, we also need to recognise it as an aspect of thinking well, a multilayered activity linked to creative processes and to what might be referred to as 'intellectual sympathy' – our focus for Chapter 4. For now, I want to consider in detail ways of advancing traits of criticality with a view towards the goals of what Ronald Barnett terms 'critical being'.

What is critical being?

Reasoning ability is connected with self-awareness, and also with an awareness of the wider ramifications of your thinking for your civic and professional life: all your critical skills are integrated into 'critical being'. It means being able to readily ally abstract knowledge acquired through analysis of texts, and ideas in general, with real-world scenarios using intellect, intuition, and imagination – that is, bringing together theory and practice so as to, in Ken Robinson's words, find a 'balance between education and the wider world' (cited in Hartley 2007, p. 198).

The faculty of reason used in textual analysis is part of a set of critical skills, all of which are essential. However, universities have a tendency to focus on just one in particular – the form which deals with gaining discipline-specific knowledge through examining concepts and theories. This approach is insufficient for several reasons. It doesn't necessarily cover the following:

1. Adaptability or inventiveness. At university you may be able to produce a satisfactory critique of a text within a particular discipline, but this is not enough if you want to be able to achieve excellent results and make some kind of social contribution. Recent thinking on the subject emphasises making connections across disciplinary boundaries and 'between generative thinking and critical thinking' (Robinson, cited in Hartley 2007, p. 202). As in life, we need to identify possibilities for different applications of ideas in unfamiliar contexts, to be able to think beyond our immediate areas of expertise. Why? Because the world is in a state of flux. Change is the only constant. In Barnett's words: '[N]othing can be taken for granted ... no frame of understanding or of action can be entertained with any security. It is a world in which we are conceptually challenged, and continually so' (2000, p. 257).

2. Perceptiveness or creativity. In work and life, we all need to be able to think of the right questions to ask about any given situation. That statement sounds like I'm describing something straightforward and simple. I'm not. Imagine you're in a new job or a new flat or have just begun a new relationship – in other words, you're in unfamiliar territory – how are you supposed to know what you need to know in order to make the best decisions you can? Take the example of the new job: Two colleagues who are in disagreement about something you don't yet know terribly much about are giving you contradictory instructions. What questions might you ask in order to decide whose guidance to trust? Or, in a new relationship, how do you think your way through to a decision to trust or not to trust this person? Or, in making a political choice, how do you work out the consequences of supporting this party rather than another?

3. Ethics. This starts with the personal. A true critical thinker – and a brave one at that – would try to get beyond self-interest and egotistic responses to the world by asking questions of herself like, Do I use overly emotive language to get my way, or to persuade people in argument? Do I tend to shut up about issues that I deem important out of fear creating dissent? Do I use my power to manipulate? Those questions apply both to everyday life and to the simpler task of writing essays – not exploiting rhetorical facility and not choosing only safe subjects for research. But more of this later.

I want to conclude this section by emphasising two points. Firstly, we need to balance several levels of criticality, because the cultural, social, and personal consequences of an imbalance can range from being merely ineffectual to being downright dangerous – as will be illustrated. Secondly, as an all-round critical animal you're always casting about for the sort of questions (or 'problem-finding') that will take you beyond the surface of things into territory which is new and fresh. It can actually be pretty exhilarating. It means you're engaging in thinking as an action – also referred to as 'acts of thinking', or 'active thinking'. This connects you with other people and the various different roles, both expected and unexpected, in which you may find yourself. So I hope that this chapter will help to widen your understanding of and ability to use your critical faculties on several levels, rather than limiting yourself to one.

Barnett's 'Three Domains' of critical thinking

CT1. When you're engaged in analytical work – as in writing essays, literature reviews, and reports, this is what you're doing: considering propositions and exploring concepts. We will examine the procedures needed to master this form of critical engagement throughout this book, with an intensive in Chapter 3, as it is a vital aspect of developing critical acumen. But there's also:

CT2. This refers to the internal world – *your* internal world. It's a form of critical thought where you think about your own reactions to the ideas you need to analyse in the CT1 process. It is a mindful practice that helps you to push beyond a purely instrumental approach so that you can become more independent and aware, and more capable of the intellectual flexibility needed in this increasingly complex world.

CT3. This relates very directly to work environments and to the external world in general. It involves active engagement with one's society. You might say that CT3 is the ultimate aim of CT1 and 2.

By the end of this chapter the links between CT1, 2, and 3 should be clear, but let's start by focusing on reflexivity: CT2.

Reflective thinking

Why second things first? CT2 is concerned with *how* we think on an individual level. It makes sense to consider our own intellectual processes early on, as the intellect is a fundamental tool for interpreting phenomena. And to help us use this highly personalised gadget to the best advantage, keeping a reflective journal is very handy indeed. Think of it this way: if you were a builder you'd need to know how to construct your walls so that they are straight and true, so you'd use laser and spirit levels to this end; you'd also need to know how to use a hammer and chisel. And consider for a moment the possibilities for disaster with a nail gun or an electric planer in untutored hands. Texas Chainsaw Massacre? Choose your own splatter movie. The point is, you need to be familiar with your tools – of thought, in this case.

The reflective journal is an ideal place for playing with ideas in an informal way. That is one of its essential functions. It is a *meta*critical tool – that is, as the writer of the journal you become the subject of critique when you begin to ask yourself why you react the way you do to ideas you examine. The importance of such questioning must not be underestimated because it is natural for any of us to favour ideas or information that support beliefs we already hold, and all too easy for our minds to be corralled into a bubble inhabited exclusively by other apparently like-minded souls. This is a phenomenon many readers will know as 'confirmation bias' discussed in Chapter 1, which serves to entrench us ever more deeply in ideology or prejudice – the opposite of criticality.

Metacriticism is criticism of criticism, involving interpretation and judgement. It is one means of coming to a better understanding of how our nature and backgrounds are likely to affect the conclusions we draw about the ideas we come across in our studies, thereby fostering critical awareness.

Reflective writing: the journal. Why do it?

Identifying deficiencies in others' reasoning is so much easier than finding problems in our own. In fact, the latter is utterly impossible without excellent reflective skills and a will to use them. This lies at the heart of critical thinking, a capacity that can only develop over time. Keeping a reflection journal helps to internalise the ongoing process of developing critical awareness, or 'criticality', to train your mind to become more *present*, if you will, to any task to hand, and to articulate what is going on in our internal world. It is a means of improving scholarly practice and 'good thinking' in general.

Journaling helps us become aware of our own predispositions and biases and then act upon this knowledge with a view to reading a text or analysing an idea without prejudice. To paraphrase the *Oxford English Dictionary* definition of metacriticism, it means considering the underlying principles that guide you in your interpretation and judgement of texts, events, concepts. This is why, in the journal, you'll be asking yourself, 'Why do I think what I think about this idea?'

> If when you ask this question you feel at a loss to answer it, try imagining a person who disagrees with your beliefs asking it. This may be counterintuitive, even a little spooky, but it can help you to probe a little deeper. It can also stimulate research to come, if only to prove your point to this disagreeable voice you've conjured up. I think of him as my cranky mate 'John'.   **TIP**

Journal writing forgoes many of the stylistic constraints imposed by more strictly scholarly genres – it's informally written. Think of the journal as an in-between zone or a bridge between diaristic and academic writing. It's an ambivalent interval 'between certainties', where you can think on paper (or the screen) about ideas, make notes about what you think, and then *why* you think you react to ideas the way you do. This may shed some light on how your thoughts may be moulded by your expectations, or your sense of obligation, or your ambitions, background, family, friends, and so on.

Journaling is a creative process that involves musing and sifting through ideas in the first instance, then adds to this a kind of mental detective work, with yourself as the subject of investigation. Some people find they take to both processes like ducks to water – either because it's natural for them to reflect in this way or because they happen to enjoy loosely linking ideas in a playful way. Others don't find it natural, or struggle to figure out their motivations or how personal history affects perceptions.

But once you get underway with journaling, a form which lends itself to experimentation in thinking and writing, it can contribute to the development of academic prose that is as insightful as it is rigorous. In part this is because it encourages you to:

1. Take chances

The journal is, paradoxically, a safe place for taking risks. If you fail to take any risks, there's a danger of getting blocked off from the further learning that only comes with valiant exploration of ideas. Say, for instance, you find that your research uncovers a concept that sparks your imagination, leading you to speculate upon its ramifications, but you're afraid you might have got it wrong, or that your examiner will disagree. I would suggest that you examine it first – in your journal. Link this idea with others you've come across, and of course conduct further research around the subject. Then, if it seems to have legs, include it when you come to writing an essay. In such an essay your stance will be inquisitive rather than authoritative, and that is perfectly fine. After all, a scholar is supposed to enquire. You might even introduce your speculation with a tentative phrase like, 'This may be drawing a long bow, however …' or, 'In this case, one might argue that …'. You don't need to pretend you're the expert when you're not. Just be sure you have the evidentiary backup you need.

2. Be uncomfortable

You have to go out on a limb sometimes, otherwise when it comes to writing essays, dissertations, or theses, your work may end up slavishly following a particular theory, or identifying with a particular ideological stance. This means you won't be able to add anything new to the conversation within your discipline.

Obviously you already know that it is essential to read widely – but vary the reading so that you cover authors whose ideas make you uncomfortable. Don't just read those who support your thesis. From time to time select authors relevant to your field whose arguments may counter those of authors you would automatically look to for support, and explore their ideas and your responses to them in your journal. You may find, paradoxically, that the inclusion of divergent voices in your essays often results in strengthening your own argument. Ways of integrating the opposition effectively to this end will be discussed in Chapter 8.

How to keep a reflection journal

Dedicate a notebook or a file to journaling. My students keep an online journal. The form doesn't matter. The main thing is to make entries *regularly*. I'd recommend you make one entry per week over a term or semester so that you can monitor your development over time. About a page for each entry will do, but if you find you want to write more – and plenty of students and experienced researchers do, once they get underway – then do so.

Don't worry too much about your grammar and style. (Journal entries are *not* essays or reports!) Use the first person, use colloquialisms. Your concern here is not literary elegance, but ideas and your response to them.

A basic template you might follow in your journal

1. Briefly introduce a point raised in a text, lecture, or seminar, or a comment made by another student or colleague. Keep it loose. Give the topic your full attention, that is, don't analyse or critique just yet; instead, save that for the following stages …
2. Reflect upon your response to it. Here is where you ask yourself: Why did I respond to the idea this way? Is it to do with already accepted beliefs or attitudes I hold? Be honest, to the best of your ability.
3. Work this idea or perspective into a synthesis with other theories, texts, or perhaps other lectures.
4. Take into account how your reading, analysis, and reflection might relate to your personal learning process in your particular field.

Under 'Reflect', I wrote: 'Be honest.' It's actually very hard to do in this context. Self-consciousness kicks in. When I started journaling I felt terribly self-conscious. So, in the spirit of disclosure, I'll give you an example from my own early attempts. I wanted to kick-start myself into reflective journaling, so I decided to:

- deal with the self-consciousness by jumping in at the deep end and trying to ignore my automatic self-editor until I'd written at least a short paragraph. In other words: I had to *just write*.
- Just write *what*? Since the exercise deals with becoming aware of our biases, I decided to start by working directly with my prejudices. Something I felt strongly about. What do I love? What do I hate? I decided to start with hate.

I gave myself two minutes to write without stopping in order to 1. Describe an idea.

A pet hate? 'MyCulture'. I hate the overuse of the 'my' on websites, in adverts, shops etc. It's all 'my' this that and the other thing: 'MyBus', 'MyHRonline', 'MyHouse', 'MyShopping', 'MyCafe' … Why this repetition of the personal possessive? Everyone's doing it now. My-my-my-my, me-me-me. Although of course I suppose it could have some practical uses in that, say, at the top of a webpage you know that it's your own account when it says 'myAccount'. But no! Not necessary! Who else's account could it possibly be? Or if you absolutely must, have 'Katz account' – that'd be clear, no? Or just 'Account' since it can only be accessed with my password for crying out loud?

After letting off a bit of steam I was up to 2. Reflect upon your response to it.

A pretty strong reaction! What in particular outrages me so much and why? Probably does go against some attitude or maybe some disposition I hold dear, as I'm quite personally affronted. What do I value, then? Humbleness rather than egotism – though my rant above is hardly humble, is it? Am I a hypocrite? But the 'My' business seems to celebrate narcissism and I've had personal experience in dealing with egotistical types. Who hasn't? I'm reminded of a particular example – a close 'friend' whose self-obsession sidelined me time and again. Narcissists leave others out in the cold. So I have some experience, but not a great deal of knowledge about this – even regarding the terminology (e.g. I've used 'narcissism' and 'egotism' as if they're synonymous, and I'm sure they're not). Look up later.

I do know that narcissism is considered to be a disease some people can't help. Maybe so, but the scale of what I'll call 'me-firstness' seems bigger than that. Is it a cultural development then? I could look into it, even write something on it, maybe call it, 'Me-oh-my: cultural change measured in proliferating personal pronouns'. Ha ha. No, but seriously, why not? Others might have something useful to say. And maybe I could join the conversation once I know more.

And so to **3. Relate** this new idea – if possible – to another theory you know.

Years ago I read Christopher Lasch's book, The Culture of Narcissism. *That was first published in 1979, and I'm wondering if the phenomenon has actually intensified since then. Ok. Quick Google search – type in the keyword, 'narcissism' – found plenty, including a newish book, Anne Manne's,* The Life of I. *I'll continue looking further after I complete this entry …*

Lastly, **4. Consider** how your reading, analysis, and reflection on this idea might relate to your personal learning process.

Strong reactions can be a strength. But also a weakness. I need to direct *my impassioned reactivity – in this case, against what I perceive as a cultural phenomenon – rather than allowing it to bury me in messy, unreflective emotionalism. If I just keep ranting, my thoughts are unlikely to go anywhere new. I'll be like an ignorant radio shock jock, venting but not creating. Need to strike a balance. Need to go into it more deeply than this simplistic surface retort.*

Allowing space to think about the idea was the initial phase of a learning process. The second phase was considering why I reacted that way. I already knew I had to watch my tendency towards going off half-cocked when my buttons are pushed. But the requirement to formally reflect meant I had to take a breath and examine my gut reaction, then whether or not the idea that had provoked me was worth pursuing. Having decided it was, I entered the third phase – theorising 'me-oh-my'. The reflective process had led me out of the moralistic trap and into a more carefully considered exploration of possible reasons behind the 'My' thing via Lasch and Manne. Then, finally, I articulated the process in relation to my own development as a learner.

I've witnessed some students doing remarkable things with journaling.
An exemplary case was the international postgraduate who set herself the task of exploring why it was that she held the belief that 'practitioners of Falun Gong are

depraved'. Coming to understand that she had never really questioned the opposition to the movement was really very hard for her. In her journal, she started with the personal, and ended up researching the political climate that contributed to her reaction, that is, the relationship between her internal world and the external became a lot clearer, paving the way towards the condition Barnett has dubbed 'critical being'. After this exercise it was a piece of cake when it came to questioning her responses to texts she needed to read for her master's degree in Strategic Public Relations.

Soon, I'll suggest you try out a similar experiment with a 'hate' or a 'love' idea and see where it takes you. You can choose anything you like. One researcher I worked with decided to write on how she hated it when people voice support for something then don't follow through – usually because it means making any kind of sacrifice of their time or money. It emerged that she'd had experience with this when she worked on a project to reduce pollution in her home city of Beijing. Unsurprisingly, everyone she spoke to was in favour of reducing the smog. So a plan was suggested to charge people who brought their cars into the inner city. Nobody was in favour. Nobody was prepared to act in any way that affected their own security or comfort. After writing quite an impassioned diatribe, then reflecting upon her reaction to the resistance to the changes suggested, she began to look for other ways of communicating the need for a radical action to a dangerous and pervasive problem. In her journal she was explicit about the need to connect theory and practice, and later she actually began to follow through with it.

Another example comes from a student who wrote about writing. How he *hated* it. (And I have to say that it was pretty interesting to read a writer writing about how he hated writing while enrolled in a writing course!) Coincidentally, in the same group, another student came up with the same topic. Only this time it was how he loved it. The contrast was amusing when both of them volunteered to read theirs aloud, one after the other.

So – choose something you feel strongly about. And keep this first entry fairly loose and free-flowing, as per my example, because in the next exercise I'll be suggesting a slightly more stringent approach.

As is clear by now I think, the journal requires authentic enquiry. It is a place where you review new ideas or experiment with concepts: thinking on paper. You can use it for sifting through ideas, and for uncovering personal tendencies that might otherwise inhibit this process. Some scholars have found that journaling helps them negotiate their way through a complex research process to find what the artist Matisse (cited in Flam 1995, p. 48) calls 'the desire of the line'.

Matisse was talking about the line in the context of drawing and painting. But we can consider 'the desire of the line' in the context of writing, that is, where is your argument tending? Where does it want to go? Where is your research leading you as you read and analyse texts in order to learn enough about a topic to construct a coherent, unbiased argument about it? In a reflective journal, you can think some of these problems out on paper without worrying too much about whether you're right or wrong. Journaling treats writing and thinking as two processes that are very much bound up with each other in a kind of creative symbiosis, an idea we'll be exploring further in Chapter 6.

Exercise 2.1 First journal entry

Describe an idea – something you love or hate.

Why do you think you react this way to this idea?

Does this idea relate to any other theories, etc.?

How might your analysis and reflection on this idea relate to your learning process?

Being in-between

The journal has been described by some as 'critical space' and by others as 'creative space' or a zone in-between – as in T.S. Eliot's formulation, 'the conception and the creation'. For our purposes, it is between academic and personal writing. It is a mode that encourages the possibility of original scholarship because it allows you to play with ideas without feeling constrained. This is the way new understandings are formed, where jotted ideas and mental siftings get sorted out. After all, how can you come up with anything new if everything you write is about pleasing examiners?

The following are examples of students reflecting on ideas related to their particular disciplines, and the comments that support them:

REFLECTIVE WRITING, SAMPLE 1

I'm getting an uneasy sensation that the field of Political Economy is infatuated with capitalism, it's a bond hatched out of ideological disgust and dare I say it disguised envy; envy that comes out of being marginalised. All the economic schools of thought that form part of that heterodox clan take a reactionary stance towards their popular brother and take great care in pointing out its failings, but like the former Australian prime minister Tony Abbott, provide no real alternatives and like him have been sidelined into relative societal anonymity. Where are our public intellectuals? Where are our true critical thinkers? The ones that are willing to explore new ideas without pigeonholing themselves in one ideological silo or another. I feel the form is there, but like many things in our consumerist, individualistic, political correct society, there is no substance. What's the point of pointing the accusatory finger when you can't answer the question, what's the alternative then?

The reason why this annoys me so is that we have an economic system that is increasingly dividing us through purchasing power stratification and destroying us through its voracious appetite for natural resources. The environmental science is telling us that we don't have much time, so Political Economy does not have the luxury any more to study the shortcomings of the existing economic paradigm. Like a drug addict the field needs to detox itself from the seductive and safe high moral ground and get to work on real-life solutions that can help people.

Comments

It is clear that this researcher's main concern is with current directions of the discipline of political economy. He's using the journal to think about why it is that scholars in his field seem to be 'infatuated with capitalism', as he sees it. If this had been an essay rather than a reflection, he'd certainly need to be more specific here – rather than referring to 'capitalism', he'd have to identify which forms or manifestations of this broad term he's referring to. But the student is 'in the flow', so to speak, and the journal is the place to allow this without getting bogged down in too much detail. So although some proponents of journaling insist on a more systematic approach, I'd argue that you need to consider the journal as a composite work in which some entries are systematic, some more free-flowing.

The student then moves straight on to his perception that it is disgust, envy, and alienation that provide impetus for this shift in direction, and he sees a pressing need for real alternatives to current thinking in economics. From later work this student produced, it was clear that he moved on from lamenting the lack of authoritative voices and sought out researchers who were in fact doing the kind of work he respected.

This entry demonstrates that the student certainly has some critical acumen, and can make links across disciplines through reading widely. However, there's less self-reflection in this particular entry. He might have considered, for instance, on what experience he bases his convictions, how he drew the conclusions he did about Political Economy, and whether other conclusions could be drawn instead. But as journals form a body of work done over time, some will focus more on the play of ideas, while others will contain more experimentation with reflection and analysis to achieve an overall balance in a journal.

REFLECTIVE WRITING, SAMPLE 2: A Case of Objective Subjectivity

Neat objectivity always gets me. I'm drawn by reason, its being so precise and impregnable. It has an appeal, doesn't it? It makes you feel in a castle protected by Hulk, Godzilla, and Daenerys's dragons all together. Plato's objective arguments for premise 1 and 2 on page 161 of the Course Reader are impeccable. Un bijoux. But then I turn the page, and read Malouf and Maugham and my heart just shrinks, only to then get bigger and lighter and go up like a helium balloon. I'd hate to be the Henry James of Maugham's critique – I wish to observe life through my own eyes and make stories. Good ones. I wouldn't have to give up on reason, would I? Wishing for a full life shouldn't go against Plato's preachings.

Hugh Mackay seems to speak of observation as opposite to experience. Is it too much to aim at getting two birds with one stone? How wonderful it would be to master an objective subjectivity! Which is different from subjective objectivity. The former gives priority to the subjective bit, I believe. So, first step: go and live; second step: put your experience into context, making what you got out of your senses as objective as possible.

Why do objectivity and subjectivity interest me? Because I think everybody, during his or her search for identity, stumbles across this crossroad. There are good arguments for both paths, but neither of them is feasible in real life. You can't possibly be a Platonically real (detached from all particular objects and persons) machine, nor can you just keep being 'itchy and hungry' 24/7 […]. It is clear we all must pave our own way somewhere in the middle of these two divergent roads – which is more easily said than done …

Comments

This international student – new to the humanities as her undergraduate degree was in science – has found herself trying to breach the gap between her respect for objectivity and her interest in subjectivity, seeking to ally them somehow. This brief journal entry may lack analytical depth but she is making connections between her own thoughts and those of other thinkers on the subject she has chosen to explore. She has also extended it beyond the context of writing into considerations of issues of identity that were only implied in the texts she has read on the subject.

She has described the points she's interested in, reflected upon her response, related it to other ideas and to her learning process. This entry demonstrates some critical ability and self-reflexivity, and the style, while grammatically imperfect, is cohesive, follows a logical progression, and her own voice comes through with confidence as she relates the ideas to her own life and work.

The next sample entry is concerned with issues of bias in academia. I suggest you make your own comments as an informal peer assessment exercise before going on to experiment with this kind of reflective journaling yourself. The criteria to help you make a judgement are simple: level of critical ability and self-reflexivity.

REFLECTIVE WRITING, SAMPLE 3

I would like to start off this week's journal by saying that I'm completely biased, I will go even further to say that I'm really proud of it. If I had an audience in front of me I can imagine half of them leaving in self-righteous indignation for having wasted their time, while the other half would be curious to see how I could dig myself out of this black hole – you know those types, the ones that can't help stopping to look at accidents. In this age of positivism and logic we have deluded ourselves into believing in a false reality, that to be biased is to have a flawed logic – this is wrong.

I'll give you an example to prove my point: imagine a scientist researching human biology by studying blood samples. You know, real science, real data, controlled environments and no pesky emotional and unpredictable humans in the equation to deal with ... So how can you possibly be biased in this situation you might ask, blood has no ethical issues to deal with, no political agenda or aspirations of being greater than any blood cell that has come before. Well ... What about the scientist? They're human, they have to deal with ethical issues, they might have a political agenda and aspirations of being a great scientist. In order words, the blood might give objective data but it is always analyzed by a subjective mind that is influenced by social and political norms and personal desires. Even the choice of methodology and the subject matter tells us what the scientist considers important ...

Please ... If you're humble enough to realize you are always biased then ... you become self-aware and are able to manage it. It's not Ok though when you think that you're being objective when in reality you're not. Just look at the damage economic neoclassicism, which claims to be logical and unbiased, has done to modern societies by erroneously stating that it is 'human nature' to be 'selfish' and 'individualistic' in its 'scientific' models.

... So I say again I'm proud to be biased, because by admitting to this I'm being objective.

Exercise 2.2 Have a go at commenting on the third student's journal entry. Bullet points will do.

A little further advice

Although many students find the reflective process extremely valuable, it is also quite hard to do for reasons I've mentioned already, and then there's the problem of trying to gain some objective insight into your own subjectivities: it is difficult to self-evaluate.

So, if journaling is not a task required of you at your institution and you do not have a tutor to help you, then it's a good idea to work with a friend, a writer-responder like yourself, so that you can swap your reflections and receive feedback from each other. Some suggested questions follow. You'll notice that the comments require almost as much thought as the entries. So choose your partner carefully.

- Do you think the writer of this journal entry demonstrates curiosity? For example, if they've chosen to write on a subject about which they don't know a great deal, have they attempted to inform themselves about it adequately? Or if they've already written a fair bit in this particular entry, have they mentioned that they intend to follow it up in another entry?
- If you think they are making unfounded assumptions, can you tell if they are aware of this?
- Does the author ask questions of the text, or of their reading of the text? Provide examples.
- If the author seems vehement about the subject they have chosen to reflect upon, have they also allowed for the possibility of opposing viewpoints?
- Can they tell the difference between fact and opinion? If not, provide an example.
- Would you say the author shows a level of originality? If so, in what ways?
- Can you tell if they are noting their own possible strengths or, on the other hand, biases or other weaknesses. That is, are they aware of their own learning process?

Socrates' philosophical approach can help you to look deeply into your own thinking and help you to distinguish between what you know, and what you *think* you know. As we've discussed already, Socratic questioning forms a system of thought that helps both in uncovering assumptions and in analysing concepts. So, use the same template as before, but AFTER you have finished the first part – *Describe an idea* – ask yourself questions along the following lines:

- Why does this topic interest me?
- Is my idea based on experience? What sort of experience in particular?
- Is my idea based on knowledge? If so, does the knowledge belong to any particular school of thought?
- If I drew any conclusions, might there be other conclusions that could be drawn?
- Have I taken anything for granted here?

I've included these prompts in the relevant sections in the journal entry template on the next page.

Exercise 2.3 Reflecting on your research

Summarise an idea.

Reflect upon your response: *Why does this topic interest me? Is my reaction based on experience or prejudice or knowledge? Do I need or want to know more about it? What in particular do I want or need to know?*

Make links between this new idea – if possible – to another theory, text, reading, lecture, etc.: *If my response is based on knowledge, does the knowledge belong to any particular school of thought?*

Consider how your analysis and reflection on this idea might relate to my learning process: *Have I taken anything for granted here? What have I learned about the way I process information?*

Conclusion

This chapter has dealt with various means available for improving critical awareness and metacritical ability so as to refine your ability to research, to write, and to adapt to different situations and events not only while at university, but in life generally. One of these means, reflective journaling, involves a kind of disciplined self-reflection designed to contribute to this intellectual and practical flexibility. The journal, as a metacritical process, philosophical in nature, is readily available to students from any and all disciplines who recognise the value of evaluating their own thoughts in a practical way.

I hope that it is now clear that scholarly analysis needs to be used in conjunction with and tempered by reflexivity and that, in fact, we need all three of Barnett's 'domains' of critical thought for the sake of balance. Without careful consideration of propositions and concepts (CT1), reflective activities (CT2) could descend into self-absorption. Without ethical considerations (involved in CT3), we run the risk of becoming narrowly vocationalist, or worse, cold-bloodedly utilitarian. A particularly extreme example of this comes from Germany, preceding and during World War II:

> Universities in Germany acquiesced in the activities of the regime: they were accomplices in the domination of instrumental reason over more humanistic forms of critical reason … At the least, the Western university must strive to avoid producing the fragmented critical consciousness that would again support such a situation. And it can only do so if, through our universities and in our institutions of highest learning, we develop whole persons who integrate all their critical capacities, across all three of the domains and at all their levels. (Barnett 2015, p. 64)

In other words: thinking well and living well are linked. Critical thinking is essential for refining analytical skills and, when used well, can also lead us to confront established ways of thinking – our own as well as others' – head-on, so as to refresh our view of what's happening within us and in the world, socially, culturally, and politically.

Critical Analysis of Texts

Chapter overview

This chapter contains:

- A broad discussion of logic, which like reflection, is an essential tool of the critical thinker
- Discussion of the practice of deductive and inductive logic
- Pitfalls in logic
- The importance of being able to identify a writer's theoretical position and how to go about this
- Different frameworks for thinking about critical thinking, from logic and analytic philosophy to the critical theory school of thought
- Evaluative tools based on critical thinking
- A quiz designed to evaluate your own critical facility.

In Chapter 2 we looked at how our personal backgrounds and therefore our understanding of any given situation will affect our reading of a text. This chapter continues the work of identifying both our own biases and those of other writers in order to analyse and critique effectively. Where previously we practised using the reflection journal to help deal with the irrationality that is the product of tenacious assumptions and belief systems that can occlude our clarity of thought, here we will use the fundamental critical tool of logic. Logic helps us to diagnose a text's reliability and usefulness, and assists with the essential work of identifying underlying assumptions – beliefs for which no proof is offered – and implications of arguments. Also, after reading this chapter you may be able to see more clearly in which areas of critical accomplishment you ought to feel confident, and which might need further attention.

Like reflection, logic is a thinking tool. It is most commonly associated with mathematics and the sciences for its emphasis on formal and structural considerations, and in the humanities, with philosophy – the study of reasoning or of theories and measures of validity of arguments and inferences. Logic is used as a means of identifying instances of false reasoning (which we'll look at presently). It also helps develop certain extremely valuable intellectual habits. I've mentioned elsewhere the downside of habitual thinking, as it can anchor us to conventional mental routines and received ideas, but there are instances where routine practices become a good thing, particularly when allied with other critical dispositions as discussed in Chapter 1. In this chapter we'll look at some of those routines.

Logical mental processes assist us to develop and evaluate theories, and then to compare and contrast them with other theories. Logical analyses of ideas, of texts, enable us to see in different ways how problems and concepts connect with each other. For instance, say you've just come across a new and unfamiliar idea that you think may feed into your current research project. You'll use logic to draw conclusions regarding what this new concept seems to be telling you. To do this, you must firstly disengage from that idea to some degree so that you can think about different possible interpretations of it and its potential usefulness to your project. After this, you then re-engage with the idea in a more personal way. So you're juggling what Greg Restall (2013, pp. 10–11) calls 'distance' from and 'presence' with the idea. This 'presence' he eloquently describes as 'a kind of empathy in "trying the theory on for size"'.

To illustrate the everyday relevance of this process, here is an example from personal experience:

Distance and Presence

I recently watched the 2015 Netflix docuseries *Making a Murderer*, in which a man seems to be unjustly accused of a crime, his conviction being based largely on prejudice and spurious evidence. At least, this was my interpretation – and I could be fairly sure that that is the conclusion the directors, Laura Ricciardi and Moira Demos, wanted me to draw. I was predictably outraged at the sentence the man received. Here we have *presence* in operation. I then attempted a thought experiment in which I distanced myself from personal and, I think, directorial bias. This involved mentally reconstructing and reinterpreting events and statements so that a different reading of events would be possible, a reading that would leave room for me to conclude that he was guilty rather than innocent. It was actually a horrible feeling, going against my previous reading which included a strong gut reaction to what I had witnessed as the ten-episode programme had unfolded. Still, I looked again at the prosecution's evidence while attempting to put aside my aversion to the characters who were determined to 'slot' the man, and my sympathy for him and his family. I did a little research into the making of the film, the events themselves, and the characters involved. What was the outcome of the experiment? Ultimately it was the same as my original verdict – as it happened. But I felt more confident that it was the best conclusion I could draw, rather than one based entirely on what the film-makers had intended for me.

This juggling of distance and closeness is something we'll revisit throughout this book, particularly when we get into our discussion of research processes. For now, I would simply like to say that logic is essential when it comes to engagement in the critical processes of interpretation, making inferences, and evaluating texts.

Practice of logic

If you're going to write a persuasive paper that is cohesive and convincing, then you need to think about logic, premise, and argument. We'll look at argument and premise first. So, to begin:

Q: What is a premise? **A:** It's a beginning statement of an argument.

Q: And what is argument? **A:** Actually, that's a big question. Here's how Lamm and Everett (2007, p. 4) describe it:

> Argument changes the world. It shapes the way people think, offering them alternative ways of seeing what is 'true'. It motivates people to behave differently, providing them with reasons to take action or to halt. As a result, countries wage war or seek peace. People gain or lose civil rights. Those accused of crimes are convicted and jailed or acquitted and freed. Business deals are made or broken. Personal relationships form, break up, or mend. Politicians are elected or defeated. All these activities are set into motion and resolved through a dynamic process of change known as argument.

That's one longish answer. I wanted to include it because there's always a danger in an instructive book like this of falling into the trap of becoming overly reductive, and as Lamm and Everett point out, the activity of argumentation can indeed have massive influence. That said, a more concise (and somewhat reductive) answer that will do for our purposes for the moment is simply this:

A: An argument is a group of premises leading to a conclusion.

If your premises are fair and accurate, all well and good. But if not, your argument is invalidated and your conclusions will be false.

Deductive reason is dependent on its premises. Here is a much-cited historical example.

Premise 1: All men are mortal.
Premise 2: Socrates is a man.

The conclusion can only be that Socrates, specifically, is mortal. This simple statement is true because the premises are true.

Let's experiment. What if we wrote instead:

Premise 1: America's power is greater than that of any previous empire worldwide.
Premise 2: Power is the foremost measure of greatness.

The conclusion can only be that America is the greatest country in the world.

But only a limited understanding of the notion of power can lead us to believe that America is the greatest country in the world. If we look further we discover that although the United States may lead the world in its ability to wield political and military clout, it is also listed as having the world's second largest prison population rate. Nevertheless, it does do quite well in The Economist's Quality of Life index, but not as well as the dozen countries that precede it, like Ireland and Singapore and Finland, nor does it appear among the top-ranked in the United Nations' World Happiness Index. Therefore, if you wanted to argue that three basic criteria for measuring greatness included a low crime rate, a high quality of life, and overall happiness, then the United States is certainly not the greatest. So deduction doesn't always work. In this case, one of the premises was false because it was subject to the vagaries of a particular belief system. We need to beware of false premises as they lead to false conclusions and the promotion of misinformation.

> Because the conclusion is often the most easily identifiable part of an **TIP** extended argument, if you're reading a complex piece of work that's hard to get a grip on, then try starting with the conclusion and working back.

Deduction is commonly used in the sciences, but at this point I want to move beyond deductive reasoning based on premises, to inductive reasoning. It's somewhat different and is commonly used in the humanities.

So what is the difference between induction and deduction? In inductive reasoning the premises still support the conclusion, but unlike deductive reasoning, they do not necessarily lead us to the *only* possible result – only the *likelihood* of truth. Remember the Socrates example above? Here's another version:

Premise 1: Socrates was Greek.
Premise 2: Most Greeks like olive oil.
Conclusion: Socrates was likely to enjoy olive oil on his bread.

With deduction we can't really go beyond the information contained in the premises, but with induction we can. If we want to think where no one has thought before, we need this more open-ended and exploratory form of reasoning. Two basic forms of induction are analogy and generalisation.

Analogy

Within the analysis of an analogy we use evaluative skills of comparing and contrasting. Analogies are aids to discovery, that is, heuristic means by which problems may be solved. Consider a complex question such as, 'Is the Lilliputian nation-state likely to recover from conflict at the same rate as the Brobdingnagian nation after a crisis?' To answer that question, we need to consider if there are parallels to be drawn between these two countries. If we find correspondences, we'd then extrapolate from the Brobdingnagian situation what the outcomes for the Lilliputians might be.

Physicist David Bohm (2004, pp. 50–51) refers to the example of Newton who arrived at his theory of universal gravitation through his perception – or his imaginative vision supported by the logical process of analogy – of the similarity between the behaviour of earthly and celestial matter. This is a lovely instance of an insight arrived at through drawing an analogy, or inductive reasoning used in a referential process to extend knowledge.

Indicators of arguments through analogy

- Is there a comparison being made between one object, or system of objects, and another?
- If so, does the comparison allow for inferences to be made with respect to the topic under discussion?
- Does the comparison play a part in supporting a conclusion?
- The author may also use metaphor in order to link ideas across domains, so check that also. For example, 'a tsunami of spam floods my inbox daily' ('tsunami' – geomorphic domain and 'inbox' – workaday communications technology domain)

Generalisation

This form of inductive logic focuses less on comparing and contrasting and more on contextual considerations. An argument based on generalisation assumes that if you have a decent sample to begin with, you can infer that the same result is likely to occur on a larger scale also. But there's a particular pitfall to be avoided here – that of making an unwarranted generalisation. So make sure the original sample is well chosen, and that the evidence supplied to support the discussion point is substantial. In order to create an argument with solid premises, we need reliable evidence.

As it is common for essays to move from the general to the specific, here's some structural advice on building on a generalisation. Let's imagine your topic is: 'Globalisation and higher education.'

1. Start with your generalisation: Although globalisation is not a new historical phenomenon, over the last twenty years its contemporary forms affect every area of human endeavour. It involves the exchange not only of trade and capital worldwide, but most importantly, of knowledge. As centres of education and knowledge-production, universities have been powerfully affected by, and in turn have a powerful effect on, the distribution of knowledge.
2. Add backup to support this contention, and provide examples you intend to develop in the essay to support it – an overview of the analysis to follow.
3. Home in on specific examples one by one, thus forming the body of your analysis.

Indicators of arguments based on generalisation

- Does the author start with a specific example which is then expanded into a general claim?
- If so, is the claim supported with evidence?
- Does the author use language that refers to quantity (e.g., a majority, several, few), frequency (always, frequently, generally), and levels of certainty (undoubtedly, presumably)?
- Does the author qualify his claims?

Returning for a moment to Socrates and the olive oil question, how would you go about persuading your reader of your point? You'd probably provide some figures to support the second premise – about the Greek taste for olive oil – and if that evidence was sound, you'd still need to clarify the part about the bread. Perhaps Socrates was more of a potato than a bread man? Perhaps he even had a Classical Greek version of gluten intolerance? Yes, I may be splitting hairs here, but it's in the interests of dealing with possible objections or counterarguments. There are three main approaches recommended here. We'll focus on the oil rather the bread for this experiment.

First, you might **make a strategic concession** where you acknowledge possible oppositional viewpoints. You might admit that some will argue with the qualification that most Greeks then and now may only *appear* to be fond of olive oil. Perhaps you've uncovered a particular researcher – let's call him Nathaniel Dobbs – who cites a lack of options available to Greeks for lubricating their bread: it's easier to grow olive trees in the arid Greek climate than to graze large numbers of the sort of livestock capable of producing a lot of butter, which Greeks might prefer to spread on their bread if they had a choice.

You can also **refute by showing weaknesses in the possible counterarguments**. After establishing that Dobbs' argument is fair, point to a greater body of evidence demonstrating that regardless of any question hanging over the oil preference, it is still true to say that most (not all!) Greeks have been shown to like olive oil very much indeed.

The third approach is to **demonstrate that the counterarguments might not be entirely relevant**.

One of the beauties of inductive argument is that it is rich in possibility. In academia we complexify rather than simplify so as to examine wide-ranging prospects and probabilities. Academia encourages the curious-minded to enquire, to get involved in the conversations that are constantly going on a global scale. But the academic community is also competitive and full of rivalries – which keeps people on their toes. So it's necessary to show that not only are you aware of other viewpoints, but that you're capable of using them to strengthen your own case. We'll look at this form of persuasion more in Chapter 8. You need to be able to anticipate other possibilities and then deal with them in such a way that your point becomes more convincing in contrast to those of others.

What we've been looking at here are examples of reasoning processes, where conclusions are inferred from previous statements, or premises. Clear, logical reasoning is a fundamental skill, although we tend to use a mixture of both deduction and induction when researching and writing, as in life, because thinking critically is a multilayered business. But if we have the ability to reason well we can develop a strong thesis while avoiding the traps of logical inconsistency, which can weaken the argument of a paper. These include:

Logical fallacies (some examples)

Probably the most apt example at this point of our discussion on logic is the *non sequitur:* The conclusion does not follow logically from the premise. Example: Adolf Eichmann was a highly organised and skilful bureaucrat, therefore he would make excellent decisions as a Security Service officer.

Cognitive bias too can distort our reasoning. **Confirmation bias**, as previously mentioned, describes the way we are prone to notice evidence that confirms our preconceptions. **Congruence bias** is when we too readily accept a theory without properly critiquing it. Both of these can affect our reasoning during research and writing, leading to the maintenance of beliefs that need amendment, or might actually be better discarded.

Hasty Generalisations occur when we make a judgement based on too little evidence, or on evidence that is biased. Example: 'After being in London for a week, I can tell you: Londoners are rude.' Or, 'According to the statistics available, it is reasonable to say …' Any statement beginning this way that is not followed by a citation should immediately ring alarm bells – what statistics? From whom? When? And why only one source? It might be best to put this article aside and start reading something else instead.

Either/Or Fallacy: Only two options are presented when in fact several exist. This fallacy eradicates the possibility not only of nuance, but of any discussion, full stop. A real party-pooper. Example: 'Embrace coal seam gas mining, or watch your children freeze to death in winter.'

People sometimes resort to using **red herrings** in order to win an argument, whether on paper or in company. Have you ever been involved in an argument with someone – let's say you're discussing whether or not the latest budget is a fair one – and found that you were winning, then have your interlocutor assert, 'Well, I'm entitled to my opinion'? That's an example of a red herring – distraction from the point by referring to an irrelevant issue. The issue being discussed is the budget, not freedom of speech.

Straw Man: Like a person made of straw, a straw-man argument is when you set up a thin version of the opponent's argument and then knock it over. As in, 'Some local residents might argue against the proposed high-rise in their neighbourhood because, amongst other things, it will overshadow their houses. But a loss of a bit of light is nothing in comparison to the loss of revenue if this development application fails.' Here, only one part of a more complex argument is acknowledged, and a certain rhetorical advantage is exploited unfairly.

Ad Hominem: Arguing against the person instead of against the issue. Example: 'He doesn't really believe in freedom of the press. He just wants to defend his right to watch porn.' Attacking a person's religion or race instead of engaging intelligently with the ideas they are putting forward is another form of this fallacy. Conversely, one might accept a proposition based on the belief that the person proposing it has credibility, possibly for personal or cultural reasons, yet claims made by such apparent authorities might be seen as questionable if we look only at *the claims*, not the person making them.

That said, we do need to try and establish where the author is coming from when reading a text because the author's background will inform the thrust of their arguments. This brings us on to a sub-focus for this chapter, so let us segue into a brief discussion of how and why to identify the author's position and note the signals.

Identify the author's position

You need to consider what the author of a text wants you to do, to think, to believe. (Remember my *Making a Murderer* example?) Therefore, you need to look for the premises upon with their conclusion is based. In other words, knowing the author's theoretical perspective enables us to recognise any gaps in their reasoning and to identify any unstated assumptions or biases. For instance, a fundamentalist creationist Christian may observe Mount Everest and see evidence of God's mighty creative power. Conversely, an atheist scientist looks at the mountain and sees geological plate tectonics at work. Same subject, different theoretical position, different bias, different vision, and different 'facts' emerge, including the age of Mt Everest. For one it is thousands of years old; for the other, millions. In the example I've just given, it's a matter of making a judgement based on reason rather than faith, on critical thought rather than dogma or ideology.

In academic thinking, elaborated systems or 'schools of thought' are based on critical analyses of previous theories and research. For example, in writing this book, which is concerned with critical thinking, I was aware of several different approaches to the subject. Logic and Analytic Philosophy are the overarching traditions governing this field in the English-speaking world. Logic you're familiar with; Analytic Philosophy also – even if you don't know its name – if you've ever had to provide thoughtful reasons for an opinion, substantiate your theories with evidence, identify rhetorical ploys, or make valid inferences and judgements. Another influential tradition in this field is the Critical Theory school of thought, which emphasises the use and misuse of language rather than the mechanics of constructing an argument. The idea here is that once you've broken down an argument and seen how it works you can spot how the text may have been used to mislead rather than elucidate. Different schools have different starting points for analysis.

Margaret Atwood (2009), who is better known for her fiction, explains the effects of disciplinary difference and authorial positioning rather well in her book *Payback: debt and the shadow side of wealth*. She wonders: Why is it that in this society wherein, historically, men have wielded the power and continue to do so at higher levels, is our symbol of justice female? She then proceeds to come up with plenty of reasons based on a multiplicity of perspectives. She first mentions that if you were a primatologist looking at the world through that lens, you'd point out that among the chimpanzees it's often the older females who are the king-makers. The boss male can stay in power only with their support: so justice is feminine. Or as an anthropologist you'd see the female elders in hunter-gatherer bands who had a lot to say when an animal was being shared among families according to need: the justice of fair division in this context also is feminine. A Freudian might talk about child psychological development and how the first food comes from the mother, as do the first lessons in justice and punishment. Ergo, justice is ...?

You know what discipline you work in, so you should also be familiar with the key approaches and main schools of thought in your field. If not, you really ought to find out. For instance, if the scholar you're reading at the time comes from a tradition of Humanism – a system of thought wherein the agency of human beings is emphasised – they will seek rational ways of solving human problems. But if you happen to be reading the work of, say, a scholar of Psychodynamics, they too rely heavily on empirical research but the perspective will be different. They will see the interrelation of the unconscious and conscious mental and emotional forces as main factors determining personality and motivation, a perspective focused less on the humanistic notion of individual autonomy and more on our propensity to fall prey to hidden fears and desires. This psychologist would have a very different departure point for thinking on any personal, societal, or cultural issues from a Marxist, say, who would explain social dysfunction in terms of economic factors rather than psychological ones, or for a Feminist, for whom the role and position of women informs the thinking and interpretation of events and texts.

Ok. Enough isms. In sum: as a writer you need to be able to direct your writing to those whom you would like to persuade. As a reader, you need to be able to recognise where an author is coming from.

Note the signals

I'd like now to be able to produce a simple checklist for identifying authorial position. But readers of this book will come from a range of disciplines, so it's impossible to provide academic examples that will be relevant to all. Instead, let's look at an example of an everyday equivalent of theoretical positioning with which we are all familiar: the advertisement. Ads are designed to appeal to particular individuals, markets, or interest groups in order to sell products. They need to identify a version of the *readers'* theoretical position. Reading the following ad it is possible to recognise to whom it is directed by spotting certain signals in the text. Further, we can probably work out, to some degree at least, where the intended audience is situated politically or culturally or economically.

JOHN CAMERON SWAYZE: CAMELS AGAIN FIRST IN SALES! FIFTY AND EIGHT TENTHS OVER NEXT BRAND! "I'VE STUDIED THE FIGURES. THEY SHOW THE DECISION IS AGAIN FOR CAMELS – MORE THAN EVER THE FIRST CHOICE FOR AMERICAN SMOKERS" For mildness – for flavor – CAMELS AGREE WITH MORE PEOPLE THAN ANY OTHER CIGARETTE.

- As this is an advertisement from the 1950s and from a particular country, you may not know Swayze. I didn't, and wondered if he was perhaps a statistician, a scientist, a marketing expert, or a celebrity. On checking, I found that the last was true. He was an American news commentator and game show panelist. So, signal one: this ad is directed towards people who would consider this person a trustworthy authority on the subject. So authoritative in fact that he can simply claim to have 'studied the figures', but is not compelled to say what figures or where he found them. This then gives us an idea of the advertiser's idea of this market's opinion regarding the constitution of authority. In turn, this may indicate some of the presumed values of the intended audience.

- 'Camels again first in sales'. The assumption here is that if sales are good, then the product must be good. In other words, success in the market signals quality. Again, what value judgements might the audience to whom this ad is directed be supposed to make regarding the concept of quality?
- 'Scientific' proof including that uncited figure is offered. So, perhaps it is presumed that this audience will have a respect for the value of scientific research, and respond to figures regardless of whether they are substantive?

What might be the assumed theoretical position of an audience that is expected by the authors of this ad to respond positively to endorsements from celebrities, to respect the ability of market forces to ensure quality, and to be satisfied with uncited figures and an allusion to science?

The point here is simply this: How advertisers and anyone else attempts to appeal to those they wish to persuade depends upon their understanding of the worldview of the audience. As previously discussed: In academia, the way we read the world depends upon our perspective, our 'school of thought'. It will be easier for you to recognise the author's perspective, or identify the approach they have to the subject under discussion, by taking into account the author's theoretical framework. The framework will be comprised of concepts and explanations of these concepts and their relevance to the study being conducted, or the ideas explored. Some authors will overtly state their theoretical assumptions. In articles, reports, theses, and so forth, the theoretical position is usually indicated early on in the paper. If it isn't, or if it is unclear to you, you will need to familiarise yourself with the area they're exploring by reading more widely. There are no shortcuts here, I'm afraid! Start by checking the author's research hypotheses, the main claims they make, the other theorists they've referred to in the text, and the literature they have selected. Look at the abstract (for an article) or foreword (for a book), scan the introduction, and take note of the authors listed in the bibliography. It is only possible to identify an author's position and the framework within which they're working once you have familiarised yourself with the field.

When you're engaged in a research task yourself, it's a good idea to **TIP** categorise texts according to their theoretical position. That way you'll be better able to sort that information for analysis of the literature, and to track how one piece of research builds on previous research and where each belongs, conceptually. Identifying and grouping according to theoretical position will also help clarify why further research has been undertaken, as you gradually acquire a grip on the bigger picture. And tag the information that comprises your research under headings that help to clarify your understanding – this means working out a system for filing and cross-referencing that suits your purposes.

Early questions we need to ask of any text are:

Is it true? Is it useful? What is its value?

These questions seem to have a venerable provenance, though where they actually originated is uncertain. They've been attributed to Gautama Buddha; linked to Christ's teachings; referred to as means of defeating what in Jewish law is referred to as *lashon ha-ra*, or wrongful speech. But most commonly they are accredited to Socrates. The story goes like this:

A man – let's call him Demetrios – comes up to Socrates and says he's just heard
  something interesting about one of Socrates' students. Before the man has a
  chance to elaborate, Socrates asks him if what he's heard is true. 'I don't know',
  Demetrios admits. 'I only just heard it – haven't had time for any fact-checking.'
'Well then, you may not know if it's true, but perhaps it is something good you have
  to report about my student?'
'Erm … well no, it's not good.' Being a bright man, Demetrios realises it's best not to
  snicker at this point, and besides he's starting to feel a little bit too embarrassed for that.
'And is this information you have to impart of any particular to value to me? I mean,
  will I benefit from hearing it?'
'Probably not', answers the deflated Demetrios.

Although they are often cited simply as a gossip filter, two of these three questions lie at the heart of critical enquiry. If what we read or hear is not true, or useful, then it has no value to us in everyday life or academically. And in order to establish veracity, quality, and usefulness, there are processes we can follow. Following Richard Paul's advice on textual analysis, and with reference to Bloom's Taxonomy, here is some guidance for analysis of a text:

Advice for textual analysis

First of all, when you come to read a new article or book you need to **identify the main claim presented, and also the secondary issues**. These are pretty easily established by reading the abstract and scanning though the subheadings (or chapter heads if it's a book rather than an article). Then, if after this basic perusal you've established that you're clear on what beliefs the author has stated overtly and that this text is actually of interest to you, pay more attention to the explanations and evidence provided for any claim to see if sufficient backup is supplied.

    Attend also to the language that's being used, identifying any rhetorical strategies used by the author. (We'll discuss rhetoric in more detail in Chapter 9.) And make sure, right at the start, to take note of *when* the text was written, as considerations of timeliness may inform your analysis. By no means am I saying that only the most recent material is relevant – historical data and ideas are essential so that you understand what the newer information is based on, and it contextualises more theories or studies – but you must also keep up to date with recent developments in your field. And if the author you're reading seems unaware of either historical background or recent changes then you might want to move on to another.

Assuming that you're continuing to read the text, you then need to **attend to any meanings that are less overtly stated**, that is, consider implicit rather than explicit meanings and try to identify any unstated beliefs underlying the claims. Also, does the author seem to assume any particular knowledge, background, or biases on the part of yourself, the reader? At this stage you'll probably find you're coming to grips with the author's purposes in writing the text, and that you're on the way towards knowing whether or not you agree with them. If not, then try and articulate to yourself how your point of view differs from that of the author, and reflect on why that might be.

Do you think this text is proving useful to you so far? **Consider if you would like to borrow from this author's thoughts**, whether that be to support your own argument, or to use as rebuttal of another's.

Think also about implications for the text. Can you discern what possible consequences might ensue were the reader to pursue the line promoted in the text? For example, I mentioned the logical fallacy of the *non sequitur* and illustrated the concept of a conclusion not following logically from the premise with the following example: *Adolf Eichmann is a highly organised and skilful bureaucrat, therefore he will make excellent decisions as a Security Service officer*. What could be the moral implications for writing such an article before or during World War II? How might others use or misuse these arguments?

Continue to pay attention also to the argumentative techniques employed, and consider whether you might like to emulate them or avoid them. Throughout your reading it's important to remain aware of the author's attitude, which is often indicated by their tone, and the way they use rhetoric to persuade the reader to their point of view.

By now you'll also **be aware of how the parts of the text work in relation to the whole**, where the claims, evidence, and explanations appear and how they relate to each other. You'll be able to tell if the argument is progressing logically. So, after this analysis, or 'breaking up' the text to examine it, you proceed to the phase of synthesis, or 'bringing together', that is, of relating it to other texts. Earlier in this chapter I mentioned the importance of knowing where ideas fit in the greater scheme of ideas. You need to identify to what collective belief system or school of thought the text might belong. It will be easier to address if you first consider if the text brings to mind any other/s you have read. It is also necessary to identify what other arguments there might be apart from those of this particular author, and how they compare to this one. Overall, it is during this

(Continued)

synthesising process that you'll find out what other texts, if any, this particular one relates to.

The last part of this evaluative process is judging the text. By this stage you'll have probably read it more than once if it seems key to your aims, and you'll have read others that relate to the ideas you're exploring as part of your research. You'll know how well, and how usefully (to your purposes), the text presents its major and supporting claims; also how valid and timely the evidence is, and how effective the rhetorical strategies might be. So, you'll know whether or not you agree with the writer, and if not, why not.

In brief, as you read a text and, if possible, discuss it with your peers, try to answer the following questions as you go:

1. What is the **main issue** or claim, and what are the secondary issues of the text in question?
2. What, in your opinion, is the **purpose** of the text?
3. What **evidence** is supplied in support of the ideas being developed?
4. Does the author make any particular **assumptions** with regard to the issues discussed?
5. Whose **point of view** is advanced in the text, if any? It's likely that someone's point of view will be present, as you can't have a 'view from nowhere'.
6. Having identified the key **concepts** with which the text is concerned, and considered the validity of any claims and evidence provided, would you say the argument progresses logically?
7. Are there are any further **implications**?
8. Can you make any **inferences** based on the content, or on the author's tone or attitude, as you perceive it? Does the author use persuasive language to help strengthen their argument? And are you able to draw reasonable conclusions based on the material you're reading?
9. Overall, how successful is the text, do you think, in terms of presentation of main and supporting claims, validity of evidence, and effectiveness of any persuasive tactics used?

As this is a generic book, and readers will come from different disciplines, I'll leave it to you to select texts to practise on.

Further advice for textual analysis

I strongly suggest that, if possible, you form a study group with friends – or at least work in pairs – so that you can make comparative analyses. Exercises in logic and academic analysis are much more effective if you have others to bounce your ideas off. You might choose to focus on a particular theme or argument, and then with your peers look at it from a range of different theoretical positions. Research indicates that the best choices of texts for such an exercise are likely to be those that involve a level of disagreement. According to Brookfield's (2015, p. 537) survey results, students report that,

> the most dramatic leaps forward in … understanding of material are usually triggered by having to resolve some sort of disorienting dilemma, that is, having to reconcile two antithetical yet valid responses to a question, or having to incorporate into their frame of understanding a new piece of information that calls into question much of what they had previously held to be true.

Based on my own experience, I think the same applies to researchers in general. So, bear in mind this advice when selecting texts to work with. Now, the process:

1. Select a range of books and articles on a particular subject – choosing texts that explore an issue relevant to your discipline from a range of angles, including those by authors who disagree with each other.
2. Distribute the reading material among your group members (or pairs).
3. Read and annotate your text/s, and refer to the questions supplied in the box, starting with identification and then definition of the main issue/s explored. Also consider the following: As discussed in this chapter, you'll know that your way of thinking will be informed to some degree by disciplinary perspective, and also by your personal world view. So, if you find that you are now reading an author whose viewpoint clashes with your own, you'll need to control your biases. It's likely that at this point you'll want to look up further references in order to obtain clarity on issues raised by the author.
4. Write a summary and analysis of each text.
5. Distribute for group discussion.

Self-evaluative quiz

(With 1 as the highest and 4 as the lowest score you can give yourself.)

QUESTION	SCORE from 1 to 4
In my reading and analysis I am open-minded and truth-seeking.	
I manage to avoid making unfair assumptions and consider oppositional voices.	
I am able to manage any biases I can recognise in my thinking.	
I can avoid errors in reasoning and logical fallacies.	
I can differentiate between fact and opinion.	
I'm able to extend my analysis to apply further content from my discipline.	
My approach to reading and analysis is systematic.	
I seek further evidence to support or refute a point where necessary.	
Any further evidence I use is of a high quality.	
The conclusions I draw are fair and valid.	
I am able to come up with further questions for enquiry based on what I've read.	
I can justify my own opinions.	
My thinking is original.	

Creative Critical Thinking

Chapter overview

This chapter includes:

- Creativity in research processes and when working out:
  - what to read, and why to read it
  - how to make connections between ideas
  - how to identify patterns of thought in what you read
  - how to use your creative faculties in topic selection and drafting
- Practical creativity in academic work:
  - sympathetic reading
  - systematic believing (as opposed to the more traditional doubting)
  - rhizomatic mapping
  - 'clustering' ideas
  - freewriting
  - outlining
  - the first draft.

Our imaginative faculties enable us to think and write and do things in ways that otherwise would remain pedestrian and limited, closed off to further development. The simple, common nouns 'creativity' and 'imagination' represent complex and profound concepts. In the broadest sense, imagination is a perceptual faculty, or a way of seeing and responding to phenomena, and this includes images, texts, and ideas. But before exploring ways imagination works in tandem with critical skills so as to invigorate research and writing in an academic context, it will help to firstly take a look at what the terms 'imagination' and 'creativity' actually signify. I also want to prepare the ground for this discussion by banishing certain erroneous beliefs surrounding creativity in institutions of higher education.

Three misconceptions of creativity in universities

Means to an end? Ironically, the first and most pernicious problem occurs when creativity is embraced. It is often used synonymously with 'problem solving', whether in academia or in the workforce, particularly in 'creative industries' where Richard Florida's (2012) meagre formulation that 'creativity is the new economy' is popular. This is a particularly odious misconception that puts creative endeavours in the thrall of market fundamentalism, when they should not be in thrall to anything. While creativity is indeed needed to solve problems and can help us attain predetermined goals, it is misguided to see it solely as a means to an end. One cannot necessarily predict its results: creativity is a risky business. Imagining is a risky business, as it takes us into unfamiliar territory, intellectually and psychologically.

Superfluity? In complete contrast to the claims outlined above, others worry that exercises in creativity might act as a distraction from or even a hindrance to academic study and, by extension, to career prospects. Conversely, this chapter shows how imagination and creative actions will allow your ideas to progress in directions that fascinate. This is possible precisely because they are *unexpected* directions, which is why I mentioned earlier that when approaching any writing task, it is *not* a good idea to decide beforehand exactly what you want the specific outcome to be. That would be akin to a scientist deciding before an experiment what the result will be – you only end up ignoring evidence that counters your original assumption, which is not only antithetical to the value of openness upon which scholarship prides itself, but can lead to false conclusions.

False dichotomy: Although the arts do not have a monopoly on creativity, it is often situated within that domain, where one might pursue either 'creative writing' (fiction) or 'academic writing' (scholarship). This is a false dichotomy. In Chapter 3 I referred to the logical fallacy of the 'either/or' argument? Well, this creative/academic split is an example of a commonly held fallacy, often wrongly supported in higher education in general. Think of it this way: How is a derivative painting, or an aimless novel devoid of insight, or a clichéd poem creative? And how is a beautifully constructed, elegant, expansive essay containing profoundly insightful ideas that excite the intellect and the imagination *not* creative? Regardless of your discipline, it is necessary to use both critical and creative faculties to produce good work, including strongly argued and persuasive essays and articles.

From imagining to creating, or from imaginative vision to rational insight

To be creative as a scholar means allowing your senses and intellect to work together in an imaginative correspondence where one moves from what is known to what is, as yet, unknown. In other words, a creative writer (whether working with fiction or academic theories, in arts and humanities disciplines or elsewhere) needs to be able to absorb and then extend ideas and information acquired into new knowledge, or new ways of thinking about old knowledge. This idea could be expressed as a kind of formula:

Imagination plus criticality makes for creative scholarly work.

According to physicist David Bohm (2004, pp. 50–51), acts of 'creative perception' encourage the possibility of insights through which we might develop new theories on any subject. They allow us to see aspects of the world *as it might be*, rather than being restricted to simply seeing it *as it is* at the moment. It is upon this ability that any possibility of human development rests; it is never enough to say of any situation or any knowledge, 'well, that's just the way it is', implying that this is therefore how it must continue. That is logically weak, and the way of the hidebound traditionalist. The example I mentioned in Chapter 3 of Newton's use of analogy resulted in what is sometimes referred to as a 'rational insight'. Rational insights are dependent upon a certain clarity of vision that perceives what is relevant in a study of ideas or phenomena, and discards what is not; imaginative insights also require reason to be effective. In other words, critical reason and imagination work together so that new ideas, artefacts, and theories may be created.

Although Bohm shies away from actually attempting a definition of creativity, he does pose questions as to its nature, and also to that of 'originality' – a discussion well beyond the scope of this book. Instead, I'll refer to educator Ken Robinson's description of creativity as 'applied imagination': a meld of imagination, intellect, and practical functionality.

Creativity and criticality and thinking well

Time to practise what was suggested in the previous chapter: working with oppositional voices with a view to improving criticality. A good starting point will be to critique the notion that seems to be the basis for this book – that critical thinking should be at the centre of all academic practice.

Some consider that to doubt the centrality of critical thinking verges on heresy. However, this really isn't the case. For some years scholars have pointed out certain problems in critical thinking pedagogy. Before entering the debate, let's briefly summarise what critical thinking may achieve: Through reflective and analytical practices critical thinking develops the intellectual faculties needed to read with discernment, including dealing with fallacies and broadening readers' perspectives; it prepares students to become engaged citizens by encouraging a questioning attitude to authorities and commonly held beliefs; it provides an edge when it comes to dealing with this 'supercomplex' world where jobs are precarious and the nature of work itself changes as modes of operating become outdated. It involves examining and analysing and searching for hidden flaws in others' thinking.

What's wrong with this picture? There is the argument that in the habits of critique is a level of assertiveness, even aggression (think of the torture-chamber implications of the commonly accepted phrase 'textual *interrogation*'!), that can lead a reader into the trap of becoming simply a habitual debunker, which may result in cynicism rather than open-minded scepticism. Another argument is that the critical process may tend towards certainty that is premature, and given that premature judgements typically lack nuance and sensitivity, this can actually inhibit deeper engagement with a text. Further, Kenneth

White points out how criticist discourse, now so integral to the higher education system, results in 'a vast accumulation of studies and statistics that … get nobody anywhere'.

Why not simply acknowledge that there are limits to the critical paradigm? And having accepted it, consider that criticality has to be developed in conjunction with creative attitudes and practices. Not as an adjunct to critical thinking, not as an afterthought, but together. Right from the get-go and throughout the research and writing process criticality and creativity feed each other in the same way as image and text respond to each other in illustrated books or magazines. Ken Robinson (2011) put this idea beautifully when responding to a suggestion that improving literacy and numeracy in schools had to take precedence over teaching creativity, to which he replied that this was 'like saying we're going to bake a cake and if it works out, then we'll put the eggs in'.

This next section introduces approaches that feed into practical strategies for increasing creativity in how you respond to and appraise texts: sympathetic reading, using belief instead of scepticism to test the validity of an argument, rhizomatic mapping, and freewriting.

Sympathetic reading: a seduction

I mentioned in the previous chapter the importance of gaining distance from a text in order to interpret and evaluate it, giving the example of my reading of the docuseries, *Making a Murderer*. I emphasised the importance of moving back from a highly charged, emotionally loaded story in order to view the facts objectively. It is a balancing act. Start close, then move back. Having discussed the value of an objective, distanced, purely critical approach to reading already, in this section we'll touch upon the opposite: subjectivity in reading, which creates more of a relationship between the author and yourself as reader.

When you first approach a book, article, film, and so on, rather than immediately attempting to distance yourself from it by summarily breaking down everything the author has claimed in order to examine it critically, do your initial reading with a generous spirit and do your best to get into what they are trying to convey. That is, absorb it and try to do justice to their point of view before attempting to analyse it. Allow yourself to muse with the author. In other words, *be seduced*. Working this way not only means wholehearted, practical involvement and active, personal immersion in the text, but the generation of a sympathetic and imaginative relation with the author. Critic Brian Ott (2004, p. 194) refers to the visceral aspects of reading – or 'the erotics of reading' – as a practice, not a methodology. In fact, he goes so far as to refer to 'method' as stifling. He proposes we attempt an imaginative engagement with the text, which has the added benefit of allowing more opportunities for actually enjoying what you're reading! This argument for the reinstatement of pleasure in reading (i.e. subjective connection) is a way of becoming engrossed before dealing with a text objectively and disinterestedly as a carrier of meaning or container of knowledge – in other words, reading in a way that evades being dichotomised and that is both analytical *and* empathetic.

At this juncture I'd like to add another thought – an unorthodox one which will go against the grain for some readers: There may actually be situations where you don't want to critique a text at all. That book or article or film might represent something very dear to you, and you might feel that too much scrutiny would spoil its poetic or aesthetic purpose. In such cases, you might prefer to exercise a kind of intellectual humility, and simply leave it. *Don't* dissect it. Move on to something else that might serve your scholarly purposes. I know this statement is likely to annoy some readers who hold to the idea that it is that very subjectivity that needs critical attention. So I'd like to propose a peer discussion point here:

'*There are certain no-go areas for critical thinkers*. Agree, disagree, or a bit of each.' That's the suggested topic, but save the discussion until later, after reading through more creative strategies for developing ideas to be outlined below. And now, a return to methodologies, albeit non-traditional ones.

From sympathetic reading to the effortful work of 'the believing game'

A related approach is that of Peter Elbow (2008), who experiments with what he's dubbed 'the believing game'. To clarify: where a critical approach requires the use of '*doubting* as a tool to scrutinize and test' to uncover flaws in arguments, illogical conclusions, contradictions, and so forth, he attempts to use '*believing* as a tool to scrutinize and test' (emphasis mine).

Elbow's 'game' disrupts the usual process of doubting, but as he points out, 'It's easy to doubt what is dubious, but the whole point of systematic skepticism is to try to doubt what we find most obvious or right' (p. 4). We already know we need to test notions by using the tool of doubt. We have yet to work out how to utilise the tool of belief.

Exercise 4.1 An uncomfortable thought experiment: doubting what you believe

Following Elbow, I suggest that next time you come across an argument you find repellent for one reason or another – maybe it represents a political stance you find ridiculous, or it discusses with sympathy a social attitude that you find disconcerting – anything that goes seriously against the grain for you intellectually or morally, try to believe it. This does not mean simply listening or resisting the impulse to become combative. It means actively attempting to find some merit in in the argument that offends the assumptions, tastes, or beliefs you hold at the moment. Your goal is to attempt to believe something you would normally dismiss as wrong-minded. It is unnatural and feels very awkward, but that is why humans invent tools – to help us with the hard work. This activity may allow your mind to enter into strange territory so that you can test an idea's validity from the position of belief rather than scepticism. It can be a humbling experience.

Rhizomatic reading and writing

We have moved from consideration of intellectual doubt through sympathy and humility. It will now be interesting to reflect further on possibilities for writerly daring! This was referred to obliquely in Chapter 2, when I suggested that in order to produce work that is vigorous as well as rigorous – and possibly even original – it is necessary to take chances. Here, what comes into play is 'rhizomatic thinking' – a sort of 'non-methodical method'. Rhizomes are the underground stems of a plant that send out roots which, as they spread, sprout other shoots from new nodes forming a complex interweaving root system. This is the image used in *A Thousand Plateaus* by Deleuze and Guattari back in 1987 as a metaphor to describe the non-linear pathways that are constructed in a research methodology in which writing is part of the research, a form of thinking-on-paper.

The discursive model commonly employed in the English-speaking academic world requires that an essay or dissertation, article or book, guides the reader from the introduction through sections or chapter headings, sub-headings, and so forth to the conclusion which summarises all that precedes it (as per the book you are currently reading). There are good reasons for this – it is logical and clear. Similarly, there are good reasons for conducting research in a linear manner. It keeps you on track. But it is also useful at times to depart from this form whose structural boundaries direct a researcher undeviatingly along the pre-set purpose. Why? Because while we might gain clarity, we risk losing sparkle. We need both. And most of us, whether as readers or writers, *want* both. Diversions can lead to unexpected insights that would otherwise never get to see the light of day. Let's be clear here: a little intellectual audacity can be a very fine thing.

Rhizomatic mapping

One technique that we could refer to as 'rhizomatic' is mindmapping. Such idea sketches can be done independently, or in groups. Many of you will have had some experience with mindmaps, but for those of you who haven't, on the next page is an example of what they look like – though of course, given space, they can spread out much further. In fact, one student of mine actually plastered the walls of his room with sheets of butcher's paper all covered with an ever-expanding map of a particular set of ideas in which he was thoroughly engrossed (or some might say, obsessed!) at the time. What follows is a map exploring concepts of beauty.

Traditional mindmap:

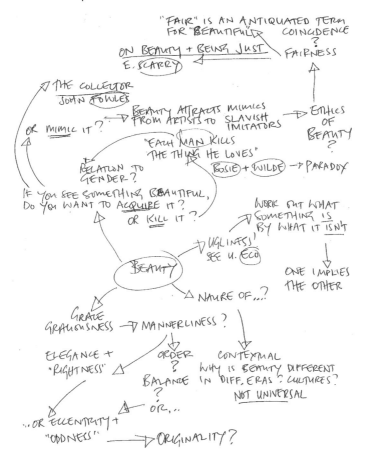

Such maps need to be loose and exploratory; they help you identify keywords for later searches (e.g. 'beauty and mimicry', 'beauty and justice', 'beauty and gender'). Don't subject your spiralling thoughts to the editing process just yet.

One student wrote in her reflection journal, 'mindmaps are a very simple method to visualise what we think about a topic'. Actually, they're not at all simple conceptually, but the process is. What follows are some notes based on my 'Beauty Map':

- The concept I was working with was written in the middle of a large page. It needs to be A3 at the very least (though I had to make do with A4, vertical, in order to fit it into this book). You might also start with a phrase or an essay topic, or the words you choose might be more arbitrary and only relate to the topic peripherally. This is fine because mindmapping is a process that takes place in a sort of transitional zone in the research process, often in the earlier stages of thinking and reading about a broad subject area that has yet to be narrowed down.

- In this instance, I had to consider the possibilities for this very broad concept I was thinking about for an article. Then, because I happen to be what pedagogues refer to as a 'negative learner', my next thought after writing the word 'beauty' was 'ugliness', so I put that down, then immediately added another arrow to point out that 'negative' is not synonymous with 'bad' – 'work out what something is by what it is not.'
- What followed was the thought that 'one implies the other'. This led to a quote I recalled but have yet to source: 'In every assumption is the possibility of its opposite'; and thence to the resolution to work through ugliness to beauty. So I moved on to an ambivalent concept: 'eccentricity.'
- If I find beauty in eccentricity, there are certain to be many who don't. So I added some other tentative definitions including 'grace', 'graciousness', and 'elegance', which looped across to balance, and thence to the golden mean … and so forth.

If you examine the map you will see the links from idea to idea, and also to other authors whom I recalled had worked on beauty and ugliness. The thoughts of scholars Elaine Scarry and Umberto Eco are likely to provide more insights into the concept, as might those of novelists John Fowles and Oscar Wilde. Therefore, one of my next steps was to revisit their books, and in the case of the academics, their bibliographies also.

You will also notice that some of the nodes form clusters of related ideas. Examples of idea clusters include thoughts on the nature of beauty; what is prompted by beauty; the opposite of beauty. These 'clusters' will come to form themes to be explored and developed into an essay or article on the subject of beauty.

An alternative approach to mapping in this way is to:

- take a section of text from a book or article you're currently reading, and underline sentences or phrases that stand out for you because you respond to them strongly – either positively or negatively.
- Relocate these words for further consideration. After extracting the words to form new nodes, these nodes can become departure points for both wiser and deeper thinking on the subject. The difference here is that you're starting with another person's work, and taking it in your own direction by means of association, in order to explore it and to fuel further research. Below is an example of how to start such an exercise. And please note, each of the phrases I've lifted and relocated in new thought-bubbles only represents the *beginnings* for new mindmaps that would be much more extensive, as per the previous example.

Clustering thought-bubbles:

Market value

First – think about specific meanings of 'value' in various contexts. Merit? Worth? Who measures it? For what purposes? Criteria? Do criteria vary depending on field or context? Why?

ORIGINAL VERSION:

In large part narratives determine attitudes towards work, as does lexical manipulation. The meaning of a word changes and therefore our attitude to the subject and the way we respond to it, changes. For instance, when catch-all terms from the market are substituted for specific descriptors (e.g., the word 'product' for 'car', 'painting', 'health', 'film', 'tin of anchovies', 'prosthetic device', 'education', or any other object or amenity that can be sold), meaning is subordinated to market value. Such fuzzy vocabulary displaces other more precise means of expression designed for particular ideas or things, and those ideas that might have been conveyed, those stories that might have been told, are undermined.

fuzzy vocab

fuzzy thinking – fuzzy logic!

I like that. There's got to be a connection.

Room for play here. Parody of clever technologies for starters.

'Those stories that might have been told'

What's at stake here? Think of how dominant cultures overrun not only physical territory, but cultural memory …

Narratives determine attitudes …

To paraphrase: If a narrative is a story, the words we use to tell the story affect how we encounter that story, and affect that story's meaning.
The term 'meaning' implies intent. What intentions do I have in speaking of 'product' rather than 'radio programme' for example? What are the implications for this programme now that it is represented as 'product'. What are the implications for the producer of this programme, who is no longer a programmer, but a supplier of 'content'.

These processes have something in common with surfing the net. The hypertext realm encourages rhizomatic mapping. The pathways you find yourself negotiating when conducting online research are created by developing associations. You, as the mapper, create sense from the mass of possibilities through the links you make. Why click here and not there? Why select this node or direction and not that? It all depends on the partialities of you as author, or maze-navigator (Burbules 2000). There is space for chance and accident while you use your own subjectivities to advantage in order to find 'the desire of the line'.

Before finishing with this section on rhizomatic writing   TIP

You may have come across mindmapping software, but I'd advise against using it as you can become distracted from your thoughts by the formality of the software design, or limited by the options imposed by the designer. It is preferable to work freehand on mindmaps.

You may be thinking at this point that it's all very well to explore ideas in this way, but how would you actually write a rhizomatic text that would still be accepted in a traditional university context? This is a subject we'll deal with in Chapter 10. For now, it's time to consider how you begin to formalise and structure the ideas you've acquired in the mindmapping phase. This is the stage wherein, having been given a broad subject area to work with, you begin to home in on a specific aspect of this subject you will explore in an essay or article. Soon, you'll be able to formulate an actual thesis statement that you've arrived at through imaginative exploration.

One method by which you can narrow down your focus towards forming a thesis and a coherent outline is to start with the clusters you've identified in your map and lay them out clearly – though even at this stage, your configurations will still be rather loose.

Refining clusters – two examples developed from the Beauty Map

Cluster One

Could come under the heading, 'the effects of beauty: desire to kill, acquire, imitate'. Does beauty indeed prompt the desire to destroy? As in Oscar Wilde's claim that, 'Each man kills the thing he loves'? Or does it prompt an acquisitive impulse? Yes, that too. As in the collector's idea of beauty – like collecting butterflies, and in doing so you have to kill them. (Acquisitiveness and murderous impulse together? Oh dear – where is this leading me?) The butterfly's life being worth less than its beauty links to Fowles' novel *The Collector* whose protagonist ultimately murders the beautiful girl he has abducted. 'Killing beauty' again! But another effect may be less acquisitive and murderous: the desire to recreate – to make a representation of the object of beauty. Beauty attracts mimics, and can lead either to the creation of great artworks or to a million slavish imitations. Again, although the link was not willed or consciously contrived, we return again to death – not of the object of beauty, but of its representation. In summary: Beauty prompts the desire to destroy, triggers acquisitive impulses, and attracts imitators.

Cluster Two

Sprouts from 'imitators' on map. There are those who desire to imitate beauty. Who? Acolytes. Fans. Fan culture demonstrates desire to participate in the aura projected by the object of desire, or the object of beauty. Is imitating the original ethical? It can be a great compliment, but not necessarily. Some imitators prefer not to acknowledge their source. In some cultures this is acceptable, but in western cultures it is considered to be a form of theft, which is why universities in Europe, America, Australia, and so on have laws to guard intellectual and creative copyrights. Ethics come into play when one desires to imitate or even 'borrow' from another artist or writer whose work we consider valuable or beautiful, to ensure fairness. Being fair is an ethical position. And 'fair' is an antiquated word for 'beautiful'. Beauty in fairness? In justice? This may be an interesting refinement worth exploring. Some argue that beauty has come to be denigrated as a distraction from seriousness, but perhaps we can consider the possibility that beauty might attract us towards goodness or the repair of injustices. I know I came across this thought somewhere else – revisit Elaine Scarry's book, *On Beauty and Being Just*.

In summary: Beauty represents aesthetic or ethical values, and compels us to imitate it because we want to participate in it, or perhaps to learn from the person, object, concept, or text we so admire – through emulation. This impulse towards imitation is value-free in itself: it depends on how it is used.

I've been dealing with Beauty as a departure point, but the process I've followed is applicable to many investigations across disciplines. The steps I followed for the first cluster are clarified below.

'Cluster One' steps

1. **Identify foundational concept.**
   e.g. Effects of beauty: prompts desire to kill, acquire, imitate.
2. **Rephrase as a question.**
3. **Add evidence to support your agreement or disagreement with each part of your cluster. And note where further evidence will be required.**
   e.g. To kill: Wilde; to acquire: Fowles and Wilde; to imitate: specific evidence needed – refer to particular artists who desire to replicate natural beauty in film or photography, marble or paint. Or more general desire to acquire replications on tea towels, scarves, postcards of famous paintings – reproduced ad infinitum. Also, appropriation of artists' and writers' work by other artists and writers.
4. **Consider refinements and counterarguments.**
   e.g. 'Imitation is the sincerest form of flattery'? Or authorial 'death'? Find supporters and detractors for each view.
5. **Focus on building discussion points, pros and cons.**
   e.g. Desire to kill and to acquire cross over; replication may also result in a kind of death. Or new life in another form?

Having mapped the complexity of possibilities within this broad area you might have decided that these themes could form chapters in a book on Beauty. However, if you're not writing an entire book on the subject, then part of either one might form your thesis statement for an essay or article. Examples:

- 'The death of beauty', or 'How beauty prompts the desire to acquire and to kill.'
- 'Mimics of Beauty: how fan culture both elevates and diminishes the objects of their desire.'
- 'The aesthetic cure: the relationship between the desire for beauty and the desire for justice.' (Although I suspect when I reread Scarry she might have covered this.)

Exercise 4.2 Clustering

Try experimenting with identifying the steps in 'Cluster Two', but map out a topic that you're currently working on in your own discipline. The prompts below may help.

Your topic: ....

Identify foundational concept.

Rephrase as a question.

Add evidence to support your agreement or disagreement with each part of your cluster. Note where further evidence will be required.

Consider refinements and counterarguments.

Focus on building discussion points, pros and cons.

But before getting to the stage of outlining sections in an essay or chapters in a book, there is another useful exercise that combines criticality and creativity which you might like to experiment with.

Freewriting (finding gems in the junk)

Freewriting is often used in universities and other educational contexts as a powerful technique for developing writing skills. The theory is that writing and thinking go together, that is, you don't research and think then write, you do both together: one enhances the other, or as E.M. Forster is reported to have said, 'How do I know what I think until I see what I say?' Or Joan Didion: 'I don't know what I think until I write it down.' This idea will be explored further in the following chapter when we consider 'writing as a method of enquiry'.

Freewriting is most often used by writers of fiction and underutilised in academic writing. However, writing freely on your topic of interest while still in development stages can be highly illuminating. It's also extremely useful to resort to freewriting whenever you feel blocked during the writing process. Like mindmapping and clustering, it helps you to focus and refine your thoughts while also allowing for unexpected possibilities to emerge without conscious intent. Freewriting can be done instead of mindmapping, as they serve a similar purpose, or you can do both. See which you prefer.

There are two main forms: writing to unblock and writing to explore particular ideas. The second is a more focused version. For both, it may be best to use pen and paper, because with a computer you'll be tempted to cut-and-paste and edit as you go – which we absolutely do not want at this stage. In freewriting, editing and proofing are counterproductive.

1. Freewriting to unblock

   By the way, please note that writer's block is normal. While there may be extreme and debilitating cases, usually it does not constitute an insurmountable obstacle. Rather, it might be dealt with either by taking a break or by just writing – *anything*. This is where freewriting is very handy.

   And before you begin, be aware that you will probably start hearing horrible little voices saying things like, 'So many far more brilliant minds than mine have been here – why should I bother?' or 'Why do I think I have anything to say; I'm an arrogant idiot!' or 'People will laugh' or 'People will sneer'. You could address the voices directly if you like. Get angry – it's just you and the paper, after all. Or you could ignore them – they are just aspects of your self-editor on overdrive. Or you may not be feeling insecure, just annoyed that you have to write on a subject you're not all that interested in. Write about that annoyance, and why you feel it. It might also be useful to explore in your freewriting your motivations for embarking on the course of study, that is, return to basics – why you're here at the university breaking your head over obtuse concepts. You might want to criticise the course, the concepts, the teacher, yourself. See what emerges. If you're going through some sort of emotional difficulties unrelated to your work, then write about that too.

Don't worry about grammar or style. Don't worry about neatness. The important thing is – *don't stop* till the timer rings. Even if it means writing something like, 'I don't know what the hell I'm doing this for', that's better than stopping and checking the flow or being tempted to reread or edit. You'll find that in all likelihood you will re-enter the flow after a little while. In fact, you may not want to stop when the buzzer goes – this is not an uncommon experience.

Exercise 4.3 Freewriting

Set a timer. Ten to fifteen minutes is plenty. Begin to write about your frustration about not being able to think clearly, or compose your ideas, or get a handle on the topic – whatever it is that seems to be bothering you. You might feel like expressing anger, or you might approach your feelings with humour or any other emotion you're experiencing. Write about particular fears, perhaps a sense of inadequacy to the task.

2. Freewriting for scholarly exploration

For this exercise, you'll have to have done some initial research. Freewriting here is to help you to clarify directions you might take in your essay or article. The material you've read as well as your early thoughts on the subject will inform what comes next.

As you write, you might also find that the freewriting wants to become a mindmap – if so, follow the desire of that line of action. Map the thoughts out as you go. You'll probably ask yourself questions too, like 'What is the main thing I want to convey here?', or 'What do I really mean by my phrase, ...?', or, 'Is there another way of putting it that would make it clearer?' Again, don't worry about style or structure and *don't stop*. Don't take your hand from the page; just *keep going* till the buzzer goes off.

Exercise 4.4 Freewriting

So set a timer again, and begin to write. Put down the first thoughts that occur to you regarding the topic as you understand it, based on the research you've conducted. There might be some idea that's only partly formulated that you'd like to develop but you're not sure how – write about that. If you know that your essay will need some sort of careful introduction and justification but you're not quite ready for that, then skip it, and just keep writing about the idea that wants to emerge. You might find that your writing starts to turn into loose ideas in dot points or linked by dashes – fine – forge ahead; you can add asterisks if you think you want to develop those points later.

After you've finished, read though what you've written. You may well find that that there will be some 'gems in the junk' that you can use in your essay.

Outlining

At this point you need to start organising your ideas into a cohesive whole, that is, to draft your outline and work out your text's 'best structure'. Having decided upon a thesis statement, you must let that statement control the direction of your argument. Do not lose track of it. Everything you write must relate back to that statement, which might be:

Beauty represents value. It is context-dependent, and associated with power and desire.

i. Begin by putting your thesis statement at the top of the page. For rhetorical impact, make it a strong statement. (Persuasive tactics like this are detailed in Chapter 8.)
    Introduction: At this stage it's only necessary to (1) write a rationale as to why you've approached the subject from the angle you've chosen – this will clarify it in your own mind; then (2) state your contention that concepts of beauty are culturally circumscribed, and inform your reader of the culture/s you're referring to in your essay; and (3) explain that you're going to be looking at the relation of concepts of beauty to power and desire. Don't be too concerned about providing a detailed overview of how you intend the essay to progress just yet, because the order in which you arrange the sections will change as you go through the drafting process.
ii. Lay out the sections you intend to cover in order to prove your thesis. Write a short paragraph for each. Conclude each of those paragraphs with a lead into the one to follow. If they don't follow clearly or if, say para 9 can go where para 16 is, then be aware that you may have to rework your structure, because ideally there should be only one place for each paragraph. This can take a while – and it can't all be done before you start drafting. At this stage you might not be 100% sure of how the essay will pan out. It will evolve during the drafting process. But when you can answer 'yes' to all the following questions …

  - Are all my points relevant to my thesis?
  - Is a logical sequence beginning to emerge?
  - Have I provided enough evidence to support my points so far?
  - Conversely, have I included too much backup so that my own voice is becoming lost in a sea of quotes?
  - Do my ideas flow coherently creating a well-considered and thoughtful argument?

… you're ready to begin your first draft. It is best to do so while the ideas are still fresh in your mind.

Drafting, revising, and giving and receiving feedback

If the task you're working on is relatively short, say a 1500- to 2000-word essay, it's a good idea to get your first draft down in one sitting. Yes, it will still be loose; it will have grammatical, stylistic, and structural flaws – all fine – it's only a first draft. First drafts aren't refined documents. They are just one step further along the track from a freewriting exercise. But it's an *informed* freewriting exercise. So have all your research material ready to hand, *go offline*, and focus all your attention on the task to hand.

If your assignment is a longer one, then obviously you can't get a draft down in one sitting. Choose a section. It doesn't matter which section. It might be the introduction, though it's more likely to be a piece from the body of the text that you feel most comfortable with. It's only later that you have to start linking the sections up in a way that reflects your outline – which, as mentioned, is still loose at this stage. You may well find that new ideas will occur to you as you plough through this part of the process – note them down and file them – they may come in handy later.

When you have a fair copy – and by that I mean a text that you deem accessible to people outside your own brain – it's a good idea to get some feedback from your peers. That study group I mentioned before? Very helpful here, because this is the stage at which you can really use some fresh eyes, no matter whether you like to work alone in the main.

It goes like this:

Exercise 4.5 Study group activity

1. Each group member brings his or her paper along to your meeting place. You'll need to select a timekeeper, and allocate a time limit for each person. Be strict with timing so that others don't start getting restless or feeling neglected. Say, 15 minutes.
2. Distribute copies to each of your peers. One person reads. Don't rush. The others need time to take notes or jot down questions as you read.

    Q: Why reading aloud?

    A: Mistakes and inconsistencies often become more apparent. The ear may pick up what the eye misses.

3. The reader finishes then asks something to which they want an answer, like 'Are you clear on my thesis? Any questions about where I'm coming from?'
4. The others respond.
5. The reader might then ask, 'Do you need any other information or explanations?' or 'Is there anything I could add (or subtract) to improve flow or clarity?'
6. The others respond.

As group members, you have to make sure that the questions you ask are actually useful. Not much point in saying, 'I like it', or 'it sounds okay to me'. Slightly more helpful might be something like, 'I thought the way you qualified the concept of critical thought in relation to creative process was eloquent'. An actual question would be better though. Like, 'Can you give an example to illustrate the relationship between critical and creative thinking?' And a really good question might be, 'I was intrigued when you moved from the discussion of objective intellectual engagement to subjective involvement in a topic, but can you clarify how these two perspectives can work together?'

Revise your draft based on responses as soon as possible after the peer review. And ask yourself such questions as,

- Can my thesis be clearer? How might I go about making it more succinct?
- Does the order in which ideas emerge in my draft work as well as it could?
- How could it be improved? Maybe the transitions between ideas?
- If one of my friends was confused, could it mean something's missing in my outline?
- Do I need to do further research on any of the aspects I've covered? (The answer to this question will probably be yes, as it's rare that you will have covered everything you need in a first draft.)
- Is my language refreshing – or a bit on the turgid side? (A good sign of this is if anyone dozed off while you were reading!)

You will certainly find you need to amend your outline and rewrite – this is only a first draft and therefore bound to be imperfect.

Exercise 4.6 Discussion point

I mentioned a potential discussion topic earlier, one that should be relevant to all readers of this particular book, regardless of discipline:

There are certain no-go areas for critical thinkers. Agree, disagree, or a bit of each.

I chose this based on Brookfield's assertion from the previous chapter which is worth reiterating here:

the most dramatic leaps forward in ... understanding of material are usually triggered by having to resolve some sort of disorienting dilemma, that is, having to reconcile two antithetical yet valid responses to a question, or having to incorporate into their frame of understanding a new piece of information that calls into question much of what they had previously held to be true.

(Continued)

However, you and the members of your study group may decide that there are other contentious topics more worth your while exploring; if so, please go ahead, as you'll need to do some reading in order to have an informed discussion. The previous chapter's advice on group textual analysis ended with the distribution among the group of each member's summary and analysis of the text. It was upon these analyses that the group discussion was to be based. But in the interests of consolidating a couple of the practices explored in this chapter, instead of launching into discussion after reading each person's contribution, map out the ideas rhizomatically, then cluster them. If there are three to six or more of you in a group, give one member the role of scribe. If you're working in pairs you may prefer to take turns. Either way, experiment with mapping and clustering and see how this affects the nature and quality of the discussion that emerges.

Conclusion

This chapter began by mentioning three mistaken beliefs surrounding creativity, because the term is often misused and the concept itself misapplied. I do not want readers of this book to harbour the idea that creativity is just a means to solving short-term pre-set problems. To hold to such an instrumentalist attitude is to grossly limit the possibilities for intellectual and imaginative exploration. I also set up the major concern of the chapter, by firstly clarifying the meanings of criticality and creativity and then showing how these conceptions work together to produce clearer – and potentially more original – thinking. New understandings of the world occur when creative and critical faculties work in tandem. Only then might we achieve 'rational insights'. Methods of approaching reading and writing using critical thinking, creativity, sympathy, the (seemingly perverse) activity of Elbow's 'believing game', and intuition together were explored, as was 'rhizomatic' mapping and freewriting. These aids to scholarly exploration inform the preliminary writing phases of outlining and drafting, and assist in the development of strong and coherent academic writing, approaches to which will be developed further in the following chapters.

Research Practices

Chapter overview

This chapter on research practice considers:

- An integrated approach to writing and research. Very brief historical background about the separation of writing and research – and the ascendancy of objectivity over subjectivity – is firstly provided
- How different writers require different approaches to writing and research
- Building a body of annotations, and assimilating subjectivities into research material
- Searching the literature for a research topic using 'the concertina effect' – development of strategies outlined in the previous chapter
- Disciplined writing exercises to concentrate your reading and refine analytical and critical skills.

The focus of this chapter is research practices within the context of expanding critical awareness. Chapters 2 and 3 set the scene by reviewing essential attributes of a critical thinker, then discussing particular 'tools' of reflection and logic that support intellectual work. Chapter 4 discussed how creative and critical processes align when forming a thesis based on the sort of broad topics set at postgraduate level. This chapter now looks specifically at the processes and skills required to conduct research for extended self-selected writing tasks, from longer articles and essays to dissertations and theses. Here, writing and research are treated as complementary aspects of one multilayered process, so writing begins as soon as you start reading, that is, at the very earliest stages while mapping out ideas towards the finished written product.

I'd also like to point out here that while the discussion points and examples provided in this chapter may appear more relevant to those involved in non-empirical or desk-based research, all writers need to be able to conduct a research project effectively and to present a case persuasively, whether composing a scientific report or presenting the findings in a series of case studies or writing a paper on Shakespeare's handling of madness in tragedy.

'Writing: a method of enquiry'

Sociologist Laurel Richardson (2005) claims that often enough within her discipline, the literature available on topics that sound fascinating can appear on the page in a form best described as boring. Like many of us, Richardson had been taught not to start writing until she had organised and outlined all her points and proofs, and to maintain an objective stance throughout. But many find this approach constraining. Arguably, the reason for the insistence on this rather mechanistic approach is a reflection of the adoption of quantitative methods from the sciences by humanities researchers in an effort to make their work seem somehow more reliable.

To put this in context, scholarly work wasn't always hard-line regarding method and objectivity. It was in the 19th century that professionalisation of academia started to occur. A case in point: After being appointed a place at Harvard University and coming to enjoy professional status, the acclaimed amateur scholar Charles Eliot Norton criticised other scholars for what he termed their 'feminine passionateness' as opposed to 'masculine' objectivity. He championed 'the organisation of knowledge according to professional and objective standards', a stance which has come to be the norm (cited in Garber 2001, pp. 17–18). But, as Alan Jay Levinovitz (2016) points out much later, fetishising of scientistic models in many disciplines (and he's talking about economics) does not guarantee truth – just its appearance. Many other scholars have noted the problem of the semblance of objectivity masking truth, and we'll revisit this conversation point in Chapter 10, but for now it's enough to say that this conservative attitude endures, but has been and continues to be contested even from within the sciences.

Such freedom of movement is particularly vital with regard to writing and research within the arts and humanities. Where a scientific study can employ charts and graphs and other illustrative forms and can summarise results in a way that enables the reader to get straight to the point of the study, a humanities tract tends to require closer attention and the work of an ethnographer or a historian, a philosopher or a student of comparative literature may not be best served when written in standardised, scientistic language. This is why there has been an acknowledgement in more recent times that knowledge need not conform to one fixed form in order to be considered authoritative, and students are now encouraged to explore other approaches to writing eloquently and with vigour. In other words, the style of writing needs to reflect what one is writing about – form and content go hand in hand.

Laurel Richardson refers to 'CAP', or 'creative analytical processes', used within sociology and emphasises that writing methods themselves inform the content and quality of the research that emerges. This is another way of looking at what was discussed in the previous chapter of this book: creativity and criticality as mutually supportive aspects of writing.

In 'Writing is not just a basic skill', Mark (not to be confused with Laurel) Richardson (2008, n.p.) eloquently disabuses his readers of 'pernicious myths' surrounding writing in university at all levels, and one point he makes is of particular relevance here:

> Writing is not the expression of thought; it is thought itself. Papers are not containers for ideas, containers that need only to be well formed for those ideas to emerge clearly. Papers are the working out of ideas. The thought and the container take shape simultaneously (and develop slowly, with revision).

'Know thyself': identify your research style

As this chapter looks at reading and writing together, best work out an approach to research tasks that sits well with you, personally, because the reflective and interpretative aspects of research cannot help but involve the subjectivities of the researcher, which is why reflective journals were prescribed in the second chapter of this book.

There are different kinds of writers. Creme and Lea (2008, pp. 72–76) suggest, for instance, 'divers' who like to plunge right in; 'grand-planners' who need to do a great deal of researching and annotating – often reading and writing a good more than they'll actually end up using – before they begin drafting; and 'architects' who like to formulate a structure diagrammatically before they begin. In the same way, there are also divers, grand-planners, architects and so forth among researchers. I have asked several students and colleagues over the last couple of years where they think they fit, and some say that they've found that this depends on the stage of research process, and the ideas or data they are exploring at the time. So before going any further, stop for a moment to reflect upon the kind of writer or researcher you consider yourself to be, and if you prefer to be one kind at the beginning perhaps, then shift into other modes as you progress.

How to recognise your research style?

1. When faced with the prospect of an extended writing task, do you
   (a) Go blank with panic?
   (b) Become excited at the prospect of the acres of reading stretching off into the misty distance?
   (c) Calmly begin to survey the territory, then begin to read and annotate, looking forward to when you will start to see a structure emerging?

It seems self-evident that B is inclined towards grand-planning – wanting to acquire a stack of articles and books and just read, keeping notes minimal at first. Another way of telling if you're a grand-planner is if you actually feel ill-at-ease without first amassing tons of material, even if much of it won't actually be needed in the long run. So go ahead and follow that path. Such people often find that because their concentration is so intense, they're able to recall key arguments quite well when they actually start drafting.

C, on the other hand, tends towards the architectural approach. Some researchers find themselves naturally scoping out perspectives to investigate and ideas to pursue diagrammatically, with columns and headings, subheadings and arrows to other possible points of departure.

But A? A doesn't know yet. If this is you, then rather than freezing on the edge of the terrifying precipice, the best advice is – jump. And if, after jumping in and swimming around for a while in the ocean of resources you're happy, carry on.

(Continued)

But if you find you're drowning, then get out and dry off and make a plan. Try 'B' for a while.

You might not be a natural diver, but a nervous planner who needs a push. So, push yourself.

Alternatively, you might consider jotting down notes or pieces of experimental writing like those mentioned in the previous chapter – mindmapping and clustering. And freewriting comes into its own here; even though you're not actually doing an essay yet, you're researching. Freewriting is for generating ideas and directions to follow as much as anything else. Remember, it doesn't matter where you start – just choose an aspect of the topic that interests you most (you'll have an idea of what that is by now, after all that swimming around in the resources) and begin to write. Then read some more, and begin to write informally on another related subject. In time you'll find the ideas that are of greatest value to your main topic and gradually home in on them. Not only that, but some of the loose writing you've done at this stage may well contribute to the final product.

If indeed you simply want to do some writing first before establishing what it is you really want to say on the subject, you're probably a natural diver who is happy to allow a plan to emerge as you read and gather information. Divers take quite readily to treating writing and researching together.

There are strengths and weaknesses for each approach. For instance, those who dive into the process of reading widely and immediately start drawing on extremely diverse sources will gain a broad view of the field of investigation. All well and good, but do take particular care to include bibliographic details as you go rather than skipping merrily over documenting your sources only to find that, down the track, you can't remember where you sourced that idea, from whom, and when. This is where the risk of accidental plagiarism becomes very real. 'Grand-planners', on the other hand, will find that their plan has to change as their body of knowledge grows, and it's essential to allow for this, rather than feeling too wedded to the original conception. Similarly, the diagrams of 'architects' need to remain open to amendment, otherwise a great deal of time and energy will be wasted in trying to make new evidence suit old schema. The point is that it helps to be aware of what suits you and what doesn't so that you don't try to fit yourself into a mould that doesn't work for you – square peg into a round hole situation is always painful. Rather than feeling miserable and inept, work with your strengths. And regardless of what these strengths might be, make sure you annotate texts as you go, keeping a record of all the authors whose ideas you may need to refer back to later on.

Searching the literature

Identifying a research topic takes time. While you'll already know in a general sense what it is that interests you, you may not know precisely what aspects you want to explore. It's only after you've conducted a literature search that you will be able to come up with a topic that:

1. commands your interest to the extent that you look forward to spending months (or years) thinking and writing about it;
2. is worth exploring because nobody else has approached the topic in quite the same way; and
3. will interest your intended readership.

Mind the gap

TIP

Through your literature search you'll be able to discover what others have already considered with regard to your project, and to establish whether or not you think you can add an idea or an insight to the body of knowledge that already exists – that is, is there a gap of knowledge or interpretation waiting to be discovered? The gap might be filled by some previously un- or underexplored idea, or an as yet unanswered question that you think you can answer, or a solution to a problem.

This is what we might call 'problem-*finding*' – a good deal more complex and creative than mere 'problem-*solving*'.

A way of researching that is both linear and lateral, progressive and iterative, I refer to as 'the concertina effect' because, as when you breathe, you are drawing in information, absorbing the oxygen of others' ideas, which is followed by exhaling in a concentrated stream – and this will be repeated several times throughout the research process, like the expansion and contraction of a concertina in order to make music. Research is not meant to be stultifying or intellectually exhausting, but the opposite. It is a living, breathing practice and it needs to be given the chance to invigorate the researcher's mind, to expand horizons, not enclose them or restrict then in a safe little academic silo.

The concertina effect

But how to go about this search? There is wide reading, then there is finely honed, focused reading: balancing distance and closeness in a slightly different way from that discussed previously, that is, after reading widely, home in on a particular idea or theory which will in turn lead to other related ones, so you'll expand your attention again, then return to examine a particular aspect in detail … then repeat. For example, if you were investigating a topic like, 'how we express our relationship to money and economic processes', you might come across the work of behavioural economist Keith Chen (2013), who claims

(Continued)

that language influences our attitude towards saving money. You might be intrigued to note Chen's finding that speakers of languages with no future tense (Chinese, for example) tend to be better at saving money because their conceptualisation of the future seems less distant and abstract, more *present*, than that of speakers of a more overtly 'futured' language, like English. You might then be led to explore linguistic-cultural connections in a way that is beyond what is narrowly circumscribed as 'economic', and to read authors who are not involved in economics at all. It is important to allow yourself a certain set time – with a real deadline, if you're feeling particularly constrained – for exploring divergent pathways. Then return to a narrower economic focus once more, until your research leads you to follow another intellectually stimulating and potentially useful direction.

A little more detail on what is involved in such wide reading follows, and after that, a discussion of close reading.

Wide reading

Your work will gain vitality if you allow time to go off the beaten track and read outside of your discipline, because thinkers in fields other than your own will turn up a range of ideas and perspectives, perceptions and sensibilities that you would otherwise not encounter. Don't be corralled by (sometimes arbitrary) academic boundaries. This more open-minded practice will refresh your outlook and open up the possibility for you to write something *of your own*, something no one else but you could have written, because no one else could have followed exactly the same pathways that you selected or made the connections in quite the way you have. Method is a tool. Treating it as law can take over from the writing and reading itself, estranging you from your task. As philosopher of science Paul Feyerabend (1993) insists, open-ended research practices help develop the imagination and therefore creativity within an academic context.

Wide reading aligns with the 'non-methodical method' of 'rhizomatic' research, (see pp. 54–66 in Chapter 4) which Nicholas Burbules (2000, n.p.) equates with the activity of surfing the web, and often enough it does in fact involve just that: surfing the web. So google and surf and allow yourself to follow different pathways based on purely associative connections for a while. Most readers of this book will have access to authoritative peer-reviewed articles, but don't think you must always start with the most extensively cited experts. Of course you *will* refer to them – in fact it is essential that you do read the seminal authors – but rather than making them your first port of call it can sometimes be useful to get a bit of context from more generalist trade publications, especially if you're unfamiliar with the field. Such texts are easier to read; after all, they're written for a wide audience of intelligent, educated, curious-minded people like yourself, rather than exclusively for the eyes of scholars. As are talks (yes, including TED), podcasts, and so on. Watch and listen. Visit the library and talk to librarians – they're often a font of information and many are happy to talk. Borrow books and download articles that stimulate you even though they might seem only tangentially connected to your focus, and enjoy those tangents, muse over them and start developing mindmaps; make *your own* connections. Discuss your ideas with friends and colleagues via social media or face-to-face. And all the while you're doing this, you'll be taking notes – *and noting where you got the ideas from: record full bibliographic details of each text.* If you wait till you've finished reading before you start writing you'll miss out on the sort of insights that can emerge when you're thinking on paper – and you'll also lose track of your research. Look closely at bibliographies of authors whom you've enjoyed and follow their thinking back to their sources, and make sure you ground recent research with historical background. (By the way, where I might insist on historical context, other texts on research skills may stress that because older research will often have been superseded you'll be wasting your time. This is another false dichotomy – at least within humanities and social sciences disciplines. While you don't want to get bogged down in the past, you certainly do need to know where the ideas that interest you come from. You don't want to end up working in a vacuum, 'cleverly' citing recently fashionable theories without any idea of how the scholarship got to that point.)

Bear in mind that because this kind of wide-ranging research includes material that may not always be entirely reliable, it is vital to keep interrogating texts as you read them, checking their provenance, reliability and validity, comparing them with other sources, and remarking in your notes not only on points made by authors but also your responses to them.

Regarding note taking while reading widely: *Do it.*   **TIP**

Highlighting is not enough. It is too passive. Have you ever had the experience of returning to a highlighted print-out and saying to yourself, What was I thinking? Why are all these passages *pink*? Well, you won't know what you were thinking or why they're pink because you're in a different mood now, thinking different thoughts. When you take notes, even if they're scrawled marginalia (yes, that's okay; if it's a library book, just write in pencil and erase your scribble before you return it) you are actively engaged, you're thinking purposefully, not vagueing out or thinking about getting a coffee or feeding the cat.

Exercise 5.1 Wide online search with mindmap

1. Set yourself a time limit. An hour or two will do for this exercise, though it will be repeated several – or possibly many – times as you research, depending upon the requirements of the assignment and its length.
2. Sit in front of your computer and also keep a piece of paper and pen to hand for taking notes.

(Continued)

3. Choose a broad subject area you're interested in but don't yet know much about – early planning stage of a writing project. Write the topic on the piece of paper, and draw a line outwards from it to a phrase or a word that you think might be worth exploring.
4. Go online and key in that phrase and see where it leads you. Keep jotting the connections down on the paper as they emerge. No need to go to a university database yet. Where you find an idea or source questionable, jot down your queries for future reference.
5. Highlight key words.
6. Note also your reactions to what you find, whether intellectually speculative, emotional, or sensory. You might want to take a few minutes occasionally to pursue some of these more personal reflections.
7. When you find something of particular interest, make a note to add it to your annotated bibliography later on.

Close reading

This is where you become a lot more selective and start working exclusively with particular authors whose work will contribute directly to your understanding of your topic. You will also need to identify and read the most frequently cited thinkers in the field and establish what their theoretical bases are.

Being familiar with the seminal texts within the broader context will help your research topic to become much clearer to you – and it's best framed as a question. For instance, the statement from Chapter 4, 'Beauty prompts the desire to destroy, acquisitive impulses, and attracts imitators' you might rephrase as, '*How does* beauty prompt destructiveness, acquisitiveness, and attract imitators?' Or, you might really hone it down to a very tight focus like, 'In what contexts does beauty create the desire to destroy?'

Usually the advice given to students is that a good research question should not be too broad. This makes sense because it makes your task more manageable. Some texts will insist that a lack of focus occurs if, for example, you choose to explore the works of a favourite author rather than just a couple of books, or that you must select a narrow time frame within which to conduct your research on your topic. But such stringency can also lead to *over*specialising. It is not the best advice for everyone. Only you, with help from colleagues or supervisors, can make that decision. Following Brookfield's advice to teachers to 'model criticality' by providing personal examples of their own attempts to do so (cited in Davies and Barnett, 2015, pp. 536–539), I'll admit to encountering problems when as a very inexperienced doctoral candidate interested in liminality – or intermediate phases – I initially came up with the terribly unfocused topic of 'The In-between'. My supervisor kindly asked me first of all, in-between what and what, Louise? And is this 'in-between' a *place* or a fugal *state of mind* – you know, like when you're in-between sleep and waking?

I thought it could be either. So I looked up other writers who had investigated transitional zones that are geographically real (like politically contested territories), then psychologically real (sometimes experienced in traditional initiation rites), and others that are imagined (literary examples abound). Then a friend asked what disciplinary lens I planned to use. I decided I needed at least three – anthropological, mythical, and literary. Other questions followed, helping me arrive at a grouping of ideas over which I had some control. They did not narrow down my interests; rather, they crystallised them while also obliging me to think practically about how to manage my thesis.

Later, as a supervisor myself, I have encountered students who seem to have more tangents than hubs, so to speak. Again, asking questions to help them sort out what they really want to say has proven to be a useful practice. This is why I've emphasised elsewhere in this book the importance of discussion with peers, whether colleagues or fellow students.

The point is, if you have wide interests or your topic is particularly complex – which is highly likely if you're doing a doctorate, then a question that reflects this complexity will be in order – and still be manageable. But *only* if it is mapped out and organised into smaller segments or sub-topics that you can deal with one at a time – as per the 'clustering' exercise already provided. And always bear in mind the clusters' relation to each other and to the thesis question so that they interlink fluently. If one or more of these clusters can't be woven into the overall structure you may find that eventually you'll have to 'kill that darling'. (But never put it in a coffin and nail the lid down – file it for later use. It could be the germ of another essay, book chapter, or book.) Recently I met a student who was working on an essay on the role of the public intellectual. She had so many examples to explore it would have been impossible to deal with them all within the set word count. The most tangential 'darlings' had to die. So rather than investigating too many public intellectuals – and she had examples from the disparate fields of medicine, science, technology, arts, history, with case studies for each – she opted eventually to focus on the impact of intellectuals working in environmental and arts spheres. Her decision was led by logic (these two 'idea clusters' could be satisfactorily related) and also by her heart (these were things that she could get most excited about). She was also able to explain verbally what she wanted to do in two or three sentences. It's a fantastic exercise: *condense what you want to do into a very brief statement, or what some people like to refer to as an 'elevator speech'.*

Some of us need to test ourselves with tasks that may be difficult, but are stimulating. That said, your topic does need to be narrow enough that you're able to become authoritative on the subject, and that it links to other researchers' work, so if you *do* need to narrow it down, then you'll need to impose limiters. For example, 'How does beauty prompt destructiveness, acquisitiveness, and attract imitators?' could become, 'How does *female* beauty prompt destructiveness, acquisitiveness, and attracted imitators?' Or, 'How *have attitudes towards* beauty prompted destructiveness, acquisitiveness, and attracted imitators *in the realm of business*?'

Exercise 5.2 Focused reading

1. Identify the key researchers in your field.
2. Search out one or two of their authoritative works via a reputable academic search engine like Google Scholar.
3. Work out their theoretical base. To what school of thought do they belong? To answer this question, it will be helpful to check out their bibliography to see the background of the authors to whom they have referred.
4. Add them to your annotated bibliography: instructions on how to do this follow presently.
5. If you find one of the texts to be of particular interest, review it – again, instructions follow. If you haven't found a text of particular interest, look again until you do.
6. Find an author who disagrees with him/her and do a comparative review.
7. Consider how the ideas of the authors you uncovered in wide reading might relate to the more authoritative sources.
8. The more comprehensive your notes, the simpler the task of the literature review.

After several iterations of wide, then focused reading (or concertina-ing), you will know what others have already covered and what's left for you to contribute to the field of enquiry that will satisfy two central requirements of dissertations and theses – that the work is original and demonstrates independent thinking.

This next section includes some disciplined writing exercises that require you to think in a concentrated way about your readings, and to further refine your critical skills and your ability to encapsulate ideas with brevity and succinctness. They are,

1. the annotated bibliography
2. the article review
3. the critical literature review.

If you build the first two exercises into your research practice – as suggested above – you'll find that constructing a critical literature review will be a great deal easier. But first of all, after identifying a text that you think will be useful, critique it by following the instructions provided in Chapter 3 under the heading, 'Is it true? Is it useful? What is its value?'

To jog your memory:

- Identify the main claim and the secondary issues.
- Identify any rhetorical strategies employed by the author – these may either increase its value or detract from it. This will help you to:
- Identify implicit as well as explicit meanings in the text.
- Ask yourself what the broader implications of the text might be.
- Make a judgement as to the text's value to your own task.

Interrogating a text in this way will help to clarify the author's intentions. As you read, also consider why they make the assertions they make and their motivations. Check also whether they've substantiated all their claims with timely and reliable evidence, and that they've provided adequate context for their ideas, findings, and so on. Then you'll be able to make a judgement as to how well they've fulfilled their aims and to assess the text's relevance to your own project. As the texts you analyse mount up, you need to start keeping notes on the sources in a more disciplined way.

The annotated bibliography

An annotated bibliography describes and evaluates individual texts more briefly than a whole article review – which we'll look at next. Annotations of bibliographic references only require a brief paragraph – say 150 to 200 words – to remind you of the content and value of the text. It may seem time-consuming at first, but because you'll have to read a lot of material, having succinct memory-joggers for each text saves time in the long run. The main things to attend to, after a *very* brief summary of the content – using whatever abbreviated form you prefer – are reliability, authority, limitations, and usefulness. Here's an example:

Author, X (2011) 'Dangerous narratives: politics, lies, and ghost stories', *Cosmopolitan Civil Societies Journal,* **Vol. 3, No. 1.**

Provides refs from mythic traditions to support her thesis about 'monsterfication', first of Jews in Europe, then of Arabs by Israelis in modern Israel/Palestine – an unusual strategy, but has strong rhetorical impact. Although verging on becoming rather other-worldly at times, the arguments are thoroughly supported and are presented convincingly.

[Relevance] The most useful part of the text for me was Author's reading of Israel/Palestine as 'heterotopia' – after Foucault – as it feeds into my own understanding of contested territories in a different geographical location, the Pacific region.

I've mentioned the usefulness of grouping the authors you research   **TIP**
according to their theoretical position. Such categorisation helps when
you come to write your literature review, making it easier to navigate the
ways one piece of research builds on previous research so that you can, over
time, develop a kind of conceptual map of the field of interest. So, in your
annotated bibliography, code the entries according to the school of thought to
which they belong.

The critical review

The critical review – also called an article review (Mahboob and Humphrey, 2008) – is a useful exercise, one that is sometimes set by lecturers to ascertain students' comprehension and critical ability. It is longer than an annotation in a bibliography because it requires more information that that needed for a simple memory-jogger. But it's much shorter than a literature review, which deals with many texts. Try to keep it down to no more than about 750 words max. Quite often when students first attempt to review a text they find they want to write a good deal more, but one of the points about this writing genre is its brevity. It is an exercise in concision that refines critical ability. It summarises a text, identifies its strengths, and points out its value to your own work. Use this form for articles that you find particularly interesting.

There are three phases of summary in an article review, which refine your focus while further strengthening your ability to 'cut to the chase' in your writing.

1. In the introduction, after your full bibliographic citation (which of course you would never *dream* of omitting!) summarise the content, and what you think is the author's intention.
2. Isolate aspects of the text that you find of particular interest. Summarise each of these individually. You might choose to look at content, writing style, methodology – whatever is the most interesting or relevant to your study. Include a brief critique and evaluation per aspect.
3. Conclude with an overall assessment of the points evaluated – *not* the entire text as you've already covered that in the intro.

The following example outlines the structure of a critical review, which is based on the sample bibliographic annotation provided above. The **bold text** indicates where you'd expand the information into a more detailed critique and evaluation, also noting the relevance of each issue to your own work. The <u>underlinings</u> show which aspects of the article one might choose to focus on in the review. The word count of the example is 365, so the areas upon which you'd expand would roughly double the length of the review.

Author, X (2011)

[Summary **and authorial intent**] The article is concerned with how narratives affect the cultural imagination, thereby informing ways we apprehend the world. **Through historical and literary case studies the author attempts to cast political conflicts in a new light. 'Dangerous narratives'** takes examples from historical and contemporary politics, looking at how dominant cultures 'imagine' minorities, and how such constructed 'imaginaries' can have a dehumanising effect on those minorities.

    [**critique and** evaluation **topic 1**] **The rationale for <u>using narrative</u> as a departure point for political discussion is explained and contextualised**

(Continued)

early on with references to … [expand]. As the article develops, the connections of the literal and the mythic to the political become clearer through both concrete examples and metaphors …. [expand, noting relevance to your own work].

[critique and evaluation topic 2] Author's references to the literature of horror is apt, because she is dealing with perceived 'monsterfication' first of Jews in Europe, then of Arabs by Israelis in modern Israel/Palestine … [expand] This is an unusual strategy, but it has strong rhetorical impact and is also convincing because all the arguments are thoroughly supported. The obscurity of some examples is mitigated by the fact that they are made clear by … [expand].

[critique and evaluation topic 3] Author's prose style is worth remarking on because while it is largely handled with scholarly restraint, some might disapprove of its occasionally overly emotive departures. Personally, I appreciate this as an acknowledgement of the very real horror of the subject matter with which the article is concerned … [expand].

[critique and evaluation topic 4] The reading of Israel/Palestine as a liminal zone or 'heterotopia', a space that is both mythic and real … [expand].

[conclusion] The use of narrative, particular engagement with horror literature, occasionally emotive writing style, and the link to Foucault's concept of the heterotopia are dealt with in such a way that …. [expand] However, the most useful part of 'Dangerous Narratives …' for me was Author's reading of Israel/Palestine as 'heterotopia' – Foucault's notion – as it feeds into my own understanding of contested territories in a different geographical territory, the Pacific region.

I've observed that regardless of the fact that most postgraduates certainly understand, at least theoretically, that 'critical' here means that you are required to 'think critically' about the article, in the context of reviewing some find it hard to disassociate the term from its more colloquial meaning – fault finding. While you may indeed find faults (with research method, with writing style, with claims made, etc.) that is not the intention of this exercise, which is simply to appraise an article so as to ascertain its particular value to your research project. Thus there is no point in spending time reviewing something if you don't think it will be useful – you'd be better of focusing on other texts that would be.

The critical literature review

The critical literature review is one of the most refined academic genres. It is your formal, written exploration of the field with which you have been familiarising yourself through wide then close reading supported by annotations, brief textual reviews, and summaries, as well as mindmaps and clustering exercises discussed in the previous chapter (the latter in the context of set essay questions).

Q: What is the difference between a descriptive and a *critical* literature review?

A: The former is basically a detailed list; the latter, an intellectual exploration and synthesis of interrelated ideas that are critiqued with insight. A descriptive literature review does not require you to make an argument about what is indicated by the research; a critical literature review does. It is necessary to construct a persuasive argument as in an essay.

Q: What then, is the difference between a critical literature review and an essay?

A: An essay explores a range of arguments and supports them with evidence. With a literature review, it is the literature itself that you are exploring.

A critical literature review appraises and evaluates a range of texts, both published and unpublished, in varying detail. You have to work out which ones are worth looking at in depth and which warrant only a passing reference. It should be clear by now that making these decisions will be easier if you have already annotated your bibliography and critically reviewed some individual texts. Passing references have one of two functions: to add substance to another reference, or to demonstrate to your reader or examiner that you know the field very well. You decide which is necessary in the context of your thesis. Remember, the literature review is not a stand-alone piece of work. It is written as part of a much larger task.

Q: What, specifically, are the purposes of the literature review?

A: Multiple purposes. To:

- Clarify your overall intention for your thesis.
- Construct a framework that sets the limits within which you mean to work.
- Overview important concepts and patterns of thought in the field.
- Provide perspective – both conceptual and historical – and to situate your own research in context.
- Evaluate content and methods of previous research.
- Identify conflicting arguments.
- Identify gaps in knowledge.
- Demonstrate how your ideas or findings or perceptions relate to previous work. This last point needs to be stressed, because at this level of postgraduate work, you are expected to extend the knowledge within your field.

The structure of a critical review depends on your discipline and your research area, and of course on the research question you intend to answer. It can be arranged chronologically or methodologically, according to the level of importance to the field or by theoretical perspective.

Some guidelines for the critical literature review

Introduce your review with a statement of intent, outlining the significance of your topic. Include also the scope and limitations, previewing the main authors you intend to use and why, that is, justify the inclusion of some rather than others. Let the reader know how you plan to organise the review and indicate how each of the sections relates to your research question.

The body paragraphs will unfold according to main topics, by discussion of points of difference between them, and critical reflection upon the various theories. As with an essay, a clear line of argument is essential. Controversies in the field and conflicting information need to be dealt with, so take care not to omit viewpoints that run counter to your own. Work them into your review and discuss them in such a way that your work as a whole is strengthened by their presence – see Chapter 7 for further advice on integrating others' arguments to your own advantage. All must be arranged logically, with the more important issues dealt with in the greatest detail. Point out the relevance of each of the references you include to your own work, looping back to connect to the arguments reviewed in your thesis. Any gaps you've discovered in the literature are used to justify your own research.

In your conclusion, summarise the literature and clarify where your work fits into the polyphony.

Four reminders

1. A chronological list is insufficient for a critical literature review. So don't write a list, as in So-and-So claims this and Doctor Doolittle reveals that, while Prof Gonzo Bonzo indicates such-and-such. This is an absolute no-no. Your task is analytical and interpretive, not merely descriptive. You must continually evaluate the contributions that have been made to the field, and make connections between them.
2. Your work will be judged according to structure and organisation, the relevance of material included, quality of critical evaluation, and your interpretation of the literature.
3. Working in this genre you can sometimes lose track of which are your extrapolations based on your research, and which are the thoughts of other authors. Take care with your referencing – or fall into the trap of inadvertent plagiarism!
4. Although this may seem counterintuitive, a critical literature review is actually an easier task for many than one that is merely descriptive because you are in control of who and what to include, based on your thesis. Your topic supplies natural limits to whom and how much you need to cover in the literature review.

Integrating annotations

The annotations you make at the earliest stages will stand you in good stead later. I can't stress this enough. And as you make those valuable annotations, allow yourself also to reflect upon your own subjectivities – why you are responding to what you read in the way that you do – and include your reflections in your notes. This will affect not only the way you read, but also the end result, because reading and writing, analysing, reflecting and interpreting, are all bound up in each other.

Educational theorist Elizabeth St Pierre (2005, p. 970) gives an example of how she incorporated her personal responses in a study she was conducting by noting her sensory and emotional reactions, and what she calls 'memory data' which occurred to her as she worked. These formed other connections which in turn underwent further unplanned (and unplannable) transitions that generated thoughts about her topic of investigation that would never have occurred to her had she been overly focused on keeping to a more scientistic methodology. Even though these thoughts were her own, she found that some of them 'startled' her. That is a wonderful prospect, I think – a research practice that enables the researcher to be startled by new ideas or connections she discovers.

This body of notes that you build – factual, interpretive, analytical, reflective – form the basic content of the larger work. What this means is that you will have largely written the essay/dissertation/thesis while you were researching it. You'll have much of the content already, so your task then becomes one of organising those notes and thoughts into a coherent whole.

Conclusion

Having explored the loosest, least constrained aspects of research to the most controlled – from wide reading as oxygenation to close reading and writing exercises – it should be clear that research is part of a system of complexification. Not simplification. Ideas are generated through broad research and reflection, through interpretation and loosely construed connections as much as building up a body of knowledge comprised of objective facts and data. And a vital part of the process includes making mistakes. In fact, they are so important I think I'll emphasise the point by breaking a rule: adding a sub-heading to a conclusion:

Mistakes are essential to the research process

Errors in interpretation or comprehension will happen – and so they should. They reflect your own particular ways of thinking that distinguish your thought processes from those of other individuals. Not only this, but dealing with error and our own fallibilities in writing and research stand us in good stead in professional life, which is also full of uncertainties with which we all have to contend. Adapting your behaviour and your work techniques when faced with error and inconsistency – better known as learning from mistakes – is part of being critical.

Developing Habits of Strength as a Postgraduate

Chapter overview

This midway point acts as a hiatus before moving on to a focus on the art of persuasive writing. Here we deal with:

- Time management and the acquisition of mental 'habits of strength' (Csikszentmihalyi 1997, p. 351)
- Making time to think: mindful engagement with university work
- The contribution of 'Slow' philosophy to developing creative criticality
- Pleasure, efficiency, and critical thinking
- Critical being/critical action
- Study group exercises.

If critical thinking involves developing a suite of skills and attributes essential for doing well at university, such competences are also essential for doing well outside it, on every level of social participation. Foundations for developing critical ability and creativity have been covered in the previous chapters, and we'll return to different ways of practising these again in the following chapters. But at this stage some advice for developing 'habits of strength' for improving study skills will be beneficial. This will be followed by advice on the general application of these strengths within the context of what I'll call 'everyday criticality', which like the 'habits' to follow, also develops over a lifetime.

Habits of strength

Time management

Currently there is an emphasis in universities on using time efficiently, and on increasingly standardised education programmes – even though there is no such thing as a standard student. There is also an insistence on the need to pursue 'excellence' – though the nature of this idealised goal is rarely defined. I would suggest that instead of responding to the 'excellence drive' as if it were a clear and sensible aim, students and researchers might try, in the words of Barry and colleagues (2001), to find a place 'between the Ivory Tower and the Academic Assembly Line'. So, although we have to use available time capably, it is also important to bear in mind our reasons for doing this: to be able to pursue academic interests as thoughtfully as possible. Making *time to think*. However, before listing ten strategies you might put in place to help you organise your time, and to make the most of it, here are three actions to avoid:

Do not multitask while studying. What happens is that you shift from one task to another, then you have to backtrack – and this is inefficient. Do one thing at a time. And as you are doing it, give it your full attention. Of course online activity necessarily involves multitasking. That is why it's important to go offline when studying. Even accepting email notifications while you're trying to read something is destructive of concentration. Turn your notifications *off*.

Do not listen to advice from time management 'gurus' who promote very long hours (or multitasking). If you compare yourself to them you will always come off looking worse, and this is demoralising.

Do not keep a log to monitor your hours of work. If you keep measuring yourself not only are you wasting time, but you will also increase your anxiety.

Do …

1. Remember, first of all, that it's your work and the time you spend on it is up to you. If you find yourself losing direction and wasting time feeling vaguely anxious, sit back and think of why you are doing that degree or this research project; remembering your intentions can put everything into perspective.
2. Be sceptical of the culture of busyness and productivity of most universities. Particularly if your field of research or study is in the humanities and social sciences, try focusing your efforts on understanding – not on 'knowledge production'. Heed the advice from the Slow movement: instead of telling yourself that you are 'producing something, try saying, '"I am contemplating", or "I am conversing with"' (Berg and Seeber 2016, p. 57). This may alleviate some of the pressure and remind you of why you have embarked on a piece of work: because it is valuable, and because it interests you. This mental attitude can help you sustain the energy needed to work with focus and enjoyment.
3. Try to get small tasks out of the way as soon as they're assigned, especially if they're not particularly compelling. Clear the decks for the work you care about.
4. Break complex assignments into manageable sections. In other words, convert your dauntingly monolithic task into something that resembles human scale.
5. Set yourself a daily reading goal for increasing your knowledge base, and file notes carefully. If the material you accrue daily is well-organised it assists retention and ready mental access to information.
6. Remember that if you have writer's block, just get something – *anything* – down. Not the major opus, but simply a few speculations, notes, or perhaps a piece of freewriting. Even if you change it completely later, at least you've started. The alternative is having nothing at all, which is rather sad and entirely unnecessary.
7. Lay out deadlines in a planner; include start dates and sane lead-up times for each task. We all know that plenty of tasks take longer than we hope they will, so acknowledge this and allow time for it. A weekly planner is also handy. Refer to the grid suggested on pp. 87 and 90. Include *all* claims on your time.

8. Metacognition. All this means is understanding how your brain works (it enables the metacritical activity we discussed in Chapter 2). When you're aware of what works for you then you're better equipped to work out strategies of how best to handle information and research *and* management of your time.

9. Sleep. With insufficient sleep we certainly struggle to be efficient during waking hours. As individuals, we all have to work out how best to compose ourselves for a decent night's sleep, but one thing that has been demonstrated in a range of academic studies to affect us all is artificial light. It can suppress the release of the hormone melatonin, which promotes sleep. So that means avoiding light-emitting screens from television to computers and mobile phones for an hour before bed.

10. As previously mentioned, go offline when studying. The huge importance of this was recently highlighted for me in a seminar I was conducting at the university where I work. Some of my students spoke of how they valued quiet time, time alone, contemplative or reflective or intensely focused time. Others acknowledged that they were never offline and that consequently their attention was never concentrated on one project or theme or task for more than a few minutes. They made themselves constantly available to demands from a multiplicity of sources and voices through various social media platforms, and what they set out to do five, ten minutes ago (or was that an hour ago? Two hours ago?) may not be have been achieved and was probably forgotten. This fragmented approach is the opposite of the depth of engagement needed to engage critically and creatively with your work. Be aware that it can take about fifteen minutes to refocus concentration after any form of online activity.

Concentrated textual interrogation, finding other related theories in further research, developing ideas, and also *allowing time for speculation* on different directions those ideas might take are time-consuming. But it is the opposite of time-wasting; it is creative engagement with your work. It is also the way to increase the likelihood of actually retaining what you read. According to neuropsychiatrist Eric Kandel (2006) the key to memorisation is deeply processed and systematic attention, and relating new information to that which we have already absorbed and understood. Good academic results are produced when processes of critique and evaluation and development are given enough time to enable a level of creative dynamism in research and writing.

As being connected is habitual for many of us, consider installing internet-blocking software and activate it at certain times of the day.

Exercise 6.1 Interruptions: a material illustration using role play

This can be done in a seminar or with a study group. I strongly recommend it – it's fun but also very confronting. A minimum of ten players is needed: eight to play 'Interruptions', plus a pair to act as a control for the experiment. The following steps should take between 20 and 30 minutes if eight players are involved in Interruptions (two 'discussers' and six 'interrupters'). The discussers need to be colleagues or students who work within the same field.

(Continued)

In preparation for this exercise, 'discussers' and the control pair will need to have decided upon:

- a discussion topic of mutual interest, and
- the aims for their discussion. For instance, one might want clarification on a theory from the other; or perhaps both simply want to share ideas with a view to working out a thesis statement for an essay. The goal might be finite or nebulous – it's up to you.

The 'interrupters' do not need any common ground.

1. Each person writes a paragraph on a slip of paper on any topic that interests you; e.g. a recent political event, the predilections of your favourite celebrity, an animal you like, a weight reduction remedy, a global warming event. Put these slips in a hat.
2. The discussers move to one end of the room and set a timer (20–30 minutes). They then begin the conversation about their research. They might, if they like, refer to notes as they talk.
3. The control pair go to another part of the room and do not participate in the activities that follow, but simply begin to discuss their topic together, bearing their goals in mind.
4. Meanwhile, the others – the 'interrupters' – each select a slip of paper from the hat. After the discussers have been talking for a minute or two, one interrupter walks over to them and inserts herself or himself between them. If you like a bit of added drama, the interrupter might signal the intention to interrupt by saying, 'Ping!', or humming a bar from a smartphone text-tone, or ringing a bicycle bell.
5. The interrupter now reads the content on his slip of paper to one of the discussers, completely ignoring the other one. The discusser being read to needn't respond, but may if they want. The ignored discusser must not speak at all.
6. Repeat this process with different players and topics at 2- to 5-minute intervals.
7. After all the interrupters have finished, the two discussers might like to briefly present to the whole group the results of their discussion and how close they came to achieving their aims.
8. The control pair do the same.

Taking time to think

Despite the fact that few will argue against the need to allow time to think, there are barriers to the exercise of this basic requirement over which we have little control, like conservative disciplinary traditions and attitudes to research practices – not to mention bureaucratic concerns to do with funding and restrictive time frames which may constrain critical and creative development. Working within this environment can certainly be problematic for both researchers and students at all levels, but this particular book is not the place for elaborating on possible tactics and approaches for dealing with institutional quandaries and complications. Instead we'll maintain our focus on ways of contending with the last problem, that of time-poverty which comes about due to the need to spend time on everyday non-academic responsibilities, and the price we pay for the perceived advantages of 24/7 connectivity.

Do you think you are time poor? If so, to what degree? The grid below is one I've suggested for coursework postgraduates. You might tailor it to suit yourselves. For example, some academics might add an 'overweening admin' column. But be honest with yourself about how you spend your time. Perhaps there are areas to which you might allocate more attention, and others less?

Exercise 6.2a Add hours spent in each activity

	Mon	Tue	Wed	Thu	Fri	Sat	Sun
lectures							
seminars							
private study							
exercise							
spending time with friends							
paid work							
social media							
television							
sleeping							
domestic work, e.g. childcare, housework, shopping							

Fallow time

It may seem counterintuitive to suggest time out as a strategy for dealing with time poverty. In fact, many students and academics are likely to say they're simply too busy to even think of taking time out. If you think this way, I'd like to mention that there are strong counterarguments available from recent research into efficient use of time; in fact, many insist that trying to concentrate for more than five hours over a day is counterproductive. You become mentally tired, go over old ground, read inefficiently, lose focus, and so on. In other words, you're better off working well for five hours than badly for ten. In the long run, taking time out fosters the sort of mentality that helps researchers and students alike not only to contend with time pressures, but to develop habits of mind that enable one to approach tasks with the care and attention they need.

> Bear in mind that busyness is not an end in itself – and also, that it requires a foil: time which is *not* crammed with activity.   **TIP**

Fallow time is time for unfocused, undetermined activity necessary to rejuvenate oneself. It can be recuperative time that is scheduled in after you've finished a major project. It may also be an interval during the course of a long and arduous task where you allow the thoughts to settle, so that when you return to the work, you can review your research with a fresh mind. According to research in the field of creativity and happiness 'fallow time' is strongly recommended as a means of building creativity – and also efficiency. Psychologist Mihaly Csikszentmihalyi insists on the importance of making time to reflect and to relax. Some find that taking this time results in patterns of ideas becoming clearer, sequences of ideas arranging themselves – 'falling into place' – problems seemingly sorting themselves out without too much effort. It can be a part of every day when you might listen to music, for instance, or engage in a soothing repetitive task like gardening or walking or running (and although treadmills at the gym may suit some, for many of us they are usually less effective than being outside or in a place that fosters calmness). What fallow time is *not* for, however, is concentrated reading and writing. Neither is it for watching television or catching up with the news or with friends on social media or updating your Facebook profile.

Incubation

Fallow time might not actually be a clearly distinguishable slot. It might occur when you need to clear your head a little while you're working on a project. Therefore, if you feel you need to get away from the desk (and maybe do that mindless filing, housework, or simply stare at the ceiling for a bit), then it may well be the right thing to do. This is not necessarily procrastination. It is time out for musing. While some might refer to it as 'idling', others call it 'incubation'. It occurs when we cease the intellectual work of consciously and deliberately analysing ideas or seeking solutions to problems. Idling or incubating allows the conscious mind an interval in which it desists from mental control and allows the unconscious to do its work.

There is a quantity of scientific research to back up the idea that the unconscious mind will contribute a huge amount towards the success of idea development, if only you will allow it the time and space. Neurological studies investigating large-scale brain networks include what are referred to as the executive attention network (which as its name implies, is exercised when you are focused on solving a problem or concentrating – for example when delivering or listening to a lecture) and the imagination network (active when we are mentally constructing images, projecting ideas into the future, remembering, or trying to enter into someone else's thinking). Brain imaging makes visible what might be the imagination in action – interpreting another's words, picking up inferences, possibly even drawing analogies. Yet – and this is where it gets really interesting – while all this activity is occurring, the subject of the study is in a passive state. The cerebral metabolism is vigorous *whether cognitive effort is being made or not*. These networks are part of natural default mechanism, or the state the brain reverts to when unfocused (Buckner et al. 2008).

It seems that the imagination network is the part of the brain which is engaged during the incubation phase necessary to any creative endeavour – and by creative, I am of course referring to any work that involves the combining intellect and imagination in order to produce something new, like writing, whether fictive or scholarly. Although the question of whether the unconscious contributes to creative thinking during incubation, or if it is just that conscious effort is relaxed at these times, there is evidence that 'the unconscious is able to "close in" on the correct answer [in test situations] some time before the answer is accessible to consciousness' (Ritter and Dijksterhuis 2014).

How do we enable this process? Preparation is essential. Ideas do not come out of the blue, no matter that it may seem like that when you emerge from the shower or from a good night's sleep with clarity that you lacked before! The ground was already prepared. So, a caveat: in order for fallow time or the incubation period to be effective it is essential that it is preceded with sustained periods of concentrated effort. In other words – a balance of labour and rest. The length of the incubation period is also a consideration, and will vary depending upon the person and the kind of work in which they are involved. It may be a few minutes (daydreaming, wool-gathering, mind-wandering), an hour or so (that routine filing I mentioned), several hours (after a good night's sleep), or a matter of weeks, that is, sometimes a lengthy break may be needed.

And bear in mind that even if you're not 'incubating', you still need to give your cerebral muscles a rest. Allow fallow time, exactly as a farmer does for a field if he wants to produce a good yield in the future, or as an athlete does for her body after a serious workout.

Exercise 6.2b Add this extra activity to the grid in Exercise 6.2a

You may find you need to adjust the amount of time spent on other activities in order to include it.

	Mon	Tue	Wed	Thu	Fri	Sat	Sun
Fallow							

Coping with stress

Fallow time can also help relieve the stress from which many hard-working people tend to suffer. What is stress and how does it come about? It is a simple mechanism of survival and extreme forms of it, like panic, ought to be reserved for confrontations with approaching trains, sharks, or crocodiles. Nevertheless, because the part of the brain that deals with threats is not particularly prone to making subtle distinctions, the prospect of a job interview or a deadline often causes similar 'fight or flight' reactions. We get a glucose fuel-injection and blood pumps fiercely through our heart, whose acceleration increases markedly. When we feel threatened by deadlines our immediate survival may not be at stake, yet the symptoms of stress still arise and not only that, they endure, infecting daily life with unnecessary psychological and physical difficulty, including anxiety and insomnia and other unwanted nervous symptoms. Some of us actually live in a condition of constant red alert, meaning that we are unable to absorb information or learn, unable to think with clarity or precision, let alone write something thoughtful and incisive. So, what to do? The obvious advice first of all is deep breathing when assaulted by unnecessary stress symptoms. Yoga and Pilates too are effective; and if you can manage it, get out of the city for a couple of hours. Doing plenty of aerobic exercise is yet more wise advice for counteracting ongoing physical stress-effects. As well as all this, we need to employ strategies that enable us to regain control – because feeling like a helpless victim is one of the worst stress catalysts. So:

1. Talk to people. Socialise with like-minded friends and colleagues.
2. Itemise your tasks. Give urgent projects priority over those that are important, but can wait. In some cases this will mean turning down certain activities so that you can do a better job of others. 'Less is more': it may seem paradoxical, but less work can often result in your being more productive. Trying to keep up with pressure from peers or with a work and study culture that insists on cramming one's schedule increases stress, which results in inefficiency, which leads to more stress. So try and break this vicious cycle.
3. Use available time slots wisely. When feeling overwhelmed, it seems as if there's no time to study. This doesn't actually reflect any objective reality – just personality type. Study time doesn't necessarily mean acres of time. A well-used fifteen minutes is more effective than a wasted two hours. Short time

slots: bus and train journeys of half an hour or less, for example, are useful for reviewing lecture notes, completing short readings, or – probably most useful of all – just jotting down ideas that occur to you as you stare out the bus window. Longer slots of more than three hours can be set aside for more concentrated work.

4. Subdue your inner critic. That's the evil little voice that interrupts your writing with comments that denigrate your abilities or the ideas you're exploring. This critic can become particularly active when you're thinking about ideas that may be tending towards the experimental. Instead, remember that you need to get the words down before the legitimate self-editing process can begin – otherwise there will be nothing to edit. Creative engagement with academic study can also mean recognising that at times you'll need to suspend the 'strict rules of inference and evidence in order to envision new possibilities, innovative procedures, and fresh, potentially fecund, problems' (Brodin in Davies and Barnett 2015, p. 265).

5. Never mind perfection. A very common cause of procrastination is perfectionism, a favourite technique of avoidance employed by both students and professional writers, including academics. Putting off starting a task because you won't be able to produce a 'perfect' result. Why? Because writing is in fact hard work, and we always feel like there's a lot at stake – and sometimes there is. But instead of aiming for perfection, aim for reasonable results. Then, after completing that piece of work, once again, 'go fallow'.

6. Create manageable tasks. Sometimes we tell ourselves that we can't start that assignment now because we're too 'busy' with other things (like arranging your highlighters in order of colour or cleaning the fridge). This is *not* incubating: remember, you need to have spent a substantial amount of time on research first! But sometimes the work feels so overwhelming or difficult that you can't face it. The solution, as previously mentioned, is to break up work into as many small, achievable tasks as you see fit. Then you are not facing a huge, daunting pile of work, but just the first small task. After completing that, 'go fallow'. Take the time you need for rest and rejuvenation.

Csikszentmihalyi suggests the following strategies to help us cultivate what he refers to as 'flow', a profoundly engaged state where the sense of time passing evaporates. In this state, regardless of profession, we are in less danger of getting anxious about commitments, less likely to waste time, more likely to be happy in our work, and more able to achieve creative results:

• Every morning, have a specific goal for something you'd like to achieve. This need not be huge – just reasonable. Such goals may be to do with a specific project you're involved in, or the pursuit of a particular line of thought, that is, they relate to developing your knowledge base in your field.

• Note that the quality of any experience tends to improve in proportion to the effort invested in it. Again I'm referring to the importance of finding a balance between activity and passivity.

• To keep enjoying something, it is necessary to increase its complexity and to believe there's good reason for doing it. This last point links to Csikszentmihalyi's theorising of creativity. He insists that to be personally satisfied we have to become involved in increasingly complex thinking and to be working towards goals that are socially useful.

Exercise 6.3 A metacritical activity to assist intellectual progress and to reduce stress

The first point mentioned above – goal-setting – relates to self-regulation, a practice encouraged in the literature of critical thinking. A self-regulatory tool we've covered already is the reflection journal. We've already discussed how to engage in the metacritical process of reflection on your responses to ideas and texts, a fundamental tool for the critical thinker. Here I would like to suggest another kind of journal in which you keep track of your progress through self-evaluation and review. Or perhaps reflections in the front of the journal and space for this self-regulatory exercise at the back, or vice versa.

   Each week or so set aside space where you note how well you've managed to meet the goals you've set yourself. Research indicates that learners' motivation and self-satisfaction increases when they monitor their own progress in this way (as opposed to a punitive regime of hourly or daily self-surveillance) and tends to increase confidence in one's abilities rather than the reverse. This is largely because an awareness of your personal evolution as you accrue knowledge and make meaning of it – the development of a kind of individual epistemology – increases autonomy and the level of personal control.

Towards creative criticality: 'make haste, not speed'

In the intensely information-laden context of contemporary higher education, digital learning researcher Theresa Anderson (2011) discusses the difficulties associated with dealing with the sheer mass of ideas so readily available – and how to do so critically, reflectively, and creatively. Anderson concurs with a remark made previously, that insights – what she calls 'eureka moments' – that seem to come from nowhere actually come after a great deal of hard work. This means time to read and to think, time to absorb what we've read and considered, and time for the evaluative and reflective work that a critically minded researcher needs to move into new territory. Anderson also reflects upon ways of using that phase of uncertainty while accruing knowledge and learning, so that in due course, revelatory ideas may emerge. Chapter 10 will examine the role of uncertainty in more detail as part of a discussion of divergent research practices; at this stage I simply want to flag that this ambiguous, ambivalent condition is to be embraced rather than avoided as it is conducive to creative and critical scholarship.

   Anderson (2011, n.p.) cites Paul Virilio's concern 'about the primacy of immediacy and instantaneity that he attributes to the growth of digital information flows' so that, daily, many scholars have to contend with the 'political economy of speed' which has a deleterious effect on creative thought – in fact, on human reasoning itself. She refers also to other authors who recognise that we may in fact have reached a crisis point regarding our thinking about work and work practices, and that it is essential to slow it down if we are to be able to engage effectively with any kind of problem-solving activities. One such author is Gendlin, who refers to a technique he calls '*thinking at the edge*' which encourages 'a softer, slower kind of groping for a way of articulating something that is currently, tantalizingly, beyond our linguistic grasp'. Anderson sees the value of this 'slow thinking' to her field of information studies, recognising the need to think carefully about the questions John Howkins raised in his 2010 book, *Creative ecologies: Where thinking is a proper job*, about *how* we want to think, and what the best thinking environments might be. Anderson also suggests that others in her field need to 'engage with information in inventive ways to not only support the creativity and innovation of others, but to be creative and innovative ourselves'. And as has been emphasised throughout this book, criticality itself is intimately linked with creative faculties.

A perspective that can help comes from the Slow movement. It is important to note, first of all, that Slow is far more than mere temporal deceleration. In their book *Slow Living*, Parkins and Craig (2006, p. 67) point out that taking the time needed to do what you do well, and with pleasure, amounts to 'an issue of agency'. That means being in control of the decisions you make regarding your work practices, instead of automatically reacting to pressure and complying with demands. Rather than a mindless rejection of speed, or an invitation to laziness, Slow encourages *mindful* use of time. By this I mean occupying the present moment when engaged in any task, and striving towards an awareness of your own thought processes. As Carlo Petrini (2001), the founder of the Slow Food movement, wrote, the aim is to find the *tempo giusto* – the right speed for the task. Petrini's idea opens up Slow beyond escapism or nostalgia, suggesting something more radical, and it has developed into a multi-tentacled cultural phenomenon, whether interpreted as a social movement, a subculture, or a critique of the dominant narrative that uncritically accepts busyness as a virtue and accepts time poverty as an inescapable fact of working life.

In response to this Slow has taken many directions over the past few years: slow cities, money, travel, parenting, media, living, and only very recently, slow study. A number of principles have emerged in the thinking and practice of the Slow movement including:

- Quality rather than quantity
- Mindfulness
- Ethical and critical considerations in education
- Pleasure – a key principle of the Slow movement, one that was apparent in the original Slow Food manifesto in 1989: 'A firm defense of quiet material pleasure is the only way to oppose the universal folly of Fast Life.'

What does pleasure have to do with study?

Drawing upon research conducted in the fields of sociology, labour studies, medicine, and others, proponents of Slow argue against today's celebration of 'overwork and the culture of speed' (Berg and Seeber 2016, p. 13). They insist that it is pleasure in the work that we do that enables us to sustain the effort, and also to achieve efficiency which neuroscientists claim we humans experience as pleasure.

In other words, along with feeling, pleasure is what actually enables us to learn. From a psychological perspective, results of Csikszentmihalyi's studies show that when one enters the mental condition he calls 'flow' – that state of concentration or absolute absorption in an activity – the distinction between pleasure and work becomes irrelevant. Time too, is forgotten. And if we return to the ancient Greek origins of critical thinking, we find references to the critical search for understanding as creating a profound sense of pleasure. Possibly these conscientious Greeks were under less pressure than are today's researchers, which is why a fundamental need is to establish a style of study that suits you in particular, in today's cultural climate. While some people do work fast and enjoy the stimulus of continual interruption, many of us find this distracting and fragmenting and therefore need to find a pace that *does* allow us to work well, and happily.

Another suggestion for increasing the chance of actually enjoying study, whether you're a student enrolled in course work or a researcher largely working alone: turn up to lectures and talks. There is a growing body of research indicating that active participation in live lectures – as opposed to relying on vodcasts or other media – can increase the pleasure of learning, which in turn affects the amount of material that is absorbed and retained. Knowledge is acquired not only through the eyes or the ears (onscreen) but bodily, and through the emotions. Neuroscientist Antonio Damasio has remarked wryly that the body is actually more than a life support system for the brain. 'It contributes a *content* that is part and parcel of the workings of the normal mind' (cited in Berg and Seeber 2016, p. 35). Roland Barthes takes it a little further when discussing his reading practice, 'The pleasure of the text is that moment when my body pursues its own ideas – for my body does not have the same ideas I do' (cited in Ott 2004, p. 204).

Some final advice that may seem blindingly obvious but is often overlooked: Choose to study something you truly care about. This way you will maintain your motivation and remain eager to develop and complexify your research. Writing well and finding a critical focus are very difficult if you're performing out of a misguided sense of duty rather than feeling compelled out of a driving interest. You have to be able to enjoy it. In fact, Berg and Seeber (2016, p. 34) claim that 'it may the case that pleasure … is the most important predictor of "learning outcomes"'. So allow yourself to be driven by your own native inquisitiveness – at a speed that allows you to be focused, mindful, and engaged rather than anxious, for anxiety has nothing to do with pleasure, and is a state that will certainly reduce both criticality and creativity. The next two exercises may help consolidate the advice provided so far for mindfully managing your time. The first exercise is aimed to specifically support conditions that enable 'flow':

Exercise 6.4 A reflective activity

From time to time take a moment to ask yourself the following questions:

1. *What's the most important thing for me to be doing now?* When you find yourself automatically reacting to pressure by trying to do several things simultaneously, e.g., taking a phone call, scanning a document, answering

(Continued)

an email, *take a moment* to work out what you need to do first. Then, in whichever order you deem best, give the person on the phone your undivided attention for as long as it takes (and your interlocutor won't feel miffed, because it's pretty obvious when someone isn't really listening properly); scan the document, and if you find that it needs closer reading, do so; answer the email, giving full attention to the issue the sender wishes to alert you to so you won't find later that you have to reread to clarify something you missed in your hurry. As we all know, emails are notorious for causing confusion or being offensive if they're brusque. (And a further point regarding emails: it's hard – I know – but do try to deal with them just daily, or twice daily, rather than feeling obliged to check constantly and respond immediately.) This call to attention and mindful use of time gives you the satisfaction of feeling that you have control over what you do, rather than being at the mercy of others' demands.

2. *Maybe I'm tired (and not – as the inner critic says – stupid or lazy)?* When the words you're writing or reading lose coherence and start to resemble incomprehensible beetle-tracks, it's probably because you've reached your capacity for the moment. Don't harry yourself. As you did manage to get into this course/job/doctoral programme, by any external measure you're probably quite bright and hard-working. So if the text has stopped making sense, it is a signal for you to *take a moment* for a cup of tea or a walk or a conversation with a colleague. Muse on the ideas you've been exploring rather than continuing to cram in more information or trying to produce something when you're mentally exhausted.

3. *Why am I doing this?* When you're feeling overwhelmed, *take a moment* to return to first principles: What is the value of this project to myself/to the people I work with/to my academic community or society in general? If you come up with a satisfying answer, continue; if not, you may have to reconsider your motives. Asking this question may alert you to the need to change your direction (which is why we often prefer to avoid it).

Exercise 6.5 Further reflection

I mentioned earlier that it's a bad idea to monitor your work by keeping an hourly log, but that it *is* useful to keep track of your progress (including reading goals, as discussed) through any given project. Not by the hour, or by treating time as if it were stock, but by reflecting in a journal on what you've learnt and how your ideas are developing. Now that you're half-way through this book, here are some prompts to help you keep track of how your skills are developing.

1. In the previous chapter I asked you to consider what kind of writer you are. Has this awareness affected the way you approach writing and research?

(Continued)

2. Do you think you're more aware of how your own subjectivities affect your reading of texts? If so, jot down a few notes on how this increased attentiveness affects your process.

3. Assess how you manage balancing critical distance with what I've referred to as 'sympathetic reading'. Give concrete examples.

4. While engaged in formal writing, what do you think might be your main strengths and weaknesses regarding textual interrogation, interpretation, and evaluation?

5. If you've attempted to do any of the more open-ended writing exercises recommended, how did you go? Write a brief self-appraisal.

6. Review a writing project you struggled with and which is now complete. What measures did you take to deal with the difficulties? How effective were they? (Kathpalia and Heah 2008)

7. Would you take the same approach next time? If not, what other strategies might you put into play?

8. Kathpalia and Heah also suggest that you identify what project you learnt the most from over the past year and whether you achieved anything that surprised you? Why was it surprising? Ask yourself also what part of research or writing you find easiest and why. Be specific.

Critical being/critical action: applications of 'everyday criticality'

Finding the right speed for each project is not just for helping us to achieve better results in academic work – although obviously this is very important. Beyond this, working mindfully and engaging in a more complex relationship with what we do increases our ability to make a valuable contribution once formal studies are completed, that is, to properly utilise the privilege of a higher education, taking learning skills beyond the academic. This section starts from the premise that the point of learning how to think critically – and also taking on a level of autonomy regarding your work, including expectations in the time-poor context of the university – has clear applications in the everyday. We now consider ways of transferring skills learned at university to the workplace, to professional and social life.

We hear a great deal of talk about 'vision' and 'creativity', but these terms remain hollow buzzwords unless we give them meaning through action. In Chapter 2 we established that critical being means 'being able to readily ally abstract knowledge … with real-world scenarios … with an awareness of the wider ramifications of your thinking'. In other words, mobilising all modes of critical thinking – analytical, reflective, socially engaged. This is also the reasoning behind the inclusion in 'graduate attributes' listings at many universities worldwide, of the need for students to be able to acknowledge the social and ethical implications of their actions.

Workplaces have their own particular norms and power-balances. On entering a new culture we need to be aware of these, and while respecting the experience of those already working there, it's also essential to maintain a sense of identity within one's chosen profession. This means being able to balance critical agency and intellectual autonomy with perceived professional obligations. I can't stress enough the importance of maintaining this level of independence, for according to recent research by Andre Spicer (2016), there are many 'organisations [that] enshrine collective stupidity and employees are rewarded for checking their brains at the office door'. Spicer and his colleague, Mats Alvesson, assumed that the brightest employees would get ahead when they embarked on the study of hundreds of organisations from banks to universities, media to government departments. This assumption proved to be misguided. 'Talented employees quickly learn to use their significant intellectual gifts only in the most narrow and myopic ways', 'leadership' qualities were recognised in those who 'toed the corporate line', and in many cases the main job of a consultant is not to solve problems, but to give the impression of doing so.

However, having refined your awareness through the acquisition of skills in critical thinking, you are likely to be more willing to question assumptions and examine requirements within the workplace. You will also be more readily able to identify sub-structural values and assumptions that buttress an organisation and to read from this the social implications of an organisation's actions.

The purpose of the following critical and practical exercises (edited from the Griffith Graduate Project 2011) is to emphasise that while developing criticality is about doing well at university, it is also about preparation for functioning at a high level, intellectually, imaginatively, and ethically, within whatever social or professional sphere you become involved in after you complete your studies.

Exercise 6.6 Challenge! (a meeting)

1. Select a topic of interest to yourself and others in your field – one that has potentially controversial solutions. Do it before the meeting to allow the participants time to think about it.
2. When you meet, one group member takes the floor and offers a way to solve the problem. When another group member disagrees with the solution – and strong disagreement is often the best sort for this exercise …
3. … he or she calls out 'Challenge!'.
4. They then swap places with the original speaker and are given the chance to express their view.
5. Others may follow suit.

The discussion that ensues may uncover a range of possible solutions, and it's likely that it will be lively and may require a mediator. Whether or not you decide a mediator will be needed, some suggestions for conducting this exercise successfully are: make sure all group members are prepared to contribute; that more extroverted participants might try not to dominate with over-long monologues; that when a new speaker takes their place they briefly summarise what the previous speaker said; that members of the group need to be willing to change their minds in the face of persuasive evidence. Also, do avoid *ad hominem* arguments: critique the idea rather than criticising the individual presenting it.

Exercise 6.7 Dilemma

Propose to your group a discussion on an ethical dilemma in a work situation, but before you actually begin this conversation, do be aware that there are several ways to examine problems as they arise. You can look at it through the lenses of:

1. Virtue – in which you consider the ethics of the situation.
2. Utility – identifying which of two possible actions will produce 'the greatest balance of benefits and harms'.
3. Rights – which requires the understanding that a policy is immoral if those affected by the decision are being taken advantage of and are not adequately informed.
4. Common good – which defines an ethical action as one that is best for all – meaning not just those within the company, but the society.

Your discussion topic will depend upon the discipline and the field. But as an example, imagine that you are working in the area of tourism. A colleague has come up with a fantastic way to encourage tourists to visit a particular holiday destination, and they cite the profits that be made for the organisation and the potential for economic development that increased tourist trade can bring to the local people. There are problems with this proposal though. The locals may be negatively affected by a sudden incursion of visitors; the economic improvements themselves may damage the way of life, or there may be environmental issues that require some thought. In other words, regardless of the topic chosen, in the discussion that ensues you will need to apply your critical intelligence to the social and ethical implications of the project, and be mindful of the community responsibilities as well as responsibilities to your potential employer.

Exercise 6.8 Solitary reflection

The following is a private, written exercise, a kind of moral examination that would be suited for inclusion in your reflection journal. It involves critiquing the moral grounding that informs the way you make decisions. So, choose a scenario – it might be professional or personal – and work out what you think is the ethical course of action. You will need to consider 'consequences, self-interest, duty and intentions'. As you write, expand upon the reasons why you think this is preferable to that action, and also articulate why one concern might carry more weight than another.

Conclusion

Bad news first: This chapter started with a discussion of working with the constraints that are part of contemporary university life, including time-poverty in particular. We also looked at the fact that although universities emphasise the importance of developing critical skills, and some acknowledge that critical practice is linked to creative and reflective processes, the fact remains that universities feel an obligation to educate people to meet the perceived social requirement of 'effective operators who serve instrumental and pragmatic agendas' (Brodin in Davies and Barnett 2015, p. 268). Or, as mentioned in Chapter 4, rather than envisioning aspects of the world *as it might be*, the thinker is restricted to simply seeing it *as it is* at the moment and working within that paradigm.

And now the good news: There are ways of working and attitudes of mind that can act as a counterbalance to the problems mentioned above, some of which we've covered in this chapter. Strategies grounded in solid research have been provided to help you manage your time well so as to enhance your ability to produce valuable work. We discussed how to make time to think, how to increase intellectual autonomy, how to engage mindfully with academic work, and how to enjoy study rather than agonising through the process. We found ways to ensure that critical reasoning is not used simply to refine ways of interrogating texts, but to extend knowledge. We established that reflective skills can be taken beyond the realm of immediate self-interest by noting ways to invite unexpected patterns of thought. We considered how to apply critical thought ethically so that it is much more than just an intellectual game. Rather, it can be used as a sophisticated form of problem-solving for bringing about valuable contributions to the workplace, and when needed, can be used to effect social change.

Negotiating the Literature and Joining the Conversation

Chapter overview

This chapter on critical writing, voice, and style explores:

- Conventions of scholarly prose
- How style works with content in academic communication
- Discussion of the relationship between thinking well and writing well
- Rhetorical strategies as background for detailed development in Chapter 8.

To begin, this chapter briefly revisits the concept of 'thinking well' to set the scene for a discussion of writing well, because only with clarity of mind is it possible to say something useful, let alone insightful, about our chosen areas of expertise or to excel in study or research. It is impossible to engage or persuade a reader without being clear yourself about what you mean. In fact, often enough, unfit prose is the result of just that – the author herself being unsure of exactly what it is she wants to convey, or to whom, or why it is important. So our concern here is with developing clear, lively, persuasive writing, which involves beginning an ongoing exploration of style.

Style is sometimes thought of as a kind of 'add-on' to the meat of discussion, which is categorically wrong. Ways in which content and style 'speak to' each other in any discussion will be explored over the next three chapters. We'll also look at how a researcher's personal style and overall ability to express ideas clearly and persuasively improves with an evolving identity as a writer, increasing confidence in conveying a sense of writerly intention, and ownership of one's own words within the larger conversation.

The analysis of arguments and argumentation style in which we've already engaged in Chapters 2, 3, and 5 strengthens critical ability, and the authors we read provide models of how to write academically. Yet not all examples we come across during the research process are necessarily good specimens of academic prose, regardless of the fact that the articles and books might be authored by esteemed scholars. For example, you may have some difficulty working out the meaning of the text below:

> The triumph of mediated experience is in evidence both within the information technologies arena and without it; indeed, it is apparent in quotidian reality across every domain, whether commercial or purely philanthropic, because communicative events grow exponentially and there is no game-master in control! This reification of once-insubstantial images and

impressions is, or is at least becoming, a reality based on a thanatic impulse derived from an ontology of horror we accept along with the paradoxically clear opacity of untruthfulness, which is the hallmark of late twentieth and early twenty-first century meaning-making.

Exercise 7.1 Decoding terrible prose

Even if you don't quite understand the text above, try to identify as many of the problems you can that contribute to its inaccessibility.

Perhaps by the end of this chapter you'll be able to recognise more of the flaws and name them, so if you struggle with this exercise now, revisit it later.

In her article 'Dancing with Professors ...' Patricia Limerick theorises (with only mild irony) that one reason for using such mystifying language and convoluted construction is an anxiety among certain scholars that if they make themselves clear, they *will* be understood. Once you're understood you're open to criticism. Her point is that 'dull, difficult prose can function as a kind of protective camouflage' (1993, p. 22). But there are other ways – apart from confusing the reader – of safeguarding yourself from negative criticism which we will discuss in due course. For now I'll mention the most important one: *meaning what you say and wanting to say it*, because the ideas and your desire to write well take precedence in your work – not your ego. That is, your academic intention and your sense of self should govern the way you write, not a desire to impress.

Style is not just a matter of surface impression

Hiding behind grandiose or obfuscatory language or jargon can be a problem in academic prose, and Dennis Fox (2009) is particularly concerned with the ramifications of academics' tendency to write in ways that passively resist criticism. He highlights the problem with what he refers to as the 'pose' of academic neutrality. In fields such as psychology and sociology and other areas which directly impinge on the understanding of personal and political realities, the assumption of neutrality can reduce the impact that researchers could otherwise have within their fields. He maintains that although '*people* still care about things' problems arise when 'the appearance of objectivity masks, and often dampens, that passion that initially drives many academics' (n.p.). Limerick and Fox both criticise academic diffidence as reflected in writing style, the former focusing on how it can interfere with clarity, the latter because a fainthearted approach to scholarship coyly expressed is hardly likely to extend boundaries or to provide new insights. Actually, it has the opposite effect.

Fox claims that 'academic norms drive timidity', and he deplores that hackneyed phrase used to conclude so many reports: 'more research needs to be done.' This too, is really just playing it safe. When you think about it, when can more research *not* be done? It goes without saying. Many authors who conclude in this way would better serve the academic and wider community by making a judgement and stating it clearly – no matter that it may be provisional. Also, inculcating in students this level of reticence is in no one's best interests. Earlier I mentioned the necessity to take risks in your research; well, the same goes for writing, whether as a professional or as a student at master's or doctoral level.

Matters of style and content in the context of communication and conception

Eva Brodin (2015) has done a great deal of research into the reasons for ongoing reticence among postgraduate students in particular. When analysing material for dissertations and theses, and in communicating the results of their research on paper, she found that although students may be aware that now is the chance to express their 'individual voice in their writing, many feel they have to restrain their creativity as it would otherwise impair the critical quality of their work'. Here is the hub of the matter for certain students – and I might add, for plenty of professional writers also: 'They often experience that their individual voice is hampered by predetermined style and form of scholarly texts'. Most understand that in an extended piece of critical writing it is essential that they clearly articulate the theories and methods under discussion. Many also engage in self-reflective practices such as those discussed in Chapter 2, but in the case of students Brodin interviewed, these tended to focus on an acknowledgement of their perceived scholarly failings. What this means is that a focus on defensiveness and avoiding criticism still endures, so people return to the traditional modes of scholarly expression, even though by doing this they endanger a far more valuable attribute – 'their most powerful tool for criticality, namely their individual expression' (Brodin, pp. 271–272).

It may be true that scholarly norms are meant to ensure that what is written and recorded is fair, unbiased, and reliable and is conveyed through concrete argument. Yet they tend to focus on identifying flaws in others' argumentation instead of developing the skills needed to build a strong case. Therefore, fears regarding what you may say and how your thoughts are expressed are, to some extent, justified. Those traditional expectations are most limiting when they are imposed on criticality itself. This can happen when norms go unquestioned (and for those interested in academics who critique academic customs, I'd recommend, apart from those mentioned already in the chapter, Hannah Arendt, Ronald Barnett, Henry Giroux, Paulo Freire, and Toby Miller). Yet one of the liveliest critiques of those in the scholarly community that I've found comes not from an academic tract on critical thinking or styles of scholarship, but in a novel by Karl Ove Knausgaard (2013, pp. 113–114) when relating his school experience. Although students were exhorted to use their critical faculties, this did not mean that independent thought was actually encouraged. In fact, students were not encouraged to extend on the concepts they were learning, but to regurgitate knowledge from different schools of thought in a critical *style*. Only years later did Knausgaard come to question his teachers' notions of what it truly meant to be critical, to be radical, or even to be good.

Knausgaard's exasperation with the way the premises of critical thinking go unchecked in the very environment purportedly dedicated to intellectual enquiry, relates to the limitations of expression many students feel obliged to impose on themselves. *What* you are prepared to say is affected by perceived restrictions on *how* you might express yourself and vice versa. If the individual voice is constrained, impositions on the breadth or depth of critical thought affect the possibility of critical action in the broadest sense. Part of the reason for this – as Brodin points out and which I emphasise throughout this book – is that creativity, though universally touted as an essential attribute, is not in fact actively encouraged at a deeper level in traditional higher education. The result can be a compliant repetition of ideas rather than generation of bold insights and actions, and when this happens, academic work can be reduced to something rather prosaic and dull when it ought to be both stimulating and – yes – enjoyable.

How to invigorate both content and style?

Watch your thinking

In the previous chapter, while offering advice on dealing with time and pressure constraints in an academic context, I mentioned the development of a kind of individual epistemology to increase your level of autonomy – that is, I suggested self-regulatory activities of monitoring how well you've managed to keep to your reading goals and provided various prompts for use in a reflective journal, which was advised for tracking skills acquisition and the progress of your thinking. So, do maintain these practices; they increase awareness of your thinking processes – your metacognitive ability – and this knowledge informs what and how you write. Yet another useful strategy to employ while researching and also as a preliminary task before an essay, is to set yourself the following questions, which I've based on Iris Vardi's presentation at a 2012 conference on pedagogy. These questions encourage you to look quite deeply into your motivations and to try and identify your place within the broader conversation on your topic:

Strategies for improving scholarly thinking

- Consider your focus: Ask yourself what in particular you wish to achieve in any given task, and identify key issues you want to address as clearly as possible. I'd add that it is also important to ask yourself *why* you have chosen that particular focus, because without a strong motivation, it will be harder for you to do justice to the topic.
- Identify your frame of reference: Work out if your thinking is allied with any particular theoretical position or set of assumptions, as discussed in Chapter 3. Consider the possibility that you may need to broaden your perspective.
- Establish to the best of your ability why the information you're accruing leads you to draw particular conclusions, and whether you may have taken anything for granted as you research. This is not easy, as, paradoxically, you are the subject of this objective question. Journaling helps here, as does seeking feedback from peers individually or in a study group. You may find you need more information to increase your knowledge and understanding and to balance your thinking on the subject with which you're dealing.

Thinking well: acts of intellect and imagination

It is much harder to write clearly if the thoughts that nourish the writing are unclear or misguided. Therefore, I want to stress that critical thinking in its most basic, instrumental form is not synonymous with 'thinking well'. It is simply a way of examining phenomena, and is not owned by any particular intellectual or political persuasion. Critical skills may be mobilised in a private enterprise to analyse the current economic climate to discover whether an executive decision will increase the likelihood of profit for a company. There is no concern here with testing the assumptions of the business framework. Similarly, in universities, the basic premises supporting conventional critical thinking can also remain unchallenged. People use critical skills to function as traditional historians or scholars of celebrity culture, as politically conservative economists or as Marxists, to market drugs for global pharmaceutical companies or to run businesses for the Neapolitan *camorra*, or to work as psychoanalysts, economists, advertisers, political activists, teachers, and so on.

However, high-level criticality attempts to look through ideologies and other shiny surfaces to understand the factors that motivate our own and others' actions and belief systems. Within the context of higher education, you cannot really claim to be a critical thinker if you are not prepared at least to attempt this act involving both intellect and imagination. It is also necessary to ally critical and imaginative actions with sympathetic reading. As discussed in Chapter 4, you may find yourself better equipped to understand the intentions and subjectivities of an author if, first of all, you try to disengage from your personal, political, or aesthetic purposes to read a text with wholehearted curiosity. Probably the acid test of a true critical thinker who is thinking *well* is the ability to change your mind when faced with a compelling argument that disagrees with your original position. Good writing will reflect your understanding, your motivation, and your intent.

Receiving and giving support

Often another set of ears or eyes can help you to work out the best direction in which you might take an idea, whether for an essay or for a large a research project. But if, as a student, you find that feedback is not automatically offered by academic staff, then the first advice here is: seek it out. Make an appointment with your supervisor or lecturer and ask their opinion, or engage them in conversation about your intentions for your work. Support of this kind can be very valuable, but if it is not forthcoming then that study group I mentioned can be used instead, whether in person or online. While the disadvantage of this is that you are not receiving advice from people you feel are best qualified to give it, the advantage is that it opens up a way for useful exchanges between yourself and your peers.

Re-examining referencing

We tend to take references for granted, so it is well worth considering for a moment what references actually are. In-text notations, footnotes, or endnotes – what do they actually signal? That you're acknowledging a source – yes – and more. Your citations are signs that indicate where you locate your unfolding ideas as you engage in a dialogue with those you have read, and those who will read you. They indicate your place within ongoing global scholarly conversations.

Referencing is related to the development of critical skills and – as will be discussed in Chapter 8 – the art of constructing a persuasive argument. Correct citation, you might say, is the heart of fine academic argumentation. Following Vardi (2012), it is a means by which you:

- Develop an argument
- Develop your understanding of the literature
- Borrow authority to support your views
- Allow the reader to tell which school of thought or theoretical context with which your argument is aligned. Your citations illuminate whose work you are building upon, thus helping the reader to trace where your thoughts have come from and where they might be tending.

Authorial voice, referencing, and critical writing

An essential factor to help enliven your writing involves developing your own particular voice. Many of us, whether master's or doctoral candidates or academics, would not necessarily say we have a particularly strong authorial voice. Some reasons for this have been referred to already; they include – in the case of students – anxiety about straying too far from referenced material, or worry about your markers' attitudes towards any attempts at 'originality'. These are reasonable concerns, but such reticence can result in keeping learning at a fairly surface level, and also inhibit professional writers in the academic community.

However, as we've established, you can use referencing as a technique by which you not only enhance your authorial credibility but also progress your argument, and ultimately extend on the work of others. According to Vardi's research, an effect of shifting the focus of correct referencing away from its role of safeguarding academic integrity and towards intellectual engagement, frees referencing up so that it can be used as a means towards:

- becoming engrossed with texts in profound ways
- mobilising higher order critical skills with regard to choice of sources
- evaluation of these sources.

Be aware that an inquisitive rhetorical stance is as valid as an authoritative one. It signals to your reader that you're thinking critically and imaginatively about the topic. Uncertainty fuelled by intellectual curiosity is a creative way to proceed. Creativity is not based on certitude. It requires a level of uncertainty where you play with ideas and thus develop them – and referencing is part of this process. While you are 'delving and digging' you are, as Vardi emphasises, responding to your sources with a critical eye; you are evaluating the evidence provided in what you read, situating the ideas within different schools of thought, and comparing, contrasting, and synthesising the relevant ideas and accruing evidence as reflected in your references. This is the way to gradually arrive at an informed position and a strong argument.

Using your sources effectively

First of all, work out what it is you want to say about the topic. Then, having found references that help you negotiate your way through the progression of ideas related to your study, work towards integrating the 'voices' of all the different authors you are drawing on to construct your own argument. Make sure that your own voice is the strongest one. What I mean to stress here is an attitudinal shift away from cutting-and-pasting together a patchwork of borrowed notions to demonstrate that you know the territory. Instead, use others' thoughts only to support your own, never to replace them. Referencing goes well beyond shoring up an argument or helping you to avoid inadvertent plagiarism. It is an essential part of your critical writing practice.

Exercise 7.2

Read the following passage not for content, as you normally would, but for the way it has been constructed. Note:

- How many sources are cited.
- How many quotes are used, and why those quotes were selected rather than paraphrases.
- Do you have any difficulty identifying the voice of the author?
- If not, what differentiates the author's voice from others' voices?

"Uncertainty is an essential aspect of creativity – not simply a tiresome phase to be borne before somehow emerging into the glorious light of certitude. Uncertainty is much more than this. In Eric Eisenberg's phrasing, it is 'a source of possibility and potential action' (2001, p. 540). In explicating the relationship between uncertainty and creativity, Nicholas Burbules (2000) focuses on Plato's 'transitional stage', or *aporia*, that moment when we admit that we are stuck at an intellectual impasse. This, he claims is 'the moment ... where a clean terrain now exists for the reconstruction of knowledge'. Although one may experience the feeling as paralysing, it is here – in Turner's 'realm of primitive hypothesis' – that we are forced to work with the possibilities of accident, of chance, and to seek what Matisse has called 'the desire of the line' (cited in Flam 1995, p. 48). Matisse was discussing visual art, but the image may be applied to writing: one may follow a linear direction of thought or one may enter a system of interconnections that Deleuze and Guattari (1985) have described as 'rhizomatic' – that is, like a root system, branching out as it spreads through this fertile in-between ground, and which Burbules likens to the process of surfing the Net, creating sense from the mass of possibilities through the links one makes between them. The connections one chooses to make – why this nub or node and not that? Why this direction and not another? – will depend on the subjectivities of the author, or maze-navigator."

Exercise 7.3

Select a piece of writing you're currently working on. Review it while taking into consideration the role the citations play in both elucidation and evidentiary support. Checklist:

- Have you included more than necessary to either explain what you mean or to strengthen your argument?
- Note also whether you might integrate quotes or paraphrases more effectively.
- Ask yourself if you have any more ideas or turns of phrase that might enrich your argument or prose.
- Swap texts with a friend and conduct an informal stylistic analysis; see if you can differentiate the author's voice from among those that support it.

Transforming information into knowledge

At the earliest phase of your research, annotations and summaries of texts (including only main points, concepts, facts – with attention paid to authorial emphasis) need to support your individual voice. This is where you begin the process of transforming information into knowledge. Adept paraphrasing is also indispensable. The following examples should demonstrate the difference between an acceptable and an unacceptable paraphrase. First, an example of where a student has absorbed the information given by the original author, then rephrased it so as to integrate it into her own text. The underlined text is the student's.

Original text

In Judaeo-Christian and Islamic mythology it is the spoken word that creates the universe. The earliest narratives, from *The Epic of Gilgamesh* onwards, emphasise the creative power of a proto-language that calls reality into existence. Belief in the power of the text and of storytelling continues in folklore and in other forms of popular culture through contemporary writers, from fantasists such as Ursula le Guin to self-help writers who enjoin their readers to recite life-affirming avowals of strength and purpose in order to control the course of their life stories (Katz 2014, pp. 257–258).

Paraphrase

The author reminds us that in monotheistic creation myths the universe comes into being by way of the spoken word, citing examples of how ancient stories show the intrinsic power within a prehistoric language to create reality. We can find examples of the belief in the power of language and storytelling not only in folk tales but in contemporary forms of popular culture. Modern writers working in genres from fantasy to self-help encourage readers to control the direction of their lives through 'life-affirming avowals of strength and purpose' (Katz 2014, pp. 257–258).

The student's voice is the one we are hearing, which is what's important. It is also important to note that even though the idea is not original – the student is citing another author – paraphrasing in this way means that throughout an extended writing task you are integrating already extant knowledge or theories with your own developing ideas on the subject. In order to be able to use your own words, you need to thoroughly understand the intention of the original author. Rephrasing it helps in the process of transforming the information that you are acquiring through research into knowledge that in a sense, you too now 'own'.

> **TIP**
>
> When paraphrasing, make sure you don't diverge from the author's point of view. In an essay it has to be completely clear which words and ideas are those of another, and which are yours. So be sure to save any speculation or development of your own for *after* you close the paraphrase.

Below is an example of 'patchwriting', a form of plagiarism. Exactly what we *don't* want.

Bad paraphrase

It is the spoken word that creates the universe, according to Judaeo-Christian and Islamic mythology. (THE AUTHOR OF THE ORIGINAL IS NOT MENTIONED. ALSO, THE ORDER IS SIMPLY REVERSED WITHOUT SUBSTANTIAL CHANGE TO THE WORDS.) The earliest ~~narratives~~ stories, from *The Epic of Gilamesh* onwards, ~~emphasise~~ stress (SOME GUIDES ON PARAPHRASING RECOMMEND SUBSTITUTING A SYNONYM – THIS IS *NOT* ENOUGH!) the creative power of a proto-language that calls reality into existence. Belief in the power of the text and of storytelling continues in folklore and in other forms of popular culture through contemporary writers, ~~from fantasists such as Ursula le Guin to self-help writers~~ (STRAIGHT-OUT PLAGIARISM, WITH SOME OF THE ORIGINAL TEXT SIMPLY DELETED) who ~~enjoin~~ demand their readers (POORLY CHOSEN SYNONYM CHANGES THE EMPHASIS INTENDED BY THE ORIGINAL) to ~~recite~~ chant (SAME AGAIN) life-affirming ~~avowals~~ declarations of strength and purpose in order to control the course of their ~~life stories~~ lives. (WHERE IS THE CITATION?)

Paraphrasing well is not always easy. The following steps should help:

- Read the passage – probably more than once. It is impossible to paraphrase properly if you do not thoroughly understand the text.
- Put the text aside.
- Write your paraphrase without referring to the passage.
- Return to the original to check that you have not misinterpreted either content or emphases of the original, and that the paraphrase accurately represents the author's intention.

> Announce the paraphrase with a reference to the author to alert the   **TIP**
> reader to the fact that it *is* a paraphrase and that you are not laying
> claim to the idea yourself.

Some students like to avoid any danger of inadvertent plagiarism by quoting frequently, but over-quoting is no solution. The text starts to look like a cobbled together piece of gobbledygook and the voice of the student drowns in an ocean of inverted commas. That said, of course quotes are sometimes needed, especially for particularly striking or original phrases. You might allow the quote to stand alone, as in, 'Boggle claims that, "blah blah blah"'. If Boggle's claim is particularly striking, then allowing it to stand alone is a good choice. It draws attention to something important and creates drama. However, if overused, it will only interrupt the flow of your prose. Integrating quotes into your own sentences is usually preferable. As in, 'It is clear from Boggle's argument that "two many cooks spoil[ed] the ... broth" at the time of writing, which was over a decade ago. With the new knowledge that has since come to light, one might also argue that ...' (2004, pp. 4–5)

More advice on developing your voice stylishly, but without sacrificing clarity

Some writers (often inexperienced ones, but as we have seen, not always) like to employ strategies they believe will somehow make them 'sound more academic'. But rather than 'sounding', it is far better to 'be'. Wanting to give an impression of being academic is a hollow self-marketing gesture. Good academic writing is concise, crisp, and clear, and it embraces concrete formulations. Take care with the following:

1. **Abstract nouns**
   Avoid sentence structures that require 'there was', or 'with regard to'. They are fussy formulations and the result is often passive prose at its clunkiest and most syntactically awkward. Abstract nouns invite this gracelessness and are often overused in the service of giving an impression of erudition rather than actually *being* erudite. Of course, we do need ways of talking about concepts like beauty, intelligence, evil, honesty, pain, love, ability, liberty, parenthood, slavery, and so forth – that is why abstract nouns exist. Their purpose is to convey an abstraction. But using them when a simple verb would be stronger and more expressive is a mistake. For example, rather than, 'There is an expectation amongst the organisation's leadership that ...' one might use concrete language and write, 'The organisation's directors expect that ...'.

   You'll note that the second version also signals that the directors have independent agency. They may therefore be called upon to explain why they had this expectation, and if it was an unreasonable expectation they will need to account for it. The first version is vague, and allows the 'organisation's leadership' another degree of abstraction. Similarly, you might change a phrase like, 'With regard to his appraisal of the text, the conclusion drawn was ...' to 'Smith appraised the text and concluded that ...'. *Make a point.* Hold Smith to account for his conclusion. Then say what you think of it. Possibly you may then be criticised by Smith or by those who agree with Smith. This is one of the aspects of risk-taking I mention throughout this book. So make sure you have enough solid backup for your argument.

2. **Active or passive voice?**

While on the subject of calling sources to account, the choice of passive or active voice is worth discussing. The passive has its virtues: it allows a certain distance, implies impartiality, imparts information with a cool, scholarly tone. However, it is also used to evade, to play it safe. For example:

The window was broken.

This formulation is not terribly strong – it is being used here as a tactic of evasion. What if, instead, we write, 'I broke the window'? Or, perhaps in an essay: 'John Smith broke the window.' But now you've pointed the finger! Supporters of Smith are taking aim. Bombs may soon fly. So back it up, as in: 'According to Brown (2013) it was John Smith who broke the window.' Or, alternatively: 'Many scholars (Brown 2013; Jones 2014; Abercrombie 2015; Bongiorno-Campden et al. 2016) argue that it was in fact John Smith who broke the window.'

You may find that if you upload this article of yours, 'John Smith and the window', to a website like Academia.edu you will find others interested in this debate. Some will agree with your point that Smith was entirely responsible, and others may point out that although Smith was caught, the actual responsibility for the breakage lay elsewhere; yet others may introduce the fascinating complexity of the cultural or political context of the breakage, or qualify the judgement against Smith by pointing out the positive repercussions of the loss of that particular window – and like you, they will take care to cite their sources. You are now participating in a conversation.

As you can see, there are many implications for the use of the passive voice. It is part of what Fox has referred to as the 'pose' of neutrality, and it protects the author against criticism. It can hamper truthful expression when it is used to intentionally obscure truth. Another example, beyond the window: In 2002, former US Secretary of State Henry Kissinger was questioned regarding possible war crimes and crimes against humanity in the matter of Operation Condor. (Condor was a campaign of political repression and state terror resulting in the deaths of at least 60,000 people, and in which the US government was implicated.) Kissinger stated that it was quite possible that

Mistakes were made.

In a 2011 interview with the late Sir David Frost, the British prime minister, David Cameron, observed this about UK Middle Eastern policy: *Yes of course mistakes were made and of course you know what happened at Guantanamo Bay, there were mistakes made.* If actors were named, Kissinger might have had to admit to the implication of the United States and the CIA in Operation Condor and David Cameron would have to say *who* made the 'mistakes' at Guantanamo Bay.

While you may not be hiding a truth or evading criticism for responsibility in atrocious crimes, if you eschew the personal completely and rely on passive formulations, you may end up distancing yourself from the reader and, worse, retreating into authorial timidity. Helen Sword encourages 'those who favour third-person, impersonal prose … to ask themselves what they are trying to achieve by suppressing personal agency' (2012, p. 43). In order to be able to feel secure when expressing your scholarly opinion in a way that reflects your own feelings and thoughts – in your own voice – research thoroughly and allow your citations to support you. Then go out on a limb with an active formulation. It really encourages you to read more critically and cite more carefully – because so much more is at stake.

3. **Caulking or bombproofing?**

   Both of these terms refer to ways of protecting yourself from criticism. It is best to back up your argument to the best of your ability – with evidence – rather than weaken its thrust with overly qualifying language or repetition. This will only enfeeble your style, losing your message in verbiage – as per the examples on the first page of this chapter. Less confident writers sometimes make the mistake of making a statement, then reiterating it in a slightly different way. My advice would be to say it once and be sure you've backed your claim with sufficient evidence, that is, bombproof your argument. It's not always necessary to outline every argument in support of what you are saying. It can be done like this, for example: 'Many scholars (Black 2016; Green 2011; Pinkerton 1999) argue that a stitch in time saves nine.' That said, an overly long list of in-text citations is not advisable, just a few particularly relevant names, then move your essay on to engage in discussion with other authors' thoughts on your topic.

4. **Verbs**

   A matter of something as apparently simple as verb choice can have an impact on the effectiveness of your prose. For instance, 'claim' might become 'insist'; 'insist' might become 'contend'. So, consider not just *what*, but *how* the action was performed, how potent or weak or sloppy or elegant was that act? And choose just a simple verb to illustrate it. Did she 'avoid' the confrontation, or did she 'evade', 'dodge', or 'elude' it? Maybe, in fact, she 'absconded' or even 'fled'? Possibly, she actually 'escaped'! Then, once you've made your point as succinctly as you can, don't qualify yourself or repeat yourself – unless, of course, you are doing so to create a powerful emphasis.

5. **Jargon**

   Jargon is a valuable tool of academic writing when it is allowed to function as the 'highly efficient form of disciplinary shorthand' it can be (Sword, p. 118). It is specialised language useful for conveying information very succinctly to others in a specific field. However, it can also be misused – to impress or obfuscate. Before employing jargon, remind yourself of the fundamental reason for writing *anything*: to communicate. And take into account your audience. If it is discipline-specific you may be more profligate with jargon than you would be if you intend to communicate with a more generalist audience. The rule is: if your word use interferes with clarity, then use another.

6. **Hedging your bets**

   Some guides will advise 'hedging', that is, using phrases such as '*tend* to effect' or '*may* influence'; '*seem* to be' or '*likely* that'; '*generally*', '*usually*', '*often*'; and so on. The purpose of hedging is accuracy and fairness: your claims need to be proportionate to your evidence; you also need to mitigate criticism of another person's research. The downside of hedging is that it also has the effect of diluting the force of an argument. I have heard it referred to simply as 'fuzzy syntax'.

This *may be* an *overly* harsh criticism. Nevertheless, I *sometimes tend to* shy away from absolute statements when writing academically *probably* because I *might be* inaccurate, and also I *would like* to be able to indicate *some* scholarly humility.

Now, let's try the above paragraph again, this time without the hedging: *This is a harsh criticism. Nevertheless, I shy away from absolute statements to avoid inaccuracies, and also I like to be able to indicate scholarly humility.* How much is too much?

Exercise 7.4

See what other instances of hedging you can find in this chapter, apart from those I've indicated under the hedging heading. There are *likely to be* a few. (Actually, looking under the next heading, I can see some already.) Use your own judgement to establish whether they weaken or strengthen what I have written.

Exercise 7.5

Below is an example of writing from Literary Studies that suffers from multiple disorders including excessive use of abstract nouns, adjectives, adverbs, and jargon. Identify these and try to rewrite the text in a form that is comprehensible. I should mention that this task will probably be impossible for many, if not most readers.

"Replicating the post-Mendel application of Lamarck's apparently superseded scientific theory by non-empirical social scientists, Vernon Lee's fervent and intellectually original use of scientific paradigms across different fields in order to further a specific literary and creative heuristic offers an exemplary narrative trace, replete with hybridized methodologies and the rhetorical deployment of scientific language in non-scientific discourses" (example from Sword 2012, p. 51).

Your version:

To support your developing scholarly voice, I would advise you to read consciously for style – not just content. Take note of what it is you think makes the writing flow, what makes it engaging, that is, what makes you want to read it – apart from the content. Look out for the following:

- Jargon
- Hedging
- Caulking
- Concision, e.g. sentence length, use of subordinate clauses, adjectives, and adverbs
- Use of citations
- Use of paraphrases and quotes
- Abstract nouns
- Voice – personal or impersonal or somewhere in between? This might also include use of anecdote and/or humour.

Apply the same critical lens to your own work. Before submitting to a marker or for peer review, read it through attending to not only content, but style; note how your style affects the way you convey meaning. It can help if you read aloud, or work with friends or colleagues in a study group.

Conclusion

In previous chapters we looked at how to establish more experimental reflective and creative practices that support our learning. The same applies to writing itself, and the development of a confident authorial voice.

This chapter has provided suggestions for ways you might develop your own voice in the context of others who have gone before: reading and writing critically; combining paraphrases with quotes chosen with discretion; making annotations where even at the earliest stages, your words and thoughts are distinguishable from the source. And, interweaved with others' words in your text, your own voice must come through clearly, hopefully with some fresh insight to add to ongoing debates on the subject. Such an approach should mean that you will demonstrate where your argument fits into the general conversation both historically and conceptually.

This chapter has also touched upon issues of rhetorical choice – which we will explore in more detail in the following two chapters – because making intelligent decisions about style will inform a researcher's own particular voice. As Helen Sword points out (pp. 30–31), regardless of whether or not you are expected to conform to one of the more formal structures, it is up to you to choose to write in 'clear, concise, energetic sentences or opaque, complex, passive ones. Scientists can choose to use active verbs. Social scientists can choose to introduce a personal voice. Humanities scholars can choose to eschew disciplinary jargon. Informed choice is the stylish writer's best weapon against the numbing forces of conformity and inertia.' Sword also mentions that although we humans are inclined to 'imitate the common type' without giving it too much thought, if we are to evolve, we might instead consider 'imitat[ing] the successful'. Therefore, my final piece of advice for students on this topic is to find academic writers you admire, work out what it is that works so well for them, and model your own work on those exemplars. And if you take nothing else from this chapter, please take these three pieces of advice:

1. Do not try to make an impression: say what you mean.
2. Do not hide behind obfuscation: openly join the conversation.
3. Do not try to *sound* academic: *be* academic, meaning research, think, put ideas before ego, communicate them as well as you can, express your thoughts on the subject, and back them up.

Persuasive Writing: Rhetorical Techniques

Chapter overview

The previous chapter's treatment of voice, plus the critical and creative theory that we've already surveyed, form the basis for the discussion and exercises for this chapter on rhetoric and:

- The transformative capacity of language
- The art of persuasion, including discussion and exercises which provide
  - a breakdown of the main aspects of rhetoric
  - rhetorical stance and character
  - rhetoric and story
  - rhetorical devices and strategies.
- Grammar tips.

Why is it so important to be able to write persuasively? How you respond to this question will depend on the kind of work you do and your motivations for studying or researching. So I suggest that first you just think about the question, and maybe discuss it with your peers as well. Then jot down your thoughts in the space below *before* moving on down to some possible answers.

Why do I want to persuade my reader?

Academic writing is about communicating with others, joining in discussions where we explore ideas and argue points. We are usually inquisitive – hence the turn of phrase 'academic enquiry' – though sometimes more combative, yet both are styles of 'academic argument'. Scholarship is usually (and I'd argue, *ought* to be) an effort to get to a truth, to the heart of the matter you've chosen to discuss. This is why essays are called essays – from the French *essayer*, to attempt.

In an argumentative or persuasive piece of writing you'll be essaying forth into the arena of debate. Once in position, your job is to attempt to convince your audience of your point of view. This form of scholarship dates back to medieval times when one of the main functions of the university was to train lawyers. The advocate begins with a statement he wants to prove (intro – thesis statement) by means of argumentation often constructed as point/counterpoint (body text – dissertation). He then ties up all loose ends with concluding remarks – an appeal to the jury to agree with his position (conclusion).

Arguments can be blunt instruments (not recommended!) or they can be subtle and nuanced. The need for strong persuasive ability is obvious when trying to convince your readers of a contentious or ambiguous or otherwise debatable point. It is less obvious in a purely discursive essay where you're attempting to throw a little more light on a subject rather than trying to score points, but if you're discussing rather than arguing, you still need to make your point and convince your reader of its value. This is the art of persuasion, or rhetoric.

So, why are you studying? Why are you researching? These initial questions will direct you towards the answer to the original question: Why is it important to be able to write persuasively? Perhaps one or more of the following answers will match yours:

Possible answers to the question, Why is it important to learn to write persuasively?

- I have a fascinating thesis that I want to share, and I really want my audience to get what I mean because it is precious to me.
- I need a Distinction average in order to get into that doctoral programme.
- I have a lot of ideas boggling around in my brain regarding this thesis/article/essay I'm working on. I want to clarify them. Having an audience in mind really helps when it comes to organising my thoughts coherently. So, I write. I need to set out my arguments as persuasively as I can so that I can get a decent response to help me further my research.
- I'm involved in an industry-based collaborative project with other peers/students. We need counterpoints to our points in order to highlight our ideas in context, and to develop our argument. And we want this argument to be very strong. So a few of us volunteered to write persuasive tracts and put them out there for comment. By the way, we are aware that in doing this we might turn up something that messes with our original hypothesis. So be it! Even if it sends us back to the drawing board. We do want to contribute to progress in our field.
- I think I have something valuable to say that will have an impact on my field. It could actually change how people think. I'm not being grandiose, but in its way my idea will change the world, however slightly.

Words are magic – literally *and* in reality

The idea of the transformative ability of language is hardly new. Just to give you an idea of how enduring a concept it is: To the ancient Greek sophist Gorgias, words artfully selected and arranged for rhetorical effect act as 'a means of fascination, peculiar psychagogia, spiritual seduction and a magical effect' (in Kisicek and Zagar 2013, p. 129). Occult philosopher Cornelius Agrippa tells us that 'the power of … verses is so great, that it is believed they are able to subvert almost all nature' (1650). Much later, Pierre Bourdieu speaks of language as a symbolic system that has 'the power to construct reality' (1979, p. 79), Lakoff and Johnson identify metaphor as a linguistic form that is capable of 'creat[ing] realities for us' (1999, p. 146), and Norman Fairclough's (1993) research is largely concerned with the socially transformative aspects of words, particularly how the communicative value of language use in different types of discourse may have significant ideological effects.

There is a symbiotic relationship between language and culture: language is not only shaped by social circumstances; it also has a huge impact on the shape they take. It not only reflects the realities of the world; it also helps to form those realities. Actually, it is hard to talk about language without also raising the subject of societal power structures, but the scope of this book does not allow for detailed discussion of such matters. The main point I want to stress here is just this: rhetoric, the art of persuasion, is a formidable force in the world. An adept user has the power to persuade or to manipulate others, sometimes on a massive scale, for good or ill purposes. Think of the influence of Hitler's speeches, or those of Martin Luther King. So on a lighter note, bear in mind the immortal words of that celebrated superhero, Spiderman: *With great power comes great responsibility.*

Rhetoric: the art of persuasion

Athenian rhetoricians like Gorgias and Protagoras were not so concerned with the written word, given that most people were illiterate at the time. They were primarily speakers and debaters. Yet we still base the teaching of not only oral presentations but persuasive writing on the Classical conceptions of argument. The Greeks worked out that if you want to persuade an audience – whether readers or listeners – you have to appeal on three levels: intellectual, emotional, and that of your own character.

The other three musketeers: *pathos, logos,* and *ethos*

- *Pathos* refers to the engagement of the emotions in persuasive writing. It is here where decisions regarding style become crucial, and I'll talk about that in detail in sections to follow on rhetorical devices and techniques.
- Through *logos* an appeal is made to the intellect of your audience. It requires the development of a thesis based on convincing arguments supported by logic and clear facts presented with clarity of purpose. It is the analytical and evidence-based aspect of your text. Your audience will be inclined to trust what you have to say if the intellectual aspects of your argument are sound.
- This idea of 'trust' segues into *ethos*. If you are no expert, but maybe a student in the early days of a research project, then acknowledge this and simply enquire.

Be inquisitive. Students are *meant* to enquire. Don't attempt to pretend to authority or sophistication or knowledge that you don't have. Rather, build your credibility through effective referencing.

Ethos refers to the appeal to a reader's sense of integrity. You need to take into consideration the values of your audience for this to be effective. While it is true that during the early drafts you should to be guided by your interest in the subject rather than worrying about your readership, at a certain point this changes. You'll shift gears and think carefully about *whom* you want to persuade. Different emphases are required depending upon you are talking to. For instance, say you're writing an essay on global warming: if your audience is likely to include readers who belong to Greenpeace, your arguments will be phrased very differently to those used in an essay for climate-change deniers. We have to mobilise different argumentative strategies depending upon the cultural, social, or political tendencies of whomever it is we want to convince.

The Greek concepts of *logos, pathos,* and *ethos* involve consideration of both audience and subject matter. You may also notice that these 'musketeers' can be linked to Barnett's division of critical skills into Critical Thinking 1, 2, and 3, which was introduced in Chapter 2.

- Critical Thinking 1 refers to the intellectual and scholarly aspects where you consider ideas or data and logically present propositions to mount a case. The connection between this and *logos* should need no explanation.
- Critical Thinking 2 goes beyond the intellectual engagement of CT1 by involving self-awareness and mindful engagement as well. You are required to reflect not only upon the external aspects of your argument, but its relation to your internal world. Such reflection involves emotions as well as intellect and not only is a means towards strengthening your understanding of a topic and your motivations for engaging with it, but also helps to create a bond of sympathy with your reader: *pathos.*
- Critical Thinking 3 is in a sense formed by skills and understanding developed in the other two domains, enabling the application of those proficiencies to professional and social contexts. In other words, it grounds academic theorising in the real, phenomenal world. Such critical engagement with the world needs to be tempered by an ethical, rather than a purely instrumental attitude: *ethos.*

Further note on *ethos*: the difference between rhetoric and propaganda or sophistry

Persuasive argument contains a central, ethical dimension, regardless of the subject matter. That is, persuasion in itself should not be the aim of rhetoric. Flattering the audience or reinforcing the beliefs of an audience takes us on to dangerous ground. Consider the horrifying effect of the propaganda of demagogues in times of political crisis. Neither is persuasion about using clever devices to convince someone of something simply as a stylish intellectual game. That is a debased form of sophistry. It's important to consider why you're using

(Continued)

rhetoric and why you want to persuade someone to your point of view. Ask yourself what your intentions are for the tract you're working on, and who it will affect, and how that audience will be affected.

I'd argue that excellent persuasive writers are able not only to convey their intended meaning with eloquence, but also to stimulate independent, critical thought in the reader.

Rhetorical stance

As stressed in the previous chapter, a creditable writer doesn't try to 'sound' academic. Focusing on creating an impression rather than on ideas and saying what you mean will adversely affect the clarity of your prose. It also undermines the trust that any intelligent, perceptive reader might otherwise have had in your argument. The technical term for this kind of writing is, according to moral philosopher Harry Frankfurt, 'bullshit discourse'. He mentions that there is a lot of it about in public life because it occurs 'where people are … impelled … to speak extensively about matters of which they are to some degree ignorant' (Frankfurt 2005, p. 63). He's right. Public figures rarely like to admit when they are unsure of something. Do not follow this model. Do not attempt to feign expertise, just take that honest and direct inquisitive stance, and remember that by citing well you borrow authority from your sources while simultaneously demonstrating that you know the field. 'Stand on the shoulders of giants [or those just a bit taller than you!].'

It's true that caution and formality still mark both writing style and content in some disciplines. There are reasons for this, and for the traditional prohibition against the use of the first person: you *don't* want your writing to become overly subjective and you *do* want to present only carefully considered arguments. However – and this is a *big* however – your ill-conceived argument, as Graff and Birkenstein (p. xxiv) point out, might be the starting point for a well-conceived one, and you don't want to feel too inhibited too early because this can discourage the sort of critical exploration that can lead to something interesting. Also, banning 'I' isn't necessarily a safeguard against self-indulgent subjectivity. What it tends to do is 'hamper students' ability … to differentiate their own positions from those of others'.

The good news is that most teachers are human, and such creatures often enjoy a more conversational rhetorical style to overly formal prose (which is why the next chapter will focus on narrative in academic writing). As for marking, papers to be graded come in tall, teetering piles which are not always amazingly interesting to read, so when a teacher picks one and recognises a divergent perspective or a fresh idea, however tentative, it's usually welcomed warmly. It demonstrates a student's interest in actually participating in a discussion about ideas rather than parroting discursive techniques or discourses that they may not even fully understand. Teachers are also aware that students are learners, so if you are a student, take advantage of that. Just make it clear when you are speculating or if you suspect you may be drawing a long bow. You can state overtly that you realise you are not an authority and then continue with your train of thinking-on-paper, ensuring of course that you cover the ground to the best of your ability and substantiate any claims you make with evidence. This, by the way, also increases your authorial clout.

A final word about your decision to use personal or impersonal formulations:

- Think about why you have written a text.
- Think about your relation to the ideas under discussion.
- Consider the audience for whom it is intended. In the last chapter I quoted Helen Sword who suggested that if you prefer to use the third person you need to think carefully about why. I suggest you also consider your reasons if your preference is for personal, more active forms. Think about where and how often their use serves your intentions for your writing.

Exercise 8.1

Below I have experimented with different modes of expression. The first is formal; the second is the kind of writing you might do in a reflection journal; the third is an attempted compromise. The topic is 'The Apocalypse'. As you read the samples, try and identify which of the rhetorical modes – *pathos*, *ethos*, and *logos* – are used and how they affect your reading of the text. This may inform your own writing when you do the exercise.

Academic
This chapter argues that there need be no cataclysmic bombshell, but rather a gradual decline and degeneration on the eve of the putative 'apocalypse'. Certain political, economic, and educational tendencies that seem to be directing humanity along a downward path will be examined, and this chapter presents the argument that the current malaise is enabled by the devaluation of critical and creative impulses which encourages the spread of a pervasive mediocrity that some authors have described as 'zombie consciousness'. Economist John Quiggin employs a metaphor from popular culture, zombies' eating of brains, to illustrate the persistent pursuit of ideologies which he insists have already failed, yet continue to be propagated.

Personal
Forget your cataclysmic bombshells! They're redundant in the face of the zombie invasion. Things will just keep going gradually down the gurgler. You only have to look at current political, economic, and educational tendencies to recognise that we're all going to hell in a handbasket. And why? Because we're all suffering from a disease called 'zombie consciousness', that's why! And its symptoms include the desire to eat brains and to breed no matter what, which is pretty vile and disgusting whichever way you look at it. Economist John Quiggin uses the brain-eating metaphor to describe the persistence of ideologies that have already failed, but keep on lumbering about, drooling.

(Continued)

I'd say the propagation part of the story is demonstrated clearly by the way these lifeless but thriving – undead – ideologies continue to spread and spawn more of the same, on and on.

Conversational academic
There need be no final 'bang', no cataclysmic bombshell, but rather a gradual petering out. I will examine certain political, economic, and educational tendencies that are directing us along the path towards annihilation, and argue that this is made possible by a descent into a kind of demented fantasy that might be characterised as 'zombie consciousness'. There are two powerful markers of this consciousness – figuratively speaking – the desire to eat brains and the desire to propagate. The eating of brains is a metaphor for what economist John Quiggin has identified as the persistent pursuit of ideologies that have already demonstrably failed. Propagation is viewed here as the seemingly unstoppable spread of these moribund ideologies.

Now, you try. Choose material that you have to submit for marking, and try experimenting with different voices – active or passive voice; first-, second-, or third-person prose.

Rhetoric and character

Briefly returning to ancient Greek origins: Aristotle proposed that persuasive force is anchored in

- evidence (proof);
- the ability of the words to move the audience (receptivity); and
- the character of the speaker – or in our case, of the writer (credibility).

The need for clearly referenced evidence and ways to construct a convincing argument are aspects of rhetoric we've dealt with in some detail, but 'character' of the author is sometimes either overlooked or taken for granted. Yet character is actually the most important aspect of rhetoric. Why? Well, I've already mentioned that we need to appeal to a reader's sense of integrity, but it works both ways. As a writer, you must demonstrate your own ethical integrity. The other two aspects of receptivity and proof depend upon this: if the reader doesn't trust the author, he won't trust her arguments and evidence and won't be convinced by what she has to say. Character and persuasive ability are intimately related: 'The rational structure of the argument derives its power by way of illuminating the character and practical reasonableness of the speaker' (Robinson 2006, p. 6).

  Begin your essay or dissertation boldly, with a statement that expresses your point of view or with the question you intend to explore, using clear, precise terms. It still needs to be a strong beginning even if you're not an international expert. Graff and Birkenstein suggest that opening paragraphs should consider the question of 'Who cares?'; that is, locate your argument within the debate right at the outset by framing your claim 'as a response to what someone else has said' (p. 94) and you're signalling to readers who have a stake in the research, readers who want to know more, that you *have* more to add that will interest them.

In Chapter 4 an essay topic after mindmapping and clustering was 'Mimics of Beauty'. That's an evocative title; so, having made a certain rhetorical impact, for the sake of clarity you might follow it up (after a colon) with: 'How fan culture both elevates and diminishes the objects of their desire.' Or you might reformulate it as a question – a beginning that is now accepted in most disciplines today, like – 'How does fan culture both elevate and diminish the objects of their desire?' Or, 'Does fan culture elevate their objects of desire, or diminish them?' Your first sentence might then be something like, 'Traditionally, fans have been seen simply as followers, yet recent research clearly shows that they are more active and effective cultural participants …'

However, as you begin to develop your thesis in the body of your text, do take care not to become too opinionated. You'll only put people off. How can you make strong statements but refrain from sounding arrogant, or worse, being biased? Here are two suggestions:

1. The centrality of character as represented by the persona that you are creating as you write becomes clear here. Make conscious decisions as to which aspects of your character you wish to present to the reader. In Exercise 8.1, I showed you three personas (characters) while discussing advantages and disadvantages of using the personal in academic writing. The third example (suitable for many, though possibly not all, academic publications) allowed for a certain amount of playfulness, and also exhibited signs of attempted honesty. I suspect it wasn't hard to detect that the author had strong feelings on the subject, though she wasn't particularly loud about it. The second example, however, would be the voice of a tub-thumping haranguer, so I strongly suggest you eschew exhibiting that sort of character. Not only does presenting yourself as a tub-thumper reduce your credibility in essays, it also debilitates your ability to think well. Too much emotionality distorts your thinking and you risk undermining your own argument. So while of course it's great to have strong feelings on the subject you have chosen to write about, choose your words with care. Remember, they are potent magic.

2. Include those oppositional voices I've mentioned. Not only does this strengthen your argumentation and show that you know the territory, it also requires you to think very carefully about why you disagree with those intellectual adversaries. Character enters here as well. Not only do you have to *show* that you are reasonable, you must *be* reasonable. Your rationality and practical intelligence (Greek: *phronesis*) will give your reader confidence in what you are saying. Chapter 3 suggested you consider counterarguments for the sake of fairness, and also to include them in your analysis as 'strategic concessions' that also serve the purpose of showing your own point of view more convincingly. A way to exhibit your familiarity with the work of other researchers while making strategic use of a dissenting point of view can be as simple as integrating it into your discussion like this: 'While there is a strong argument for …, evidence suggests that …'. And then going on to explore both sides with evidence and drawing your own conclusions.

Exercise 8.2

In the preceding section, 'Rhetoric and character', identify which parts of the advice provided referred to the use of *pathos* (emotional impact), which to *logos* (intellectual force), and which to *ethos* (fostering readerly trust in writerly character).

Pathos

Logos

Ethos

Rhetorical devices and strategies

Analogies and metaphors

Metaphors are indispensable when it comes to making complex ideas accessible. For instance, discussing gravitationally completely collapsed objects may have profound implications for our understanding of the origins of the universe and therefore life itself, and even how creation might end, but despite its huge significance no one outside the astrophysics community cared much until John Archibald Wheeler dubbed those anti-objects 'black holes'. The metaphor achieved an access point into astrophysics that is potent, evocative, faintly threatening. 'Black holes' soon generated massive, worldwide interest. And it isn't just a matter of making a concept more accessible. According to Lakoff and Johnson (1980) *most* thought is metaphorical. We humans tend to think in symbolic language which then affects how we act in the world. Metaphors and similes, analogies and parables, fairy tales and myths are how we make sense of the world in general, and in an academic context, metaphors assist reflection and therefore support our critical processes.

As we established in Chapter 3, analogies are useful as analytical tools for solving problems. If you can't find a solution to a conundrum, you can compare it to another similar case, once you've identified the similarities between key aspects of the two scenarios. You may then find that if a particular solution is viable for one, it may well be the case that it will work in the other. Most relevant to this section, however, is the use of analogies in persuasion. A fine example from a legal case is explained by Diane Halpern (2013, p. 53). During the hearing the defence lawyer pointed out that the chain of (largely circumstantial) evidence against his client contained weak links, and that a chain was only as strong as its weakest link. Admittedly, the strength of this analogy was probably undermined by the fact that it has been used a bit too often, which may have contributed to the success of the counterargument mobilised by the prosecutor, who used instead the image of a rope. He insisted that a rope could have some weaker strands but still be strong enough to make a conviction. Rope trumped chain.

You can use metaphors or similes or analogies and other forms of figurative writing in most papers, essays, and articles. They'll make the reading and writing more pleasurable; they'll help illuminate otherwise obscure ideas; they'll arrest attention in a direct way; they'll provoke thought – or other reactions. Just remember:

1. **Be precise** in your intentions.
2. **Be aware of your reader**. How and where you use metaphors and analogies will depend on who you're writing for. For instance, such devices won't work well if you're writing for an ethnically diverse audience as meaning is culturally circumscribed.
3. **Don't overdo it**. In her book on writing style, *Steering the Craft*, Ursula le Guin remarked, when speaking of adjectives, that they are like chocolates. Two or three are delicious; too many will make you sick. Her use of simile is enlightening when discussing adjectives, and the same goes for figurative language in general, particularly in scholarly prose. Don't sacrifice critical analysis or academic objectivity to flamboyant display. You'll convince no one. An embarrassing personal example: I once submitted to a respected academic journal an article that included a lengthy paragraph that attempted to mount a case with an extended metaphor. It became progressively more grandiose as the paragraph unfolded. Two of the three peer-reviewers claimed that I was being ostentatious and unnecessarily polemical, and when I reread it, I found I agreed. It was a case of 'a tangent too far'. The amended article was accepted in the end, and I did keep that analogy, but in a much tighter form. Rhetorical imagery should never *overshadow* an idea; instead, the idea should simply be *illustrated* with the image.
4. **Avoid clichés**. You're hardly going to refresh or invigorate your prose with an exhausted catchphrase. Nevertheless, clichés abound. For instance, universities today often use a form of managerial jargon, now common to any workplace. Many of you will be familiar with it. Its terms of reference are generic and very tired.

Exercise 8.3

Rewrite the following clichéd 'Corpspeak' (Katz 2015) passage in English. You will need to think hard about what each word actually means and what it is that you want to convey. You'll need to substitute hollowed-out catch-alls, vague but inflated descriptors, and managerial jargon for meaningful English. You may find that not only the emphasis, but the actual meaning will change.

Our market-leading institution, with its cutting-edge reputation of international standing, is committed to world-changing impact. Therefore it is recommended that all productivity units responsible for knowledge transfer in this industry

(Continued)

engage in a series of leadership workshops in order that the institution may
continue to enhance its reputation for excellence. The process of performance
assessment will be transparent, featuring exemplars as examples so as to enable
all stakeholders, including teaching and learning clients and other beneficiaries,
to better understand our processes and infrastructure.

Your version. It'll be much briefer than the above. (In case it is unclear, you are writing a document for university staff.)

My version.

Our university is currently respected internationally for the quality and influence
of its research programs. Nevertheless, the marketing department recommends
that, to further promote the university, all teaching staff participate in a series of
leadership workshops. The assessment criteria and results of the most
successful participants will be published on the university's public website in
order to convey to potential funding bodies and students the impression of an
entrepreneurial spirit among our academics. The aim is to encourage an
increase in investment and a greater intake of international, fee-paying
postgraduates.

Suspense

Suspense is a narrative device used by authors of fiction. It can be transferred to an academic context to dramatise argumentation to rhetorical effect. For instance, Donald McMiken (2010, p. 249) suggests that while mounting a case, you strategically relate one side of an argument, then rather than immediately fulfilling the reader's expectation that you follow with a critique … *wait* … Allow a certain tension to develop by instead moving on to the opposing view and outlining it in detail. Your reader is waiting to 'see what happens' as if they were reading a detective novel. The only catch is, don't make them wait too long.

Another way to cultivate suspense is to supply a wealth of examples to prove a point, stacking one argument on top of the next, or one startling statistic after another, terrifying figures accumulating towards a promised point of climax, thus captivating the reader with a veritable cornucopia of information and data that they sense is leading to a fascinating interpretation. Which of course, it will. Below is an example of this listing technique. You'll notice that accumulation can be rhetorically very potent.

The Carmichael coal mine proposed for Queensland's Galilee Basin would be the biggest ever seen in Australia … six open cut pits and five underground mines. Measuring … 28,000 hectares, the mine would be seven times the area of Sydney Harbour. The company behind the mine, Adani Group, is infamous for environmental destruction … bribery, illegal exports … Over 20,000 hectares of native bushland would be cleared to make way for the coal mine, [which] would steal precious water [requiring] 12 gigalitres (12 billion litres) of water each year from local rivers and underground aquifers … Even ten kilometres away, water tables are expected to drop by over one metre. Adani plans to build a new coal port terminal in waters that are home to humpback whales, dugongs, rare snubfin dolphins and five types of sea-turtles to export the coal from Carmichael mine. Three million cubic metres of sea-bed would be dredged up from inside the World Heritage Area and dumped in the Great Barrier Reef Marine Park to make way for coal ships and the port expansion. Scientists predict this dredging would be [disastrous] to the Reef [and that] the burning of coal from Carmichael mine would produce four times the fossil fuel emissions of New Zealand. It is a catastrophe. (Greenpeace 2014)

Pace

Many lecturers and public speakers understand a simple strategy that can be used to great effect, and plenty of academics today enliven their prose in this way also: a scholar might slowly, thoughtfully, deliberatively build up a highly erudite analysis, then follow it with a briskly delivered conclusion. A very simple but effective way to increase the readability of your text is based on this formula – just vary sentence length to your advantage. Let's test the theory:

In recognising the value of an uninterrupted, flowing piece of prose followed by a short, sharp, pithy phrase standing alone in the next sentence, some writers are able to create a composition that is neither rambling, nor choppy – and not only this, but the long sentence allows the following short sentence to emerge more emphatically. Balanced writing supplies oomph.

Did that work?

Exercise 8.4

After you've completed a few drafts of your next essay or article and have a version that seems to work, experiment a little with the composition itself. Although writing is not meant to be torture, it sometimes is, especially when you're working to a deadline. But once you've arrived at what you think is your last draft take a moment to play around with what you have. And, as I've mentioned before, it *really* helps to read aloud.

If you feel happy with this kind of activity, then use it throughout the drafting process. You can always delete later if the word or phrase proves distracting or redundant. Try it out first, remembering that play is important to good writing. Not only can it be pleasant, it can also help you let off steam if you need to. And it works by association: Your light-hearted or angry inclusions may well lead your mind onto points you might otherwise have missed while you were too earnestly focused on being objective and 'on-task'.

Repetition

I mentioned in Chapter 7 that to write succinctly it's best to say what you mean, then move on, that is, to avoid repetition – unless it is used in the service of strengthening a point that really does require emphasis. Sometimes you'll have a particularly important point that you fear might otherwise be lost in your text – especially if it's a long article or dissertation – and in this case judicious use of repetition can certainly be used to rhetorical advantage.

Please note, I did say *judicious* use. When editing your work look out for instances of accidental repetition and if you find them, rephrase, or if it is just a particular word to which you keep resorting, use a synonym. You'll usually discover that a more finely nuanced term can be found to suit each situation. The thesaurus is handy here, but be absolutely sure you know the meaning of a word before you select it.

Combinations

To make a strong point, you might combine various persuasive tactics. The example below exhibits a vigorous mix of personal anecdote, listing, and irony. When writing his book critiquing humanities education in the United States, Toby Miller (2012, p. 3) who was not born in America, thought it useful to mention some of his thoughts while studying for his citizenship exam:

> I was required [...to promise] that I had never sought to undermine another country's government. How odd, given that doing so has long been US policy. Think of Lebanon, Indonesia, Iran, and Viet Nam in the 1950s; Japan, Laos, Brazil, the Dominican Republic, Guatemala, and Bolivia in the 1960s; or Portugal, Chile, and Jamaica in the 1970s. All these countries saw elections rigged or governments destabilised by the United States.

Say what you mean ...

> The bullshitter ... does not reject the authority of the truth, as the liar does ... He pays no attention to it at all. By virtue of this, bullshit is a greater enemy of the truth than lies are ... Why is there so much bullshit? ... Bullshit is unavoidable whenever circumstances require someone to talk without knowing what he is talking about. (Frankfurt 2005, pp. 61–63)

Aiming for clarity and truth means choosing your words with care; they are the components of your sentences which form your paragraphs. Obviously! So, from word level through to the completed assignment is a process of selection, de-selection, and re-selection. Curtail clichés and catch-alls. Work out how your ideas and claims might be most eloquently communicated. These practices can refresh your academic prose and help you to identify more precisely what it is you actually want to say.

Punctuation and rhetoric

Readily available online are these two demonstrations of how humble commas, colons, and question marks can be used to create or invert meaning:

Version 1:
A woman without her man is nothing.

Version 2 reverses the meaning:
A woman: without her, man is nothing.

The next example really ought to be read aloud for maximum comedic effect.

Version 1:
Dear Jack,
I want a man who knows what love is all about. You are generous, kind, thoughtful.
People who are not like you admit to being useless and inferior. You have ruined me for
other men. I yearn for you. I have no feelings whatsoever when we're apart. I can be
forever happy – will you let me be yours?
Jill

Version 2:
Dear Jack,
I want a man who knows what love is. All about you are generous, kind, thoughtful
people who are not like you. Admit to being useless and inferior. You have ruined me. For
other men I yearn! For you I have no feelings whatsoever. When we're apart I can be
forever happy. Will you let me be?
Yours,
Jill

Extreme examples, yes. However, I've used them to make the point that punctuation can make or break a piece of writing. It is often considered as simply an aspect of the mechanics of sentence construction, but it can be used to do a great deal more: correct punctuation can make meaning clearer, but *slightly less correct* punctuation can also contribute to the persuasiveness of your argumentation, that is, while correct punctuation is often a virtue, you don't have to be a diehard stickler for grammatical perfection.

Good writers are rarely absolutist about punctuation. Conventions found in style guides are not handed down from on high by some infallible deity, and in any case, slavish rule-following is hardly the approach of a critical thinker. In the case of academic writing, it can interfere with your voice, with the aspects of an idea you wish to emphasise, with the flow of your prose.

That said, a wordsmith, like any other craftsperson, needs to understand the basic functions of their tools first of all. Therefore, although this book is not a style manual, below is a basic punctuation checklist for any readers who have doubts about what is considered by most grammarians to be the correct usage. Note – I mentioned 'most grammarians' – there is no absolute consensus of opinion regarding the finer points, and the conventions change according to fashion. I will also mention where it might be advisable to break a rule or two.

The semicolon connects two independent clauses. Some argue that it can make prose feel overly laborious. I don't agree. Here's an example:

As she lay soaking up the sun on a Bahamian beach and admiring the oil-slick tanned
bodies all around her, Meredith was suddenly struck by the revelation that of course, she

too could be famous; she picked up her phone, slotted it into her selfie-stick, rose to her feet and announced to her friends, 'It's time for me to eschew modesty and assume my rightful place on the world stage!'

The colon is for amplification: it is useful when you want to be emphatic, or to begin a list:

There are many kinds of dog: the dachshund, long and thin and vulnerable to spinal disorders; the kelpie, a farm dog bred for rounding up sheep and cattle, but with a rather obsessive nature; the poodle, said to be the most intelligent of dogs; the pug, the greyhound, the terrier, the dalmation …

Notice also in the above example how the semicolon dividing the main items in the list allows you to use commas to add descriptions to each individual item without confusion.

The comma also comes after 'moreover', 'therefore', and so on. However, I have been known to occasionally skip those so as to convey a particular sense of urgency – but I wouldn't necessarily consider it a cause for which I would want to do battle with an editor.

You definitely do not need to use a comma between two independent clauses joined by a conjunction, as in:

He tends to work with extreme concentration but can sometimes be diverted if the distraction is attractive enough.

That said, when in doubt, read aloud, and insert a comma when you feel it's necessary to draw breath.

The Oxford comma is essential, in my view. Compare these two statements:

- I love my parents, Lady Gaga and Humpty Dumpty.
- I love my parents, Lady Gaga, and Humpty Dumpty (Grammarly blog 2016).

Commas are also handy for using as a mild, parenthetic pause:

Dr Doolittle, adventurer and animal lover, was considered by his peers to be a rather eccentric person.

Dashes may be used for a longer break. The longest break is achieved by using actual parentheses. Thus:

- That said, when in doubt, read aloud.
- That said – when in doubt – read aloud.
- That said (when in doubt) read aloud.

Dashes are also useful for emphasising a point, or for linking what would otherwise be a fragment into your sentence.

Traps to avoid – *most* of the time

1. **Fragments**, which are would-be sentences that are lacking all the requisite components of subject, verb, and object, should not be found in academic prose – strictly speaking. Most commonly, fragments are dependent clauses. Those that have become disconnected from their parent sentence. That was an example. It

should have read, 'Most commonly, fragments are dependent clauses that have become disconnected from their parent sentence'. However, fragments can sometimes be handy if you want to use them as a rhetorical strategy to emphasise a point (so long as the reader is able to infer the subject of the sentence with ease). Of course, if formality is required, your would-be fragment can be incorporated into the sentence with a dash – as I am doing now – and as I did above in the first sentence of this paragraph.

2. **Run-ons** are usually ugly and can interfere with the clarity of your writing, impeding the reader's ability to readily follow your thoughts, but it is easy enough to deal with these once you've noted – usually during the editing process – that you have 'committed' a run-on, which is an overly long sentence containing too many subordinate clauses covering several subjects so that sometimes the reader has to return to the beginning of the sentence to remind herself of what the writer seemed to be intending at the outset, by breaking the sentence up into several sentences, each one dealing with a separate subject.

(Yes, that was a run-on.)

Exercise 8.5

Rewrite the above explanation of a run-on clearly. It may take two or three sentences.

---

3. **Choppy prose** is the opposite. Choppy prose consists of too many short sentences. Too many short sentences can sound awkward. Sometimes, they make your writing seem childish. Almost. Choppiness can interfere with the flow of ideas. We have discussed this.

Exercise 8.6

Rewrite the choppy prose above so that it flows. Remember the previous discussion about varying sentence length.

---

4. **Clause-play for rhetorical effect**

   Whether written or spoken, discourse is comprised of independent clauses, all bearing distinct meaning, and as creating arguments in academic writing is about convincing your audience, you will sometimes need to play around with the order of things.

Take this simple sentence: 'The English language has evolved from many languages.'

Add a descriptive modification: 'The English language has evolved from a *complex mixture of* many languages.'

Introduce your enthusiasm for the subject by adding another adjective: 'The English language has evolved from a *fascinating and complex mixture of* many languages.' Of course, you'll then have to demonstrate to your reader why you think it is fascinating.

Add a grace note: 'The English language – *which some describe as a hybrid; others, less politely, as a mongrel* – has evolved from a fascinating and complex mixture of many languages.'

Re-arrange for a slightly different effect: 'Some describe the English as a hybrid tongue, while other (less politely) say it is a mongrel; both interpretations are based on the same simple fact: English has evolved from a complex mixture of many languages.'

Conclusion

We began with questioning the importance of building on our persuasive writing skills. Possibly you already had some answers to the question, and if not, I hope you did by the end of the chapter! The section that followed looked at of the magical capability of language, that is, its ability to transform reality. Considering the art of rhetoric in this light should really bring home the fact that clear thinking and strong writing are powers in the world that are dangerous to overlook. This idea informs both what and how you write, and what and how you read, interpret, and speculate upon others' words. Having introduced the potent force that rhetoric can be, we analysed its components, starting with the Classical Greeks, then recontextualised notions of pathos, ethos, and logos for the contemporary writer. A brief discussion of the notion of essay-writing as it was conceived in medieval times followed, then how to use the notion of the essay as 'the attempt' in scholarly pursuits today. It was my intention to bring home the idea that using rhetoric to strengthen one's ability to communicate well in a scholarly context is part of a tradition that dates back to the earliest days of Western thought, and that writing persuasively has broad cultural and personal implications (For more on this subject see Katz 2014, and Katz 2016). Rhetoric has the ability to change people's minds, to develop the character of the author, and yes, to change the reality we currently inhabit.

Persuasive Writing: Developing a Narrative

At art school I modestly considered myself a rather brilliant font of startling ideas. A teacher there told me, Yes, that's all very well, but ideas are two a penny. Who cares what you think if you can't present your ideas in such a way that people *get* them? He was right, and finding fabulous ways of presenting ideas isn't actually easy for most of us. In fact, it can be the hardest part of any intellectual or creative process, whether you're talking about an art work or a dissertation on Noam Chomsky's contribution to the field of analytic philosophy or a scientific paper on the relative merits of paper and polystyrene packaging. All academic writing, whether in the sciences or the humanities, based on empirical or theoretical research, needs to be persuasive. An essay in the humanities might have more scope for rhetorical play, but a scientific treatise still needs an engaging introduction and a compelling discussion section. The 'how' of presenting a case involves careful consideration of language choices, structural considerations, and style of delivery.

We've already looked at some forms of academic communication. Chapter 7 focused on the relationship between your voice and the references you use in articles and essays, characterising scholarly discourse as conversational. Chapter 8 was concerned largely with rhetoric. Informed by this background and building upon previous discussions of style, this chapter highlights the modes of narrative and description. The latter means bringing images, ideas, characters, places, and objects to life. So at this point we'll enter into a more detailed consideration of the idea of 'argument as story', which is how I define a narrative approach to academic writing.

Narrative can help make academic writing more accessible and persuasive. We'll also look at how it can be used to make arguments more convincing and your writing more stylish. But first, I want to state very clearly and unequivocally that telling a story well does not necessarily equate with thinking well. Examples of powerful narration allied with bad thinking abound in many forms of media coverage of events and in propagandistic speeches, and seductive prose can also create the illusion of 'making meaning' in academic texts as well. As emphasised throughout this book, in order to think well, we have to balance objectivity and sympathy, distance and closeness, creativity and criticality (including skills of analysis and reflection anchored by an awareness of the cultural and professional ramifications of our work). In order to write strongly and persuasively in an academic context, rhetorical or other strategies are not a substitute for the intellectual rigour that allows for the development of a sustained and coherent argument. They are just means to that end.

Structuring your text as an ongoing story, written as you research

After you complete a first draft, or even during the process of drafting, other ideas may well occur to you, or other information may present itself, as we discussed in Chapter 8. Rather than feeling frustrated because you fear you may have missed something important, take up this invitation to complexification. It is this complexity that keeps the job interesting, that fuels creativity. These ideas and the form into which you gradually 'massage' them as you write will help give the text you're working on depth and breadth and richness.

---

1. Begin writing while you are researching (annotations, mindmaps,   **TIP**
   outlines-in-draft, drafts of the text). You can become paralysed if you
   think you have to finish your research before you start writing.
2. Continue reading and annotating while you write.

For example, in writing this book, I had a fair idea of how it would progress. I had to, because the publisher required an outline before my proposal could be considered! However, the publisher and I also knew that as I wrote, things would change. The changes would be inevitable because I would continue to read as I wrote, and therefore the original outline was necessarily provisional. That's fine; outlines are not handed down by venerable patriarchs on mountaintops. I would revisit 'completed' chapters as new ones were added, and the structure would have to be altered to encompass these changes.

The process of interweaving sub-topics within your overarching thesis as the research 'story' develops can feed your governing idea, enriching it. Without the information and commentary they supply, the text would not only be less informative, it would also be more linear and one-dimensional. It would be simpler, of course, if you could simply lay out a plan, subheading by subheading, then fill in the content – a bit like a joining-the-dots exercise. But an extended writing task is very rarely so simple. But then again, if it *were*, it might read like the academic equivalent of a boring novel – a pedestrian unfolding of unsurprising events. No panache!

Structural complexity can be handled in academic writing in ways similar to those used in fictive writing, once you have a 'storyline'.

Q: if this book were a novel, what would the main storyline/s be?

A: Criticality and persuasiveness.

Q: What stories occur within the main, overarching one?

A: There's creativity, sympathy, and ethics. There's the relation between university work and the wider world, between writers and readers. Then there are the stories that emerge through references to the ideas of various thinkers on the subjects discussed, and also to my own experience.

Academic writing is a sociable activity

Here's a very broad statement: Well-conceived academic writing, whether formal or informal, delivered as a narrative or otherwise, is *always* a conversation.

Even though writing in general tends to be a solitary activity, academic writing is actually very sociable, probably more so than most other forms of writing. Whatever you write in an essay, you cannot help but respond to what others have done before, because academic writing is research-based writing and as such is part of a continuum that refers very directly to past ideas, to current ideas and new information, and it also looks to the future: you will be keeping an eye on comments other people (markers, colleagues – whoever) will make about your contribution to 'the conversation'. Academic writing interweaves many points of view and when you join in your voice also becomes integrated into the overall weft and warp of a developing fabric of discussion. Such discussions might be cooperative and collegial; others, more combative or even polemical. There is a series of exchanges going on among a multiplicity of readers and writers over time and space, making it an essentially participatory process. Why, then, should not the form of writing reflect this engagement and interplay?

Ways of constructing a persuasive text by conversational means

The strategies below are all, in a sense, conversational devices that are used in everyday narration to tell a story, that help us participate in conversations that are ongoing, ever-developing, living communications between scholars and the broader community. Often, they are global in scale. In stories, ideas or facts are laid before your reader or listener. They are a set of interrelated ideas or events that interest you and which you want your reader to be interested in also. In order for readers to appreciate your understanding of these ideas or events, you need to explain, back up, and interpret the ideas or events as your narrative unfolds.

Metacommentary

Throughout this book I've referred to the need to be mindful of your intellectual processes. In Chapter 2 we looked at reflective writing as a means of monitoring your thinking. I suggested you keep a journal in which your aim was to informally critique your own thoughts, a reflexive activity where you take into consideration underlying principles that affect the way you read a text. You ask yourself why it is that you respond to ideas the way you do. Another example of such mindful intellectual practice – that is, another act of 'thinking about thinking' – is metacommentary, which is a way of guiding your reader through your train of thought. Graff and Birkenstein (2010) look at it as a sub-text running concurrently with your main text. For instance, if you become aware that a point could be misconstrued, you might write,

'*I do not mean to say* that one should read Casanova's poetry simply because of the charm of his witty aphorisms; *rather*, my intention is …'
Or,
'*This is certainly not to say* that Professor Frankensplurger was justified in misrepresenting his colleague's findings, *merely that* …'
Or,
'Thus it should be clear that the reasons for the industrial action were the below-minimum wages and poor working conditions. However, *it is also essential to note* …'

What you're doing in each of these cases is signalling either the direction you want your reader to pursue, or the strength of one point as opposed to another. It helps because no matter how clearly you write, other people, with their often very different interests and life experience, will inevitably place emphases differently to you, or may be provoked in ways you do not intend, or see connections other than those you intended to convey while missing points you consider paramount. You'll be helping your reader if you can clarify as you go along. Also – and this last reason cannot be overemphasised (*NB: metacomment!*) – metacommentary also helps you as the writer, because it requires you to think more deeply and more broadly about your topic. It means aligning the purely intellectual with the reflective skills we've discussed previously as CT1 and CT2 in a process where you attempt to step outside your thinking, (an action impossible to perfect, but the attempt still benefits our thinking and writing!) in order to consider what might be going on in the mind of another, as is the next strategy.

Building on two – or multiple – opposing versions

In Chapters 7 and 8 we discussed ways of integrating other voices, including adversarial views so as to strengthen our own arguments. Chapter 8 also looked at this practice as a suspense-building strategy, so I won't go into much more detail here except to say that it is also an invaluable persuasive tool. By this I do not mean setting up a flimsy straw-man argument (as discussed in Chapter 3) only to blow it down and therefore 'prove' the superiority of your position. Rather, you set forth the opposition's point of view as fairly and as objectively as you are able, abstaining from any biased language. Deal with their claims thoroughly. Only after this is accomplished do you begin to outline the problems with that position. These might be to do with an insubstantial or faulty analysis, with unsound premises, flawed methodology, and so on. The strength of this approach is that you demonstrate your ability to conduct a considered analysis, to give a sympathetic reading, and to critique thoroughly; and not only this: you are using their argument to prepare the ground upon which to set up your own argument. Your reader will, like you, now be familiar with the territory and it will be that much easier for them to appreciate what you have to say on the subject.

The imaginary friend

This is a favourite of mine. Your 'friend' might be a person who exists but is not present at the time – a colleague or a lecturer – or it might be some anonymous 'gentle reader' who is interested in what you have to say. As you write, allow them to interrupt you from time to time with comments or queries. Your job is to anticipate those comments, questions, or objections. They – or you – are critiquing your text as you progress, an exercise which engages your reflective skills as well as your critical skills. To demonstrate, I've taken the first part of an article I wrote on education for *The Conversation* journal, and inserted the sort of remarks that can help develop your argument as you formulate it.

As you read over your draft, keep an eye out for where the reader might need clarification, or where an argument requires further elucidation or backup. Your 'friend' may ask for more detail, or might draw your attention to where greater depth is required or where a more emphatic statement needs to be made in order to keep the narrative rolling along.

The bracketed, italicised sentences denote possible responses to the text. Try and identify which of the comments in the following text suggest a need for:

- more detail or greater emphasis
- breadth of discussion, that is, your friend wants you to expand on this idea
- other view/s to strengthen yours, or to show that you know the counterarguments
- clarification
- further elucidation or better evidence
- solutions to be suggested – however provisional.

Excerpted from 'Report shows consequences of monetised education system ...' (Katz 2015)

Following the Independent Commission Against Corruption's (ICAC) report revealing dodgy practices by overseas student recruitment agents and the low literacy standards some international students get away with, the Productivity Commission has released a research paper into education services. *[I suppose*

(Continued)

you're going to detail which specific education services ICAC is concerned with and what the report recommends?] The paper considers, among other things, how universities meet international students' perceived needs and expectations, and the role of government in regulating quality. It rightly recommends that 'learning standards have a greater role' and that education agents should have a lesser one in student recruitment. *[Good – thanks. And so, the education agents aren't concerned with education then?]*

Profit before learning

[Right – the sub-heading clarifies things. So the agents are profit-oriented. The title 'education agent' is a misnomer then. Seems the paper really needs to think about what education is actually about, doesn't it?]

In considering international students' major contribution to Australia, the paper makes largely reasonable suggestions but is limited by the way the value of education is constructed. The first three subheadings focus on economic impact, competition, and the sector's 'high-growth trajectory'. *[So you're telling me that the paper doesn't focus on any concerns other than economic ones. A bit like 'education agents'. What about the students?]* It is unsurprising that many students exhibit a strong 'user pays' attitude to their education. A degree from a prestigious university may count well above the actual learning experience for many: the learning process comes second to the outcome – a degree, a job, a reputation. As the ICAC report said: 'The quality of Australia's international education services is […] at risk where students […] are primarily motivated by […] employment outcomes'. *[Well if they themselves mention only 'economic impact, competition, and the sector's "high-growth trajectory"' of course a 'user pays' attitude among students is hardly surprising. Is anyone interested in learning itself?]*

I have occasionally received complaints from students receiving low marks that this was 'not what [we] pay for'. *[So the answer is no then. If I were a teacher I'd start to really resent the students.]* Imagine you are a student panicking as a deadline looms because you know your linguistic or critical skills are weak. Your intensely desired aim is to further yourself professionally, so why not sacrifice your scruples and just buy an essay? *[Okay, so I'm not blaming just the students. But I'm getting depressed. Is there no light on the horizon at all – I mean, changes of policy that reflect something a bit more humanistic in education?]*

Educators have to prioritise learning over economic aspects, but policy makers devising research papers into international education services also need to emphasise aspects beyond perceived 'productivity' – like the cultural, social, and ethical values of education. *[I'm glad you mentioned that. But I'm worried about the long-term effects of the attitude of policy makers. Tell me the worst.]*

If the central role of such aspects is underplayed, then it is likely that academic honesty, and the value attached to learning to think independently

(Continued)

and critically, will continue to decline while the 'high-growth trajectory' arcs overhead. *[You paint a grim picture. What do you think is at the heart of the issue? I mean, is there something that we can address with a view to positive attitudinal change about the role of education?]*

The problems lie with the education sector's seduction by profit, and an uncritical respect for the concept of growth. *[So you see fostering criticality in students as part of a solution? Sounds pretty idealistic to me.]*

Most of the international students I have met are honest and ethical. Accidental plagiarism is not uncommon, but overt cheating is rare in my experience and usually due to desperation. *[Okay. Again, I was too quick to criticise the students. Poor things.]* Many of these students don't speak English very well. Nor can they read it or write it. They cannot understand very much of what is said in lectures. *[So their minds are keen, hearts are in the right place, but there are huge systemic problems. A bit more detail please.]*

Yet they have been accepted to study in master's programmes in an English-speaking university, having received the requisite score in their International English Language Testing System (IELTS) assessment – or have they? Recently I mentioned to one of my students that his work did not reflect his IELTS marks. He told me pityingly, 'Oh, Dr Katz, you can buy anything in Beijing.' Other students may have been given unrealistic expectations by unscrupulous agents – as noted by the Productivity Commission – and there are other methods for frauding the admissions system. *[I wish I hadn't asked. Any light on the horizon at all?]*

Assuring quality learning

[So, the answer is yes? Good.] To make sure quality learning is taking place inside universities, money needs to be spent on increasing the ratio of staff to students, and on hiring permanent staff who have a vested interest in their students and institution. *[So we need policies that focus on student support – as ICAC mentioned – and which you're about to expand on. Okay, I'm reading …]*

'Summary and response'

Graff and Birkenstein champion the approach of 'summary and response'. They refer to Martin Luther King Jr's famous 'Letter from Birmingham Jail' which consists of repeated summaries followed by demolitions of his adversaries' arguments, one succeeding the other in eloquent waves. This rhetorically powerful approach is often used in speeches, but can also be adapted for texts that are written to be read rather than spoken. Of course, this is impossible to do well if you are not adept at summarising – which as you know, is a *much* briefer review than a paraphrase – so a practice run with guidelines based on Graff and Birkenstein's model, (p. 15) will help.

Exercise 9.1 Summarise this chapter so far, following up with your own comments.

Chapter 9 begins by situating its main discussion of......................................
....
....within the context of...
....
The author also recognises the need to include a caveat, which....................
....
....
.... before continuing to explain............................
....
'Ways of constructing a persuasive text by conversational means' are then outlined, including, in brief,...
....
....
While it is indeed beneficial to...I would like to mention that..
....
....
....
....

(OR)

These are useful strategies – up to a point – but I would like to add..................
....
....
....
It is also worth mentioning that..
....
....Overall,...
....
....
....

Exercise 9.2 Now, try the 'summary and response' style, modifying the text as necessary and inserting an author and ideas from your own discipline with whom you disagree.

In her article ...., the author proposes that................................
....
....
....
.... I would like to examine her claims
for .... in more detail. Her first
support for the notion of ....
....
relies heavily on ...., and also ....,
which based on..
....
....
....is clearly exaggerated/
/biased/incomplete/unfounded. As well as this..
....
....
....
....

Further, [Author's name] then provides evidence to justify her position of ....
....
....
.... However,.......
....
....
....
....

Upon completing her analysis of ....
....
....
....[Author] resolves
that..
While there is certainly justification for this opinion, given that ....
....
....
the conclusion does not follow logical from her original premises in that...............
....
....
....[and so forth]

The unfolding narrative approach

To write an academic 'story', you first have to recognise that your audience is more likely to start reading what you have to say if they can see its relevance to their own work and interests. This can be dealt with by introducing your ideas by a statement that shows the reader where your work is located in the conversation, as discussed in Chapter 8. You can keep this reader with you by using strategies such as those I've outlined already. However, novelistic devices will also help keep them engrossed. Like an author of fiction, an academic writer can work a narrative that emphasises not just what happened, but why, and also the connections between events. Helen Sword (2009, p. 328) claims that a piece of academic prose that lacks suspense or a sense of progression will be a good deal less compelling that one that does have some kind of narrative arc.

> [Academic prose may be] plotted, even at the most subtle level, like a good thriller (What will happen next?), or a mystery novel (What clues will the intrepid researcher/detective unearth?), or a Bildungsroman (What lessons will the protagonist learn along the way, and from whom?), or yes, even a fairytale or epic poem (Will good triumph over evil? Will the bad witch of administrative incompetence poison the idealistic young teacher's apple? Will we all live happily ever after, or do new challenges lurk on the horizon?).

Narratives may be factual or fictional and sometimes distinctions between the two can become blurred (a situation which has pluses as well as minuses, as we'll see in the following chapter) so it's important, when working in narrative mode, that you take pains to work out your purpose right from the start. Ask yourself questions along these lines:

- Do I need to provide context via a recount of the process that led me, or other thinkers or writers, to the discussion I'm about to begin?
- What is my interest in bringing my ideas to the attention of the reader? Do I want to make some kind of change in people's thinking?

Questions of sequencing require careful consideration when composing a text, as we've already seen in the previous discussion of outlining. Sequencing choices can have a powerful affect on the response your reader will have to what you say. Some guides will advise you to begin by situating your argument within the field with reference to previous scholarship, or setting yourself up against another argument; others will say that it is best to begin with a 'bang' – a strong, even contentious statement – then follow with the proofs one by one. But in what order? Order of importance? Importance to whom and important for what reasons? Perhaps chronological order is preferable? Many guides will recommend this when taking a narrative approach – but I wouldn't go so far as to say it's an absolute rule. After, all stories can involve flashbacks and other departures from the linear. The way you 'plot' your 'story' is another way of looking at outlining. Remember, you need to find the form that best enables your argument or discussion to flow as well as you are capable of making it.

Exercise 9.3 Experiment with an outline you've already begun.

Juggle the sequence of events by choosing a different order of events to highlight different aspects of your argument. (I like to print out a draft at this stage, and physically cut it up with scissors and shuffle the pieces around.) You'll see that changing the order changes the overall meaning and impact.

In academic essays the purpose is to persuade your reader to your point of view. If you decide to work with narrative, it means that you want to engage your reader in a sequence of events arranged in such a way that they will be moved emotionally. You'll be wanting to provoke, or entice, or delight, for example.

Exercise 9.4 Freewriting

Choose one of the following topics: love, anxiety, university, the job market, art, radio communications. Or, if you'd rather choose any other broad area, something in which you are personally interested, then do so. Freewrite on the topic for three or four minutes. NB: don't stop to think. Just write.

Now consider some of the basic components of a story. What are these?

Plot, of course: draft out the main 'events' of your 'story'. For example, if you chose 'radio communications' you might begin by briefly recounting the history of radio from early days to the contemporary situation where radio has substantially changed with the advent of electronic modes of communication.

Characterisation may be used in a scholarly context. Sword (2012) tells us that means seeing yourself, the author, as a character, plus all the other people who influence your thoughts in the construction of your plot: sceptics who might interfere with your ideas or perhaps stimulate you to further research, like-minded authorities whom you reference and whose ideas you are building upon, those whose theories have been superseded, abstract concepts that might be seen as characters contributing to the formation of your thesis. Your 'characters' in this essay or article come to life through their words and actions, exactly as those in a novel.

In your essay on communications technology, characters may include both people and objects or ideas. They could include Guglielmo Marconi, radio producers and other contributors, politicians and economists who support or undermine the form, a range of digital technologies. There might be quite a few of these non-human characters. In order to enrich your understanding of them and the roles they play in the discussion, try to personify them in your own mind as if they were actual people with their own idiosyncrasies and preferences, motivations and desires. Where does that tangent want to lead us? Why is this idea so provocative? Perhaps it feels awkward because it senses it's out of place? Or is it something to do with its past, perhaps, or the fact that it's sometimes been overlooked? (It might have an inferiority complex, or it might be a bossy narcissist!)

Exercise 9.5 Personification

Choose an idea you're currently working with and experiment with personification as suggested. For example, what is the relationship like between this person called Electronic Storage System and his colleague, Cloud Computing? Or alternatively, in an ethnographic 'story', how does this person, Poetry, feel about being used in an article on workplace culture? (Of course, this will depend on whether this character is Concrete, Romantic, Political, or another form of poetry.)

Conflict will naturally occur, as in any good story. It will be based on the needs and priorities and characters of the players.

Themes may be overtly stated or perhaps the story is imbued with a particular sensibility that implicitly conveys your concerns.

Details of setting – which are rarely seen to have much to do with a research plot – may occasionally be included, perhaps in the form of a few carefully selected words about the place or places in which your research took place, or if you noted a relationship between an idea that occurred to you and the place in which this happened (Sword 2012, pp. 91–94). There is certainly no rule against references to sense impressions. Even if you are writing to a particularly conservative readership, you might still include a mention perhaps of a particularly strong colour in a description of an event, say, or a sound, whether intrusive or part of the ambience, in which your 'research story' is set. Judicious use of such evocations can enliven your words and help you to maintain your reader's attention. In Chapter 5 I mentioned research conducted by educational theorists and ethnographers where the inclusion of feelings – both emotional and sensory – in annotations made while thinking or reading can contribute to your understanding of the subject matter you're working with. This too might feature as a setting for your story.

Exercise 9.6a Using fictive devices and senses

Once you've worked out plot, characters, conflict, and themes, return to the original freewriting exercise and redraft it. This time you'll be thinking about the various aspects in these narrative terms, rather than simply as an 'essay' or 'article'.

Exercise 9.6b

If you want to bring more life to what you write, for the sake of this exercise, play with sense impressions too. Put the freewriting original aside and select a draft you've been working on. Mentally return to the place you first started to think about this project. Describe it briefly. Or perhaps you prefer to describe the place where you did most of the research – the site is up to you – but do include such impressions as, for example, the sound of construction going on next door, or the infuriating buzzing of a wasp. The lights just coming on outside. The smoothness of the keys on your laptop. The slightly anxious or embarrassed feeling in your gut as you perform this eccentric exercise – it's up to you. Some find that this is best done as a freewriting exercise. You may well find that (after editing) part of it could be used to invigorate the original text.

Narrative point of view is often thought of as simply your choice of first, second, or third person. But that's just the beginning of the story. Regardless of whether you choose to use 'I', 'we', and 'you', or the utterly disembodied third person, your point of view is the idea or the school of thought that you are representing, and as such requires very careful consideration. Be aware of who are speaking for – that is, whose point of view emerges from your narrative. And, as I've mentioned before, it is absolutely essential to make sure you don't override the oppositional voices. This is commonly referred to as bias. The last thing you want is for your personal prejudices to take over. Some authors think that by avoiding first-person narration they are being more objective and truthful, imparting information rather than opinion. This is a misnomer. It is quite possible to mislead or manipulate a reader's appreciation of facts or events when using the third person. Here is an example:

> There is a great body of research available that presents the case for enhanced coercive interrogation techniques, whose efficacy in extracting true information from unwilling sources cannot be denied.

Note that although written in the 'objective' third person, the reader is 'guided' towards agreement with the author's position through reference to a great body of knowledge (uncited), the use of euphemisms for torture and for people, and an authoritarian persona employing the cliché 'it cannot be denied'. Let's try rewriting it in the first person without the euphemisms or the cliché. As no sources are cited, we have to begin with 'I think'. So:

> *I think torture is an efficacious method of extracting the truth from people unwilling to impart information which the torturer assumes they possess.*

When written in this way – unveiled, if you will, point of view exposed – the author would probably be less likely to have many people agreeing with them, and they would also be leaving themselves much more open to attack by those who find torture an unattractive option. In this instance, the conversational, subjective approach elicits a more truthful statement than the remote third person.

Regarding the issue of truth: 'Truth in fiction', an article written by sociologist and novelist Hugh Mackay (2009), puts forward the idea that 'truths' presented in well-considered but subjective ways can be more profound and thought-provoking than accurately presented facts or figures. It is an issue he considers while juggling his two hats of social scientist and novelist. He mentions that 'all social research is based on indirect experience: borrowed data, other people's accounts of what they are thinking and feeling'. The problem is that the data received depends on the questions asked, and the questions have been set by the sociologist and will be limited by that individual's understanding and professional interests. The interviewee may also feel constrained by self-imposed questions, such as, What does this researcher want to hear? (How can I help?) Or: How much am I prepared to give away to this stranger in this strangely confessional environment?

Perhaps a fuller answer might be derived from a requesting a fuller narrative from the subjects. However, the problem of time constraints now enters the equation, as do issues around efficient collection and measurability of data. Fortunately, however, when writing in the humanities, compromise between truth and accuracy is actually possible with the inclusion in essays and reports of speculation and anecdote, thus balancing quantitative assessments of situations or information with qualitative interpretation. Not only this, information may also be presented in such a way that respect is given to both objective and subjective analyses.

Argument as story

This involves an unfolding of an identifiable sequence of events, linked logically, giving the reader a sense of direction as she reads, and which ultimately resolves itself with a sense of completion at the end.

An author who has used the narrative approach brilliantly is the late, great neurologist Oliver Sacks. Several of his case study reports are narrated as stories that have attracted a massive readership. One of the best known of these is his 1998 book, *The Man Who Mistook His Wife For a Hat and Other Clinical Tales*, in which he tells the story of Professor P, a musicologist, who presented with a very peculiar neurological condition. As in all case studies, Sacks focuses on the two questions that need to be answered: What is going on? and How and why does a man come to mistake his wife for a hat? Sacks discusses the symptoms observed during the development of his acquaintance with the patient, which is how he collected his 'data' on 'Professor P', and by gradual degrees, the story emerges and the reader gradually comes to an understanding of 'how' and 'why' the patient came to be as he is. The final passages involve analysis of data and the presentation of medical explanations to support the experiential evidence, with more than one theory presented. Careful records and a logical chain of evidence are maintained throughout; thus the academic requirements are covered in detail, but in a way that is highly readable. It is at once a sympathetic narrative about a person dealing with a condition that is at times quite frightening, and it is also a case study in neurology that examines the extremely complex phenomenon of an individual's interactions and relationships.

The *Harvard Business Review* often includes reports that use narrative too, featuring case studies written as impressionistic tales with storylines, characters, and dialogue that teachers in management or organisational communications use as teaching tools to stimulate discussion, debate, and deeper understanding of various concepts. Textbooks of collected teaching case studies are popular in university courses in organisational communication and public relations and other disciplines. They are based on scholarly research but are structured as impressionistic or confessional tales.

Exercise 9.7

Sacks' story of Professor P is available online. Access it via Google Books and then identify and describe the following:

- setting
- dialogue
- characterisation
- scene building
- description
- devices used to create suspense and interest in the personalities.

Note also the decisions Sacks has made regarding:

- the order in which the events unfold
- how this fictive approach is used to simultaneously provide information and develop the storyline without sacrificing scholarly precision or rigour.
- how the character of the author himself emerges in the telling.

Further style tips

Avoid the following:

1. **Phrasal verbs** – these can constipate academic prose. This is easy enough to amend in many cases. You might just do this in your head.

Exercise 9.8 Replace the phrasal verbs with one simple verb.

- It is necessary *to go into* more detail to clarify this point.
- The author decided *to put together* all the aspects of the argument in one sentence.
- Why not *get rid of* all the surplus verbiage?

---

2. **Abuse of subordinate clauses** is another common mistake in academic writing. Don't get me wrong – you can have long sentences, but make sure that in the process of writing them you don't start performing strange linguistic contortions. You'll know when that happens if you give your text to a colleague to read and they tell you they struggled to keep track of the original point.

Exercise 9.9

The point you want to convey is this: Playfulness with words is an important reason for the endurance of Shakespeare's work. Now, rewrite the following rather rambling sentence in such a way that your point is clear and is uninterrupted by superfluous circumlocutious waffle. Remember,

- There is no need to put all the information in one sentence.
- It is usually a good idea to put the main point early on.

William Shakespeare, although arguably not one man but a multiplicity of voices or perhaps just one other single other author – the main candidates probably being Christopher Marlowe and Francis Bacon – holds the reputation, deserved or otherwise, of being the greatest writer the English language has ever known – that is, the most innovative in terms of language as well as amongst the most profound, philosophically – and his success is due in large part to his uninhibited experimentalism with regard to the use of solecisms and neologisms and other experimentations with language in general and plays on individual words in particular.

Your version:

---

3. **Inflated language** often sounds rather pompous. For example, 'By means of' is just a way of spinning out 'by'. 'Due to the fact that' simply means 'because'.

Exercise 9.10

In the passage below, look for inflated language, euphemisms, repetitions, unnecessary phrasal verbs, and stylistic or grammatical redundancies. Also look out for terms that might be dubbed 'zombilingo' (Katz 2016). By this I mean words or phrases that lack specificity but are used commonly and uncritically – dead husks of words or loose formulations that are found to mean very little when questioned. *Question every catchphrase.* Then rewrite lucidly.

Having identified that the University of Diddleby needs to take a stronger position vis-à-vis the preparation of students for the challenges of achieving their individual dreams in the global marketplace, the Vice Chancellor's office aims to implement a number of strategic changes. In order to facilitate the achievement of its goal of global excellence, Diddleby will expedite strategic actions with regard to the maintenance of transparency and accountability amongst the faculties and schools in order to assure quality. The marketing department was enjoined to find creative solutions to the challenges currently facing the University in upscaling its drive towards global excellence. The departments identified as lagging in passion for innovation and commitment to excellence were Philosophy, History, English and most of the languages. A Change Plan has been recommended as well as a follow-up campaign to be run under the banners, 'Inspire!', 'Communicate!', 'Create!' to further emphasise the aims and objectives of the University.
    Your version:

---

4. **Gender-specific language** should be avoided as it is a sure-fire way to alienate readers. The question of whether to use 'he', 'she', or 'he/she' or 's/he' now arises. Both of those slash formulations are awkward-looking things; thus my advice would be either to use 'they', or vary 'he' and 'she' throughout your paper, or announce at the beginning why it is you chose one rather than the other. You would need a very good reason.
5. **Clichés**: Having already mentioned the cliché problem in Chapter 8, no further discussion is necessary. However, I think a further exercise on eliminating

clichés is a good place to end this chapter on how to refine your writing and your argumentative strategies, as tired-out tags and idioms will exhaust your prose and also your reader. Several of these were included in the passage above. I've often come across expressions such as the following in academic papers and in student essays, but there really isn't much point in using them if you want to keep your reader with you:

'in a nutshell'
'two-edged sword'
'throughout history'
'to the bitter end'
'the writing was on the wall'
'inextricably linked'. So often items are linked 'inextricably'. Perhaps, one day, they might instead be 'intricately connected'? In some cases they might actually be 'intimately related' – or simply 'inseparable' or 'indivisible'. For further advice about using clear language, I recommend George Orwell's *Politics and the English Language*. It's an oldie but a (very) goodie.

In the meantime, here's a good cliché test: When you reread your work you may notice a turn of phrase that sounds overly familiar. You may have just found a cliché. So nuke it and rephrase.

Exercise 9.11

As I have done with 'inextricably linked', replace the five clichés above with refreshed forms. Use whole sentences as your choice will depend upon context.

Conclusion

I would like to reiterate that academic writing involves an interplay of voices, which is why this chapter has developed the concept of 'joining the conversation' with plenty of detail on incorporating narrative strategies that encourage a dialogic approach to writing. This chapter also revised the strategy of setting forth an argument as a kind of debate, and saw the addition of another metacritical tool to our cache, that of metacommentary, which helps to develop the relationship between writer and reader. Your reader is no longer an abstract 'other' but an engaged, interested colleague. Writing as if involved in an interchange with an 'imaginary friend' who supplies a patter of critique that increases your awareness of weaknesses in argument, or alerts you to where further explication is needed, also assists in this communicative process, as does 'summary and response'. All of these devices support the 'unfolding narrative approach' and how to write an academic 'story' by adapting practices from fictive writing.

10

Some More Experimental, Playful Forms of Academic Writing

Chapter overview

Chapter 10 plays with some of the more uncomfortable states of mind, including doubt and uncertainty, that arise when writing. It places less traditional forms of academic prose into historical context, highlighting their value and purpose. It provides a range of intellectual and writerly exercises for developing skills and attitudes that were foreshadowed in earlier chapters, including:

- How the alliance of subjectivity and objectivity increases readability and persuasiveness of academic texts
- The necessity of working with doubt in writing and research, and how to *relish* uncertainty
- Experimental and playful exercises in academic writing.

A postgraduate writer needs to communicate as directly as possible with the reader (that is, writing in a 'readerly' way) while maintaining rigour, open-minded inquisitiveness, and a willingness to embrace encounters with paradox and complexity with enthusiasm (rather than anxiety!). Writing well, like thinking well, is a balancing act and it isn't easy, which is one of the reasons we need to recharge our batteries with that fallow time I mentioned in Chapter 6. It is also why we need to leaven research and writing with exploratory practices that are stimulating and playful as well as edifying. Such practices are often open-ended, the outcomes uncertain. This idea will colour the whole of this chapter: uncertainty, which many scholars consider a hallmark of modernity.

The ground was laid for this discussion in Chapter 4 when I recommended 'rhizomatic' approaches to research such as mindmapping and freewriting, strategies that embrace intellectual exploration and which also encourage experimental forms of academic writing. In the spirit of this age, with its massively increased information flows, the accelerated pace of technological change, and the instability of cultural traditions, doubt has become our medium, uncertainty the air we breathe. Knowledge we may once have believed was carved in stone is found instead to be written on water. This can create such levels of anxiety that it becomes difficult to see any upside of ambivalence or of risk-taking in research and writing. Nevertheless, we have to learn to think and write in ways demanded of us by the age, which according to Eric Eisenberg involve making peace with uncertainty and doing without any totalising notions of truth. And well before Eisenberg, Nietzsche asked rhetorically: 'Have not all hand-rails and foot-bridges fallen into the water?' (cited in Marden 2015); while Hannah Arendt claimed that modern thinkers, lacking any authoritative agency to support us, must learn to think 'without a banister', meaning of course that we now have to do without the supports and props we may have had in the past. For Arendt, independent thought is a 'mode of moving in the world of freedom' (cited in Bernstein 1996, p. 41). That may sound very high-minded, but it is also realistic. Independent thought and intellectual freedom is what 'critical being' requires, first and foremost.

Doubt, uncertainty, and risk

1. Doubt
In a very real sense, doubt lies at the centre of both creative and critical practice. It forms the basis, a sort of launching pad, from which we set out on any intellectual investigation. There is nothing new in this idea. Doubt gave rise to the ancient Greek philosophy of the Sceptics, whose questioning attitude marked the beginning of the open-minded criticality many of us continue to work towards in universities today. It was doubt that inspired Socrates to develop his gentle yet revolutionary mode of questioning upon which contemporary critical thinking practices are based. As Nicholas Burbules (2000) sees it, 'doubt [is] an opportunity to learn', for it enables us to gain 'an awareness of at least some alternative ways of proceeding ... a mixture of understanding and misunderstanding, of constructive and inhibitive ideas. These constitute potential points that can be linked to something new.'

2. Uncertainty
In many ways, starting an intellectual investigation from the position of certainty (knowing what the results will be at the outset) defeats the purpose of scholarly enquiry. Theresa Anderson (2011) notes many beneficial aspects of uncertainty in her field (investigating research practices), finding that 'dealing with inconsistencies, favouring chance [and] random stimulation' support creativity in the same way that allowing apparently peripheral and 'seemingly discontinuous' information into the process stimulate divergent thinking, giving rise to the possibility of discovery. This is not to derogate careful organisation and methodical process. These are of course essential at particular stages of research and writing, but chance and accident are also elemental aspects, aspects which need not be concealed from the audience. Hesitation on the part of an author – or speaker, for that matter – often signals to the reader thoughtfulness rather than a lack of knowledge, and trying to give an impression of absolute certainty can make you appear defensive or arrogant. Attempts to eliminate equivocality in scholarly writing can be a move away from intellectual enquiry and towards totalitarian thinking. We need ambiguities; we must accept contradictions and work with them, because being at home with paradox can be a means towards forming order from the disorder of experience.

3. Risk

Risk has to be involved. We take an intellectual risk every time we go out on a limb to pursue an unfamiliar theory in research or when trying out an experimental idea in an essay; we take material and economic risks when engaged in projects whose outcomes are uncertain, but if we do not, we inhibit that possibility of discovery. And discovery is, in a sense, what this chapter is about, particularly as concerns writing practice.

Factoring 1, 2, and 3 into academic communication

If I am unable to eloquently articulate what I have discovered in my research, then the idea will do little good for anyone else. Helen Sword (2009, p. 322) conducted extensive research into stylistic attributes of academic writing, and identified those which are considered to be present in the most effective examples of scholarly prose. Desirable characteristics established included (among others) those listed below. I've added in comments where a level of imaginative playfulness or uncertainty or risk comes in – ideas that have all been touched on to a greater or lesser extent in this book. You'll recognise some of these practices and attitudes as you have probably already integrated at least some of them into your writing, either consciously or intuitively.

1. Clear expression of complex ideas (Complexity evolves through critical questioning and open-minded scepticism.)
2. Minimal reliance on jargon (You need to find fresh modes of expression or your prose can become something quite deadly.)
3. Imagination (This goes hand in hand with intellectual play, as discussed in Chapter 4 and throughout this book.)
4. Storytelling strengths (Maintaining a strong narrative requires imagination, from predicting what questions a reader might need answered to freshness of expression.)
5. Concrete language (Avoiding unnecessary abstraction or being seduced by that hoary old notion of try to 'sound' rather than actually 'being' academic increases your ability to communicate honestly with your reader, rather than merely 'performing' communication. Using concrete language can also mean taking risks with how your ideas might be received when, for example, you decide not to hide behind wordiness, or a third-person voice, or to overuse the 'hedging' device – as discussed in Chapter 7.)
6. Individual voice (This means risking sounding like yourself! There is nowhere to hide once you've decided to do this. It can be frightening to expose yourself this way, but certainly worth it in the long run, as discussed in Chapters 7 and 8.)
7. Interdisciplinary references (Sometimes the links are not obvious. You need to make connections that others may not easily recognise: imagination at play again.)
8. Anecdotes (Playfulness.)
9. Humour (As above.)

All of these will help you to provide your reader with aesthetic as well as intellectual pleasure – another of Sword's criteria for effective scholarly prose. Only a few academics in her survey of six of the highest-ranking academic journals in Sword's field (higher education) actually measured up in the above categories! In the interests of amending this sorry situation, this book has suggested exercises which, to a greater or lesser degree, work on improving clarity and concreteness, on eliminating unnecessary jargon, on developing individual voice. In due course I'll suggest a couple more exercises that mobilise the storytelling skills we practised in Chapter 9 and which encourage imaginative play, but first of all I'm going to suggest you try an exercise that combines interdisciplinarity, imagination, and individual voice. It requires you to try not one but several different versions of an extract. Choose a paragraph or two by an author from your discipline whose work you would consider stylistically 'neutral', that is, neither particularly powerful nor weak – it neither stimulates nor bores you. Then,

1. Rewrite in the style of someone you consider exemplary in your field. (We've done this before.)
2. Rewrite in the style of someone else in your field you really *don't* like, or even despise. (You may find that this version will end up being parodic and if so, that's fine.)
3. A disciplinary departure: Try and rewrite the passage from a different point of view. Imagine you are, for example, a botanist or musician – choose a discipline with which you're familiar, but not practised. You will almost certainly find that when you attempt this disciplinary shift, the emphases will shift also, because what is important to a linguist is unlikely to be the same as that which matters most to a composer or a scientist. Thus, this experiment may alter or broaden your perspective while also giving you a chance to lubricate your writing muscles.
4. Rewrite as if your readers are from a field other than your own. What would they find useful? Compelling? You may have doubts that they'll be interested, but it is your job here to write in such a way that they are more likely to be. This means finding cross-disciplinary links to engage them. It might also help to firstly revise advice in Chapters 7 and 8.
5. Write as if you are an Op-Ed columnist – that is, it is your job to communicate complex and/or specialist issues or ideas to a lay audience with clarity and brevity. Choose a favourite opinion writer to use as a model.

Exercise 10.1a Your exemplar

Exercise 10.1b A style you dislike

(Continued)

Exercise 10.1c Write as if from a field other than your own

Exercise 10.1d As if to readers unfamiliar with your field, but whom you really want to enthuse

Exercise 10.1e You as Op-Ed journalist

Divergent thinking and academic writing

At this point, I want to look at certain forms of scholarship outside the mainstream that increase the possibility of writerly authority and authenticity as well as readability, and at the potential for discovery that can emerge for writers who allow themselves to go off the beaten track. Darwin, for instance, had embarked on a study of the animal kingdom, but allowed himself to be diverted by philosophical speculations on the universal struggle for life ... and we know where that led. It's hard for us to allow for such diversions in contemporary universities; in fact today it is often actively discouraged, as I mentioned in Chapter 5. However, it is through experimentation and attention paid to tantalising digressions that we humans are able develop over time. Deviations from the norm enable us to climb out of a rut – whether that rut is an intellectual one or a dead-end job or anything else – and take a really good look at the view. See what's out there.

Playing with forms and ideas

Four practical group activities follow. They are designed to improve the possibility for new views. A caveat: Informative and stimulating though the first two exercises might be, they are limited by the participants' knowledge and understanding, therefore the players need to come prepared. For coursework students, readings need to be recommended and conducted before seminars. This is a teaching style sometimes referred to as the 'flipped classroom', which simply means that the information acquisition comes first in readings conducted at home which inform the discussions and activities that occur in the seminar. For independent researchers reading this book the same applies: recommended readings are essential to inform the discussions and games and need to be provided by the one organising the game so that participants can prepare.

Exercise 10.2 'Pointing'

Some practices that are usually thought to be limited to the domain of what is (sometimes mistakenly) called 'creative' writing – that is, the writing of fiction – are also excellent tools for qualitative scholarly work in areas concerned with communication and interpretation. The first of these Jennifer Schultz (2006) simply calls 'pointing'.

- Choose a text to work with.
- Allocate to one group member the role of reading aloud to the others, who are provided with a written copy of the text.
- As the reader reads, the others are to listen carefully and highlight any words or phrases that resonate with them. Listeners are advised *not* to stop to reflect on why the terms are particularly affective or effective at this stage, whether the reaction to them is positive or negative.
- At the end of the reading, listeners are to read back the phrases they've selected, again without explanation or interpretation. As Schultz mentions, this is difficult for participants who are accustomed to questioning, critiquing, and interpreting texts.

(Continued)

> As you will probably have gathered, when all the listeners have read out their phrases and words, the result is a highly fragmented version of the original. Different emphases from those intended by the author are likely to emerge when taken out of context in this way in a process that Schultz calls, 'pre-conceptual hearing'.
>
> When this exercise is conducted with fiction writers, this is the point at which each takes one of the words that had been 'pointed to' and begins a narrative of their own based on that word. When used as a means of reviewing essays or other non-fiction works, juggling words and ideas can lead to new formulations and interpretations that would otherwise remain hidden by the original author's governing intent. In other words, it can open possibilities for a refreshed perspective or research direction.

This departure from traditional textual analysis can be used across many disciplines. Schultz's field includes nursing and interdisciplinary studies, and she has found that 'pointing' helps students who have become 'stuck' in their subject matter when they have invested a great deal of intellectual energy in it. In my teaching of critical thinking for postgraduates I've found that it acts as a sort of pressure-release, particularly when students are researching areas with which they have not yet become entirely familiar, and which they find daunting. But it can be taken further, and used in research projects.

> ### Exercise 10.3 'Hubbub'
>
> 'Hubbub' certainly lacks gravitas. In fact, it relies on the players being light-hearted about it all. You can't be too precious when you're constantly being interrupted, which is what occurs in this game. I've played it with students of both fictive and scholarly writing. With the latter, once again the aim is to generate ideas about a topic in the early stages of development.
>
> * You need at least six others, all involved in the same area of study. Someone stands and begins with a premise or a potential thesis statement. Notes are not used. The player simply begins to discuss their topic, and then must integrate interjections as they come from the group.
> * The interruptions consist of a single word or simple phrase. This word or phrase is not a prediction of what the speaker is about to say. Its purpose is to provide intellectual sustenance to help progress a discussion. After an interjection, the speaker may take a sentence or two more before integrating into their discourse the word or phrase offered by the one who interjected. You can change the form of the word of course – noun to verb or adjective to adverb, for example.
> * A mediator is useful. They can take on the role of giving the nod to the other participants in turn, and when they do, that person must immediately offer a word that is related, however loosely, to the subject being discussed. In the following example, 'X' refers to the player at the centre and 'I' to the various 'Interjectors'.

Example of a 'hubbub' game

X: 'According to the research I've been conducting, the examination system is letting students down. Problems occur ...'

I: 'Quality.'

X: '...when learning is measured by quantitative standards alone. These are insufficient to gauge the student's knowledge. *Qualitative* approaches to assessing a student's understanding of a subject area may produce ...'

I: 'Imprecision.'

X: '... a more accurate impression of a student's ability. Now this might sound paradoxical, but *imprecision* is the name of the game when dealing with humans ...'

I: 'Accountants.'

X: '... as opposed to *accountants* – sorry – joke. But a joke used advisedly. Accuracy is the aim of a good accountant, but it is ...'

I: 'Truth.'

X: '... *Not* the same as *truth*. Thank you. The truth of, say, the reasons for domestic violence within a particular community might be found more readily in stories narrated than in ...'

I: ' Questions ...'

X: '... in a list of *questions* requiring "true" or "false" responses, prepared by a social scientist. Similarly, when trying to assess a social science student's understanding of ...'

I: 'Multiple choice.'

X '... why some men resort to violence will not be well served by *multiple choice* exams. Many advocate for these as producing a fair overall understanding of an area of study. However, ...'

I: 'Tricks.'

X: '... Really? *Tricks?* Ok, ok ... Multiple choice results may be misleading as there are *tricks* – ha! *tricks* you can learn in order to do well in multiple choice. Two of the four options are usually silly, so you can dismiss them straight off, and then you have a 50/50 chance of getting it right even if you know very little of the subject. Therefore essays or short paragraphs ...'

I: 'Teachers' workloads.'

X: '... Although time-consuming, of course ...' *And so forth ...*

Question: Identify the points that emerged in the game that could become major and minor discussion points in an essay on the examination system.

Exercise 10.4

This is the first of two activities on acquiring different perspectives even if they disagree with your position.

You'll be aware that within disciplines there are different perspectives on any given topic. Storytelling devices can be used to help come to grips with these. These can be done in a group, or in solitude.

(Continued)

1. You might invent a dialogue between yourself and an author whose work you admire. Or choose a thinker with whom you're at odds, even someone whose work you actively dislike. For example, if you were a political scientist, you might choose a politician whose ideas you find dismaying. Perhaps you have wondered about the logic of some of Donald Trump's contentions? If so, invite him to explain in a structured dialogue. Or perhaps, as a reader of philosophy or a student of psychology, you've struggled with Slavoj Žižek's claim that 'we do not really want what we think we desire'.

When done as a group exercise sometimes this kind of investigation is structured as a debate, and debates can be a brilliant way to activate or enhance critical ability. But we can also fall into the trap of just trying to convince by means of rhetoric, so for now it will be more worthwhile, I think, to choose a form that enables you to engage simply as a scholar rather than as a competitive public speaker.

2. Invent a short story about a single issue. Say you are doing a study of Easter. Decide on three to five characters who will appear in this story and what each one's function is. Please remember that you're not trying to do a marvelous work of fiction for publication, so your characters can be fairly simple ciphers for ideas. Select characters whose views are likely to vary. For instance:

- A historian who is concerned with the changes that have occurred over time regarding the reasons for and manner of celebrating Easter in specific countries.
- A parent whose Easter is necessarily child-focused. How do they approach it?
- Perhaps there's another parent who feels quite differently about it?
- A child who just wants the best chocolate deal she can get.
- A feminist scholar, maybe a linguist or an anthropologist, who wants to place emphasis on the fertility goddess Eostre that perhaps the historian finds of less import than she does.

You could keep it simple and have them discussing Easter at a party. Or you could have a couple of them engaged in conversation, then meeting up later with other characters. You might like to have them performing their ideas in actions they undertake during the narrative – although this is quite an ambitious route to take. But however you choose to structure it, you'll now have views from historical, sociological, political, linguistic, and/or anthropological perspectives. You may well find that some of these lend themselves to further, more structured research.

TIP

If you've been working alone on these two exercises, maybe you could now write a brief reflection on the experience and the results in your reflection journal.

Exercise 10.5 Critical role-playing: from devils to detectives

(Based on exercises edited from Brookfield's 'structured critical conversation' workshops.)

For this group activity one participant describes the setting and problem they're working on in a case study. It can be framed as a story as this makes it more readily accessible. For the purposes of this 'structured critical conversation' the more complex and multilayered the situation under examination, the better. The others take on specific roles. Brookfield suggests (among others) the following:

- Devil's advocate. This is my favourite. You get to take the opposite point of view regardless of what is being proposed.
- Speculator. This is also fun, but if the person who takes it on is not used to thinking this way it can be alarming, because their job is to try and come up with other possible directions the enquiry might take – for example, 'What might happen if …' or, 'What would (major theorist) say …' Depending on the topic, you may need more than one speculator.
- Evidential assessor. As the title indicates, this person looks for any unfounded claims or unsupported generalisations to keep the speaker honest!
- Detective/s. You probably need a few of these because they look out for implicit assumptions made by the speaker, and also by those whom she is investigating in her case study.

Fictocriticism and play

As we've discussed, there are limitations within traditional academic writing. Sometimes it fails to exhibit much in the way of verve or dynamism, or to deal creatively with uncertainty, or with the subjectivities of the writer. A particular academic form that has emerged as a response to such shortfalls is often referred to as fictocriticism. As its name indicates, it melds storytelling and scholarship, navigating that space between the polar extremes of invention and speculation on the one hand, and deduction and explication on the other. Throughout the 20th century other forms also emerged, from creative non-fiction to paracriticism, critifiction, and crypto-fiction. However, this is not the place to explore them all!

It is true that fiction has been used in academic writing for illustrative purposes (particularly in anthropology, organisational studies, and in the teaching of different literacies) and that storytelling devices are also employed in constructing arguments – but if too tightly harnessed to a purpose its spirit can be inhibited. Fictocritical writers strive not to lose 'the passion and romance of thought'. You know, the stuff that probably motivated you to write in the first place? When talking about his discipline of sociology, for instance, Carl Rhodes (2015, p. 290) insists: 'Without gaiety, this haunting science has no exuberance and it cannot jump or dance, condemned instead to a dismal existence of stern faced earnestness.'

Fictocriticism experiments with form in a way that celebrates hybridity and actively aims to destabilise convention. It has a venerable provenance, dating back to the 16th-century essayist Michel de Montaigne. It's worth considering why it is that more than four hundred years later Montaigne is still in print in many languages and his writing remains accessible and highly persuasive. His enduring readability and cogency, not to mention his popularity with both lay readers and scholars, has a lot to do with the fact that he worked with material that inspired and delighted him, allowing his enthusiasms to stir the imagination and intellect of the reader. It also has to do with the form in which he wrote: those insightful essays used anecdotal and autobiographical detail, poetry and speculation as well as critique and evidence-based scholarship.

This crossbreed form was rejuvenated by certain feminist writers in the 1970s, notably Luce Irigaray and Helene Cixous, who were reacting against how the personal was traditionally set in second place after impersonal, or the objective, in the academy. Fictocritical writing questions the superiority of the traditional linear, 'masculine' form. It does not aim for pure objectivity, but insists on acknowledgement of the scholar's feeling for what she or he is writing about. It 'provides its own process of self-reflection' (Gibbs 2005, n.p.) while still participating in academic discourse. That means reflection and analysis go hand in hand in fictocritical writing – as they do in your reflective journals. Stories, essays, and critiques may all be used in a single text, and this genre breakdown questions the very structures underpinning academic knowledge.

Anna Gibbs sees it as a style of writing that 'is unafraid of aesthetics, of the old-fashioned pleasure of how words can work affectively both within and beyond narrative'. Another of its proponents, Stephen Meucke, tells us it makes an argument with storytelling – or poetry, for that matter – as its vehicle. Fictocritical writing emphasises multidisciplinarity and unorthodox perspectives so that the traditional divisions between criticism, fiction, and theory become understated.

Exercise 10.6 Narrative experiment: 'I am a rock'

One of my students once wrote a piece of fiction from the point of view of a mountain range in order to explain geology and the slowness of geological time. He did this from the perspectives of various minerals; some had travelled widely (in rivers, by erosion, by changing form over time due to the action of heat and cold), others never left their homes or their original states. The result was a highly effective fact-based educational text enriched with invented memoirs (of the mineral characters) and descriptions of varied environments. As Jennifer Moon (2010) has pointed out, writing stories based on scientific ideas has become popular because fiction can be a practical way to explore ideas – and further, it can be a means of theorising the nature of knowledge itself.

You might experiment with this kind of multilayered text. Choose a topic you're currently researching, but allow yourself to depart from formal scholarly discourse at a certain point to include a subjective viewpoint (that may or may not be human).

An example of the form, and a move towards greater authorial authenticity

Michael Taussig is known for the highly provocative nature of his ethnographic studies, but more to the point here, the unconventional form his writing takes. He is concerned that anthropology maintain a power to discompose the reader as well as persuade them to his point of view: his desire to startle us is a persuasive strategy. He wants to wake us up and have us pay attention. If you subscribe to this way of constructing persuasive arguments – as some scholars do – delighting or disconcerting a reader isn't likely to happen if we refuse personal involvement and detach ourselves too much from the subjects of our analysis.

Taussig engages viscerally as well as intellectually with the people about whom he writes. A case in point: during his early research into shamanism and state terror he read certain archival reports of atrocities committed by colonisers in South America, and while reading, he found himself greedy for more horrors. He was appalled at his own eager prurience. However, rather than putting aside his ghoulishness and his guilt as irrelevant personal responses unworthy of scholarly consideration (or indeed, of a moral being) and returning to an objective academic stance, he decided to honestly acknowledge his reactions, for they might provide an access point, or 'a clue into understanding the violence' (cited in Eakin 2001, n.p.). Through experiments with form and style, he tried to feel his way into 'what was at stake, the madness of the passion'. He attempted to recreate the monstrous nature of the subject of his research and the relationships between colonisers and the colonised by including in his study lyrical evocations, personal reflections, biographical notes, original photographic images, and so forth. His aim – and this is the crux of the matter – was to enable a level of *authenticity* that would do justice to the horror experienced by the Putumayan Indians. Arguably, this represents a kind of truthfulness not accessible by means of scholarly objectivity alone.

Below is an example of Taussig's later prose, from the introductory section of his 1992 book titled *The Nervous System*, to which I've added commentary and questions.

Exercise 10.7 Narrative experiment: electric currents

I am working on the Nervous System, and it's turning out to be hard labour indeed. I suspect it's working even harder on me than I am on it … Nervous System. That's all it said, scrawled across a shed I passed on the ferry, gliding over the green waters of Sydney Harbour, whenever I went into the city, reading about the terror of the early 20th-century rubber boom in the lower Putumayo River in southwest Colombia. It was the early 1980s. The signs in the street were of unemployment, purple hair, and postmod anarchy. Apocalyptic omens … And over there and far away, Colombia was in a state of siege. Torture by the State was commonplace. Paramilitary squads were on the make. Whenever I got up from my desk to cross the sunlit bay away from my other world over there and

---

(Continued)

back then in those Putumayan forests, the Nervous System stared at me in the
fullness of its scrawled, enigmatic, might. A portent? A voice from nowhere
tugging at my distracted attention. For I could not believe let alone begin to
explain the terrible material I was reading about over there and back then, and
much less could I put words to it. Wrenched this way, then that, I believed it all, I
believed nothing.

This seems to be written in a state of heightened awareness and sensitivity, and also high anxiety, which the author exploits rather than attempting to overcome or disguise.

Q: You may have had the experience, when engrossed in some project, of seeing relevant connections to your research in the most arbitrary sights or feelings. If so, write a brief recollection of it below.

In this piece of writing, Taussig responded to a random sign or graffito – *Nervous System* – and decided to go with the image of tensions and anxieties forming a neurological system. This play on words now leads his thought process, stimulating it like a kind of electric pulse darting along neural pathways, connecting different ideas and images, or nodes.

Q: What are the 'nodes' I'm referring to in the text above?

Vitalised by this electrical current of thought and a sense of impending apocalypse, Taussig makes connections between otherwise unrelated events, images, persons, places. This comprises his lively prose which, as it develops, draws its disparate elements into a coherent series of reflections, governed by the motif of the nervous system.

Q: Can you identify any of Helen Sword's criteria for good writing in the above passage – as below? That is, what are its main strengths?

1. clear expression of complex ideas
2. lack of jargon
3. imagination
4. storytelling strengths
5. concrete language
6. interdisciplinary references
7. intellectual engagement
8. individual voice
9. anecdotes
10. humour giving of aesthetic and/or intellectual pleasure.

Final Q: I hope you gave Taussig a first, sympathetic reading. However, you may find you dislike his style; it may even grate on your nerves or offend your sense of scholarly decorum. If so, write a brief critique of it below, explaining why this excerpt from the *Nervous System* is unsuccessful or ill-advised.

Exercise 10.8 Narrative experiment: scrapbooking

This exercise is based on personal experimentation and research and also on the practices that some of my more adventurous students have introduced into their research process.

Choose a subject that you're either currently researching or would like to research. For the purposes of this activity, it needs to be something about which you feel strongly. Decide upon a thesis statement or research question and outline the main points you will cover. These points will be backed with scholarly evidence, but also include some or all of the following, at least in the planning stages:

1. reference to the way you feel about the issue now;
2. where it was that you first had the idea to research this, and how you felt at the time – physically;
3. songs or poems or pieces of prose that reflect your feeling towards or understanding of the issue;
4. some reflections upon the issue – why it's important, and to whom;
5. any interesting anecdotes you may have heard or read either on social or conventional media, or discussed amongst colleagues, that relate to the topic;
6. imaginary conversations about the topic with any of the researchers or commentators you've found during your research process whose contributions have particularly impressed you, either negatively or positively.
7. If your topic involves case studies, interviews, or any inquiry into the perceptions or experiences of others, be sure to include direct commentary from those others – not just your own impressions or interpretation.

Don't think about the arrangement or final outline while you are doing the collecting. Wait until you have several pieces to choose from. You may find that when you lay them out, other trains of thought, as well as visceral or emotional responses, will arise. Include those also.

My preference for this activity is to work with paper and to physically move the notes around on a large table or the floor so that I can see patterns emerging. If you prefer to use a screen, do so, but it'll have to be one with a particularly large monitor.

Final step in the exercise

The day after you've completed the exercise and arrived at a provisional arrangement, your mind should be fairly saturated with impressions and information regarding the topic. So when you wake up, go straight to your worktable or floor or computer before your mind has time to get involved with other workaday concerns. Write the thesis statement at the top of the page and do a 5–10-minute freewriting passage on the subject. You may find that this added material will enrich your understanding of the topic, and possibly guide you towards a more authentic written response.

Conclusion

This final chapter has brought together several foci of the previous chapters which have emphasised that:

- Sympathetic reading is required of us before standing back and judging a text.
- Acknowledgement and assimilation of our own subjectivities into research practices is necessary for academic honesty in the broadest sense.
- We need a level of subjectivity if we want to develop an individual authorial voice, and expanding on the idea that subjectivity can be used to enhance criticality and scholarly truthfulness.
- Criticality and creativity work together. As fiction is weakened when it privileges vague and wooly notions of 'creativity' over critical effort and awareness, similarly academic writing that disavows creative process is demonstrably poorer for the lack of personal engagement and expression.

We've also developed the theme of uncertainty as an attitude of mind to embrace. To this end we looked at the writing of particular scholars who work with rather than against uncertainty and doubt, even self-doubt (as in the case of Taussig) and as a result produce writing that is provocative and empathetic as well as persuasive.
We saw that fictocritical texts require that the author balance the perspective of an outsider looking in with that of a participant in the research project. For this to occur, reflexivity is essential, as is a level of empathy for the subject matter, and to a greater or lesser degree, a recognition of one's own physical and mental responses to information.

Unorthodox writing strategies were showcased as ways of working across disciplines and combining disciplinary forms to augment the persuasiveness of our writing. Exercises were based on their ability to provide an experiential foundation for understanding the concepts explored, and also to draw out particular aspects of Facione's 'ideal critical thinker': curiosity, open-mindedness, and flexibility; and also to help build a set of skills and writerly propensities that enable the fluidity of thinking necessary in this supercomplex and unstable cultural climate.

Concluding Remarks

This book began by putting critical thinking into historical context with a review of some particularly original thinkers since ancient Greece up until today. Several of those mentioned used intellectual and imaginative ways of seeing beyond the analytical or interrogative – that is, what is commonly seen as 'critical'. This factor, along with the decision to present less well-known exemplars alongside those traditionally accorded respect for their contribution to Western intellectual history, set the tone for a book that approaches the subject of thinking and writing in ways that diverge a little from other texts.

Critical Thinking and Persuasive Writing for Postgraduates links critical thinking to sympathetic reading and creative practice to illustrate a central contention of the book: that these three modes depend on each other if they are to serve the overarching aim of thinking and writing well. Critical thinking is broadened out into a wider concept of 'criticality', which involves more than refining analytical skills to suit particular fields of research. This book emphasised ways these skills are used not only to support academic study, but in the workplace and wider community, because criticality does not confine itself to theory. Instead, it can be – and ought to be – a practical activity, one which also involves metacognitive reflection that attempts to bring to our attention an awareness of our natural biases which can influence our judgement and therefore our actions.

Thinking and research practices are treated not as activities that precede writing, but that go hand in hand with writing. Thus, each chapter combines some theoretical discussion with advice, and practical exercises are not saved until the end but punctuate the discussion points throughout each chapter. This book sees the ability to write convincingly and persuasively as an activity driven by our motivations for writing. In other words,

- *how* we write is guided by
- *what* we want to express,
- *to whom* we want to express it, and
- *why*.

I've attempted to present critical skills in such a way that they are transportable, that is, showing how they may be applied to any field of study. While different academic disciplines may require particular analytical tools, it is also true that there are attitudes and aptitudes that may be developed regardless of your particular scholarly interest – the ability to balance openness and scepticism being one of the most important; thus, this book considers ways we might develop interpretative, analytical, and reflective faculties without direct reference to specific disciplinary requirements. This is because today's 'supercomplex' information-based cultures require that we all negotiate pathways through a multiplicity of truths and half-truths, disinformation and propaganda, realities contained within algorithmic filter bubbles, and new worlds opened up by technologies unthought of even as recently as a decade ago. This 'reality negotiation project' is incredibly difficult, yet it is more important than ever to try. I hope this book has gone some way towards showing that incisive judgements and truthful interpretations of concepts might occur through critical inquisitiveness and openness, allied with imagination, and that the writing exercises provided might help readers refresh written expression so as to better convey what you intend in your own way – and with spirit.

References

Agrippa, H. 1650, *Three Books of Occult Philosophy* (J.F. trans., Book 1). London, R.W.

Allen, P. 1997, *The Concept of Woman, Vol 1: The Aristotelian Revolution 750 BC – AD 1250*, Wm. B. Eerdmans Publishing Co., Michigan.

Alvesson, M. 2013, *The Triumph of Emptiness: Consumption, Higher Education, & Work Organisation*, Oxford University Press, Oxford.

Anderson, TD. 2011, 'Beyond eureka moments: Supporting the invisible work of creativity and innovation', *Information Research: An International Electronic Journal,* vol. 16, no. 1, n.p.

Atwood, M. 2009, *Payback: Debt and the Shadow Side of Wealth*, Bloomsbury Publishing, London.

Australian Mining, viewed 17 March 2016, www.australianmining.com.au/features/top-ten-trends-mining-2016/

Barnett, R. 1997, *Higher Education: A Critical Business*, The Society for Research into Higher Education and Open University Press, Buckingham.

Barnett, R. 2000, 'Supercomplexity and the curriculum', *Studies in Higher Education*, vol. 25, no. 3, pp. 255–265.

Barnett, R. 2015, 'A curriculum for critical being', in M. Davies and R. Barnett (eds), *The Palgrave Handbook of Critical Thinking in Higher Education*, Palgrave Macmillan, Basingstoke.

Barry, J., Chandler, J. & Clark, H. 2001, 'Between the ivory tower and the academic assembly line', *Journal of Management Studies*, vol. 38, no. 1, pp. 87–101.

Benesch, S. 1993, 'Critical thinking: A learning process for democracy', *TESOL Quarterly*, vol. 27, no. 3, Special-Topic Issue: Adult Literacies, pp. 545–548.

Berg, M. & Seeber, B. 2016, *The Slow Professor*, University of Toronto Press, Toronto.

Bernstein, R. 1996, *Hannah Arendt and the Jewish Question*, MIT Press, Cambridge, MA.

Bloom's Taxonomy, Adapted from *Teaching thinking skills in the primary years*, Hawker Brownlow, Australia. Bloom, B. (1956, 1964). *Taxonomy of Educational Objectives*, Longmans Green, New York, https://sydney.edu.au/education_social_work/groupwork/docs/BloomsTaxonomy.pdf

Bohm, D. 2004, *On Creativity*, Routledge Classics, Oxon and New York.

Bourdieu, P. 1979, 'Symbolic Power', *Critique of Anthropology*, vol. 4, no. 13–14, pp. 77–85.

Bourland, D. 2004, 'To be or not to be: E-Prime as a tool of critical thinking', *A Review of General Semantics*, vol. 61, no. 4, pp. 546–557.

Brodin, E. 2015, 'Conditions for criticality in doctoral education: A creative concern', in M. Davies & R. Barnett (eds), *The Palgrave Handbook of Critical Thinking in Higher Education*, Palgrave Macmillan, Basingstoke.

Brookfield, S. 2011, 'Discussion as a way of teaching', viewed 1 December 2016, https://static1.squarespace.com/static/5738a0ccd51cd47f81977fe8/t/5750ef4862cd947608165d85/1464921939855/Discussion_as_a_Way_of_Teaching_Packet.pdf

Brookfield, S. 2015, 'Speaking truth to power: Teaching critical thinking in the critical theory tradition', in M. Davies and R. Barnett (eds), *The Palgrave Handbook of Critical Thinking in Higher Education*, Palgrave, Basingstoke, pp. 529–544.

Buckner, R., Andrews-Hanna, J. & Schacter, D. 2008, 'The brain's default network: Anatomy, function, and relevance to disease', *New York Academy of Sciences*, viewed 30 September 2016, www.ncbi.nlm.nih.gov/pubmed/18400922

Burbules, N. 2000, 'Aporias, webs, and passages: Doubt as an opportunity to learn', *Curriculum Inquiry,* vol. 30, no. 2, pp. 171–187.

Chen, K. 2013, 'The effect of language on economic behavior: Evidence from savings rates, health behaviors, and retirement assets', *American Economic Review*, vol. 103, no. 2, pp. 690–731.

Couldry, N. & Rodriguez, C. 2016, 'Why the media is a key dimension of global inequality, Democracy Futures', viewed 10 January 2016, https://theconversation.com/why-the-media-is-a-key-dimension-of-global-inequality-69084

Creative Commons project, untitled, with anonymous author and publisher, viewed 8 December 2016, http://2012books.lardbucket.org/

Creme, P. & Lea, M. 2008, *Writing at University*, 3rd edition, McGraw-Hill Education, Open University Press, Maidenhead.

'Critical Thinking on the Web' 2007, viewed 11 September 2017, www.austhink.com/critical/pages/definitions.html

Csikszentmihalyi, M. 1996, *Creativity: Flow and the Psychology of Discovery and Invention*, HarperCollins Publishers, New York.

Curtis-Wendlandt, L. 2004, 'Conversing on love: Text and subtext in Tullia d'Aragona's Dialogo della Infinità d'Amore', *Hypatia*, vol. 19, no. 4, pp. 77–98.

Damasio, A. 1994, *Descartes' Error: Emotion, Reason, and the Human Brain*, Avon Books, GP Putnam, New York.

Deleuze, G., Guattari, F. & Maclean, M. 1985, 'Kafka: Toward a minor literature: The components of expression', *New Literary History*, vol. 16, no. 3, Johns Hopkins University Press, Baltimore, pp. 591–608.

The Delphi Report: Executive Summary, 1990, ERIC Document: ED315 423 'Descartes: Starting with doubt', *Britannica*, viewed 5 January 2017, www.philosophypages.com/hy/4c.htm

Dewey, J. 1933, *How We Think*, DC Heath & Co, Boston.

Dragseth, J. 2016, *Thinking Woman: A Philosophical Approach to the Quandary of Gender*, The Lutterworth Press, Cambridge.

Eakin, E. 'Anthropology's alternative radical', *The New York Times*, 21 April 2001, viewed 2 March 2011, www.nytimes.com/2001/04/21/arts/anthropology-s-alternative-radical.html

Eisenberg, E. 2001, 'Building a mystery: Toward a new theory of communication and identity', *Journal of Communication*, International Communication Association, viewed 1 September 2017, http://dd8gh5yx7k.scholar.serialssolutions.com.ezproxy1.library.usyd.edu.au/?sid=google&auinit=EM&aulast=Eisenberg&atitle=Building+a+mystery:+Toward+a+new+theory+of+communication+and+identity&id=doi:10.1111/j.1460-2466.2001.tb02895.x&title=Journal+of+communication&volume=51&issue=3&date=2001&spage=534&issn=0021-9916

Eisenberg, E. 2007, *Strategic Ambiguities: Essays on Communication, Organization, and Identity*, Sage Publications, London.

Elbow, P. 2008, 'The believing game – methodological believing', *ScholarWorks@UMassAmherst*, viewed 10 March 2017, http://scholarworks.umass.edu/cgi/viewcontent.cgi?article=1004&context=eng_faculty_pubs

Elder, L. 2007, 'Defining critical thinking', The Critical Thinking Community, retrieved 11 September 2017, www.criticalthinking.org/pages/defining-critical-thinking/766

Elkins, J.R. 1999, Proceedings from a workshop on Reading Critically, at the Association of American Law Schools (AALS), New Orleans, viewed 12 March 2017, http://myweb.wvnet.edu/~jelkins/critproj/overview.html

Ennis, R. 1985, 'A logical basis for measuring critical thinking skills', *The Association for Supervision and Curriculum Development*, viewed 10 October 2016, www.ascd.org/ASCD/pdf/journals/ed_lead/el_198510_ennis.pdf

Ennis, R. 2013, 'The nature of critical thinking: Outlines of general critical thinking dispositions and abilities', *Criticalthinking.net*, viewed 1 March 2017, www.criticalthinking.net/longdefinition.html

Ennis, R. 2015, 'Critical thinking: A streamlined conception', in M. Davies and R. Barnett (eds), *The Palgrave Handbook of Critical Thinking in Higher Education*, Palgrave Macmillan, Basingstoke, pp. 31–47.

Facione, P. 2013, 'Critical thinking: What it is and why it counts', viewed 16 December 2016, https://pdfs.semanticscholar.org/6771/46d5e0414165018af9385b62226ae7e1fa49.pdf

Fairclough, N. 1993, 'Critical discourse analysis and the marketization of public discourse: The universities', *Discourse and Society*, vol. 4, no. 2, pp. 133–168.

Feyerabend, PK. 1975, *Against Method: Outline of an Anarchistic Theory of Knowledge,* viewed 2 May 2016, http://mcps.umn.edu/assets/pdf/4.2.1_Feyerabend.pdf

Feyerabend, P.K. 1993, *Against Method*, 3rd edition, Verso, London.

Flam, J. (ed.) 1995, *Matisse on Art*, University of California Press, Berkeley.

Florida, R. 2012, 'The blog: Creativity is the new economy', viewed 23 December 2016, www.huffingtonpost.com/richard-florida/creativity-is-the-new-eco_b_1608363.html

Fox, D. 2009, 'Academic objectivity, political neutrality, and other barriers to Israeli-Palestinian reconciliation', in M.F. Salinas & H.A. Rabi (eds), *Resolving the Israeli-Palestinian Conflict: Perspectives on the Peace Process*, Cambria Press, New York, viewed 15 December 2016, www.dennisfox.net/papers/objectivity_israel_palestine.html

Frankfurt, H. 2005, *On Bullshit*, Princeton University Press, Princeton.

Garber, M. 2001, *Academic Instincts*, Princeton University Press, Princeton.

Gibbs, A. 2005, 'Fictocriticism, affect, mimesis: Engendering differences', *TEXT* vol. 9, no. 1, n.p.

Gieve, S. 1998, 'Comments on Dwight Atkinson's "A critical approach to critical thinking in TESOL"', *TESOL Quarterly*, vol. 32, no. 1, pp. 123–129.

Glenn, C. 1994, 'Sex, lies and manuscript: Refiguring Aspasia in the history of rhetoric, *College Composition and Communication*, vol. 45, no. 2, pp. 180–199.

Graff, G. & Birkenstein, C. 2010, *They Say, I Say,* WW Norton & Company, New York.

Grammarly blog, 2016, viewed 14 December 2016, www.grammarly.com/blog/what-is-the-oxford-comma-and-why-do-people-care-so-much-about-it/

Grattan, M. 2017, 'Don't deride the experts: Universities Australia chair', *The Conversation*, viewed 1 March 2017, https://theconversation.com/dont-deride-the-experts-universities-australia-chair-73795

Greenpeace, 2014, 'Top 10 reasons why Carmichael mega mine is a REALLY bad idea', viewed 14 December 2016, www.greenpeace.org/australia/en/news/climate/Top-10-reasons-why-Carmichael-mega-mine-is-a-REALLY-bad-idea

Griffith Graduate Attributes Ethical Behaviour and Social Responsibility Toolkit, 2011, viewed 17 June 2016, https://docuri.com/download/griffith-graduate-attributes-ethical-behaviour_59bf3851f581716e46c32479_pdf

Halpern, D.F. 2013, *Critical Thinking Across the Curriculum: A Brief Edition of Thought and Knowledge*, New York.

Hecht, J. 2003, *Doubt: A History: The Great Doubters and their Legacy of Innovation from Socrates and Jesus to Thomas Jefferson and Emily Dickinson*, Harper One, New York.

Henry, M. 1995, *Prisoner of History: Aspasia of Miletus and her Biographical Tradition*, Oxford University Press, New York and Oxford.

Hill, C., Corbett. C. & St Rose, A. 2010, 'Why so few? Women in science, technology, engineering and mathematics', *American Association of University Women,* http://files.eric.ed.gov.ezproxy1.library.usyd.edu.au/fulltext/ED509653.pdf

Howkins, J. 2010, *Creative Ecologies: Where Thinking is a Proper Job*, Transaction, Portland.

Immordino-Yang, M. & Damasio, A. 2007, 'We feel, therefore we learn: The relevance of affective and social neuroscience in education', *Mind, Brain, and Education*, vol. 1, no. 1, pp. 3–10.

Kandel, E. 2006, *In Search of Memory*, W.W. Norton and Company, New York.

Kathpalia, S. & Heah, C. 2008, 'Reflective writing: Insights into what lies beneath', *RELC Journal* 2008, vol. 39, no. 3, pp. 300–317.

Katz, L. 2014, 'Against the corrosive language of Corpspeak in the university', *Higher Education, Research & Development*, vol. 34, no. 3, pp. 554–567.

Katz, I. 2015, 'Report shows consequences of monetised education system, but does little to dispel it', *The Conversation*, May 5, 2015.

Katz, L. 2016, 'Feeding greedy corpses: The rhetorical power of Corpspeak and Zombilingo in Higher Education, and suggested countermagics to foil the intentions of the living dead', *Borderlands e-journal,* vol. 15, no. 1, n.p.

Kisicek, G. & Zagar, Z. 2013, 'Argumentation as polyphony: One speaker, several voices', in L. Groarke & C. Tindale (eds), *What Do We Know About the World? Historical and Argumentative Perspectives*, University of Windsor Digital Library Dissertation Series, vol. 25, Open Monograph Press, Windsor.

Lakoff, G. & Johnson, M. 1980, *Metaphors We Live By*, The University of Chicago Press, Chicago.

Lakoff, G. & Johnson, M. 1999, *Philosophy in the Flesh*, Basic Books, New York.

Lamm, R. & Everett, J. 2007, *Dynamic Argument*, Houghton Mifflin Company, Boston.

Levinovitz, A.J. 2016, 'The new astrology: By fetishizing mathematical models, economists turned economics into a pseudoscience', *Aeon Journal*, viewed 30 May 2016, AEONHow%20 economists%20rode%20maths%20to%20become%20our%20era's%20astrologers%20_% 20Aeon%20Essays.html

Limerick, P. 1993, 'Dancing with professors: The trouble with academic prose', *New York Times,* 31 October, p. 3.

Mackay, H. 2009, 'Truth in fiction', *The Sydney Morning Herald,* 25–26 July.

McMiken, D. 2010, *Secrets of Writing Killer Essays and Reports: A Manual for Students and Professionals*, Kikkuli Texts, London.

McPeck, J. 2016, *Critical Thinking and Education*, Routledge Library Editions: Philosophy of Education, Routledge, Oxford.

Mahboob, A. & Humphrey, S. 2008, 'How to write an article review', University of Sydney, unpublished source material developed for the SLATE project.

Marden, P. 2015, *The Authoritarian Interlude: Democracy, Values, and the Politics of Hubris*, Routledge, London.

Marshall, J. 2013, 'The mess of information and the order of doubt', *Global Media Journal Australian Edition*, vol. 7, no. 1, pp. 1–11.

Miller, P.L., 2008, 'Socrates' irrational rationality', *Symploke*, vol. 16, nos. 1–2, pp. 299–303.

Miller, T. 2012, *Blow up the humanities*, Temple University Press, Philadelphia.

Mills, C.W. 2000, *The Sociological Imagination*, Oxford University Press, Oxford.

Moon, J. 2010, *Using Story in Higher Education and Professional Development*, Routledge, London and New York.

Mueller, P. & Openheimer, D. 2014, 'The pen is mightier than the keyboard: Advantages of longhand over laptop not taking', *Psychological Sciences Online First*, https://sites.udel.edu/ victorp/files/2010/11/Psychological-Science-2014-Mueller-0956797614524581-1u0h0yu.pdf

Orwell, G. 1946, www.orwell.ru/library/essays/politics/english/e_polit/, 1 May 2016.

Ott, B.L. 2004, '(Re) locating pleasure in media studies: Toward an erotics of reading', *Communication and Critical/Cultural Studies,* vol. 1, no. 2, pp. 194–212.

Parkins, W. & Craig, G. 2006, *Slow Living*, Berg, Oxford.

Paul, R. 1989, 'Critical thinking in North America: A new theory of knowledge, learning, and literacy', *Argumentation*, vol. 3, pp. 197–235, viewed 24 September 2017, https://link-springer-com.ezproxy1.library.usyd.edu.au/content/pdf/10.1007/BF00128149.pdf

Paul, R. 1990, *Excerpts from: Critical Thinking: What Every Person Needs to Survive in a Rapidly Changing World*, http://assets00.grou.ps/0F2E3C/wysiwyg_files/FilesModule/criticalthinking andwriting/20090921185639-uxlhmlnvedpammxrz/CritThink1.pdf

Paul, R., Elder, L. & Bartell, T. (principal authors) 1997, 'A brief history of the idea of critical thinking', taken from the *California Teacher Preparation for Instruction in Critical Thinking:*

Research Findings and Policy Recommendations: State of California, California Commission on Teacher Credentialing, viewed 5 January 2017, www.criticalthinking.org/pages/a-brief-history-of-the-idea-of-critical-thinking/408

Paul, R. Elder, L. & Bartell, T., 2015, 'Our concept and definition of critical thinking', viewed 5 January 2017, www.criticalthinking.org/pages/our-concept-and-definition-of-critical-thinking/411

Petrini, C. 2001, *Slow Food: The Case for Taste*, Columbia University Press, New York (trans. W. McCuaig).

Pope, R. 2005, *Creativity: Theory, History, Practice*, Routledge, Oxon.

Restall, G. 2013, 'Three cultures or: What place for logic in the humanities', in https://articulation.arts.unimelb.edu.au/?p=3488

Rhodes, C. 2015, 'Writing organization/romancing fictocriticism, *Culture and Organization*, vol. 21, no. 4, pp. 289–303.

Richardson, L. & St Pierre, E.A. 2005, 'Writing: A method of inquiry', in N. Denzin and Y.S. Lincoln (eds) *The Sage Handbook of Qualitative Research*, 3rd edition, Sage Publications, Thousand Oaks, pp. 959–978.

Richardson, M. 2008, 'Writing is not just a basic skill', *The Chronicle of Higher Education*, viewed 30 May 2016, www.etsu.edu/cas/litlang/composition/documents/writing_is_not_a_basic_skill.pdf.

Ritter, S. & Dijksterhuis, A. 2014, 'Creativity—the unconscious foundations of the incubation period', *Frontiers in Human Neuroscience,* viewed 16 June 2016, www.ncbi.nlm.nih.gov/pmc/articles/PMC3990058/

Robinson, DN. 2006, 'Rhetoric and character in Aristotle', *The Review of Metaphysics*, vol. 60, no. 1, pp. 3–15.

Robinson, K. 2007, 'Balancing the books', in J. Hartley (ed.) *Creative Industries*, Blackwell Publishing.

Robinson, K. 2011, 'Ken Robinson on the principles of creative leadership', *The Creative Leadership Forum*, viewed 1 December 2016, http://thecreativeleadershipforum.com/creativity-matters-blog/2011/8/29/ken-robinson-on-the-principles-of-creative-leadership-fast-c.html

Rossiter, M. 1995, *Women Scientists in America before Affirmative Action 1940–1972,* Johns Hopkins University Press, Baltimore and London.

Sacks, O. 1998, *The Man Who Mistook His Wife for a Hat and Other Clinical Tales*, Touchstone, New York.

Saul, J.R. 1993, *Voltaire's Bastards: The Dictatorship of Reason in the West*, Penguin, Toronto.

Schultz, J. 2006, 'Pointing the way to discovery: Using a creative writing practice in qualitative research', *Journal of Phenomenological Psychology*, vol. 37, no. 2, pp. 217–239.

Siegel, M. & Carey, R. 1989, 'Critical thinking: A semiotic perspective. Monographs on teaching critical thinking', No. 1, ERIC document ED303802, viewed 11 September 2017, https://archive.org/stream/ERIC_ED303802/ERIC_ED303802_djvu.txt

Spedding, J., Ellis, R. & Heath, D. (eds) 2011, *The Works of Francis Bacon Volume 10: The Letters and the Life*, Cambridge University Press, Cambridge.

Spicer, A. 2016, 'Stupefied: How organisations enshrine collective stupidity and employees are rewarded for checking their brains at the office door', *Aeon Magazine*, viewed 1 November 2016, https://aeon.co/essays/you-don-t-have-to-be-stupid-to-work-here-but-it-helps

Stanford Encyclopedia of Philosophy, 2013, https://stanford.library.sydney.edu.au/archives/sum2013/, viewed 10 September 2010.

Sword, H. 2009, 'Writing higher education differently: A manifesto on style', *Studies in Higher Education*, vol. 34, no. 3, pp. 319–336.

Sword, H. 2012, *Stylish Academic Writing*, Harvard University Press, Cambridge, MA, viewed 15 December 2016, http://site.ebrary.com/lib/usyd/reader.action?docID=10574892#

Taussig, M. 1992, *The Nervous System*, Routledge, New York.

'The slow science manifesto' 2010, *The Slow Science Academy*, viewed 1 January 2011, http://slow-science.org/

van Gelder, TJ. 2001, 'How to improve critical thinking using educational technology', in G. Kennedy, M. Keppell, C. McNaught & T. Petrovic (eds), *Meeting at the Crossroads*, Proceedings of the 18th Annual Conference of the Australasian Society for Computers in Learning in Tertiary Education, Biomedical Multimedia Unit, The University of Melbourne, Melbourne, pp. 539–548.

Vardi, I. 2012, 'Developing students' referencing skills: A matter of plagiarism, punishment and morality or of learning to write critically', *Higher Education, Research and Development*, vol. 31, no. 6, pp. 1–10

Weiss, P. 2009, *Canon Fodder: Historical Women Political Thinkers*, Pennsylvania State University Press, Pennsylvania.

Zizek, S. 2013, We don't really want what we think we desire, Plomomedia reference clip, viewed 4 October 2015, www.youtube.com/watch?v=G2Cjd6H6RmY

Index